A FREEDOM
WITHIN

A FREEDOM WITHIN

THE PRISON NOTES OF STEFAN CARDINAL WYSZYŃSKI

Translated by BARBARA KRZYWICKI-HERBURT
and REVEREND WALTER J. ZIEMBA

Foreword by JOHN CARDINAL KROL

HARCOURT BRACE JOVANOVICH, PUBLISHERS
SAN DIEGO   NEW YORK   LONDON

Copyright © 1982 by Editions du Dialogue, Paris.

English translation copyright © 1983 by Harcourt Brace Jovanovich, Inc.

Library of Congress Cataloging in Publication Data

Wyszyński, Stefan, 1901–1981
  A freedom within.

  Translation of: Zapiski więzienne.
  "This book represents one section of the unpublished twenty-volume work, Pro Memoria, by Cardinal Wyszynski"
—Verso t.p.
  1. Wyszyński, Stefan, 1901–1981. 2. Cardinals—Poland—Biography. 3. Political prisoners—Poland—Biography. I. Title.
  BX4705.W86A3813 1984   282'.092'4 [B]   83–12878
  ISBN 0–15–133466–8

This book represents one section of the unpublished collection Pro Memoria by Cardinal Wyszyński.

The lines from Karol Wojtyła's poem, "I reach the heart of drama," are from Collected Poems (translated by Jerzy Peterkiewicz), Random House, 1982.

All footnotes in this edition have been incorporated by the editor for clarification.

Designed by Vaughn Andrews
Printed in the United States of America

First edition
A B C D E

HBJ

Freedom has continually to be won, it cannot merely be possessed. It comes as a gift but can only be kept with a struggle. Gift and struggle are written into pages, hidden yet open.

You pay for freedom with all your being; therefore call this your freedom, that paying for it continually you possess yourself anew.

Through this payment we enter history and touch her epochs. Which way runs the division of generations, the division between those who did not pay enough and those who had to pay too much? On which side are we? And exceeding in so many self-determinations, did we not outgrow our strength in the past? Are we upholding the burden of history like a pillar with a crack still gaping?

Karol Wojtyła

CONTENTS ✿✿✿

FOREWORD

On the night of September 25, 1953, Cardinal Wyszyński was awakened and arrested and without indictment, trial, or sentence forced into internal exile. Until his release on October 28, 1956, he was confined by armed guards in four different places. During the imprisonment, he wrote his *Prison Notes,* which was published in 1982 and is here published in an English translation.

Contemporaries of the Cardinal, anticipating the judgment of posterity, have already inscribed him among the great men of the history of the Church and of his country. The editors of *Za i Przeciw (Pro and Con),* headlined their June 1981 article: "Such a Primate, God Gives but Once in 1000 Years." Pope John Paul II described him as a "defender of human rights and of the Church, the protagonist of so many pages of history of his country." The former United States ambassador to Poland, William E. Schaufile, Jr., in his book *Polish Paradox,* wrote that the Cardinal "with strength and determination tempered by realism and understanding of the possible, was able not only to lead the Church, but also to affect the course of internal Polish politics." In his book *The Poles* Stewart Steven wrote: "The man who in the 1950s was sent into three years internal exile for refusing to compromise on the issue of the independence of the Church knew on his deathbed that the final victory was his. . . . His funeral compared with those of Winston Churchill, John F. Kennedy, and Charles de Gaulle in modern times." As a member of President Reagan's mission to that funeral, I was similarly impressed.

Even Poland's Communist leaders declared a period of national mourning and, in a statement signed by Party leader Stanisław Kania, President Henryk Jabłoński, and Prime Minister Wojciech Jaruzelski, stated: "We are convinced that his life, thoughts, and toil created a pattern of cooperation between the Catholic Church and Socialist State."

Lech Wałęsa, leader of Solidarność (Solidarity), said that no one he met affected him as did the Primate: "He impressed me even more than the Holy Father—isn't that strange?"

Much has been written by and about Cardinal Wyszyński. However, *Prison Notes* provides a unique insight into his character, his thinking, and his goals. It reveals a man of keen intelligence, deep faith, unshakable hope, fortitude of spirit, tempered by years of strict moral and spiritual discipline blended with prudence and moderation. He was an ardent lover and a courageous defender of truth. Intolerant of sin and error, he loved the sinner and the erring. He resisted the militant atheism of Communism, but embraced individual Communists as brothers who needed understanding and help in returning to truth. He had deep commitments and convictions, and he never doubted that the eternal truths of the Church would ultimately be victorious. As a Christian realist, he eschewed violence, but insisted on nonviolent resistance to every act of oppression and injustice. Thus in 1963, he urged parents to demand the constitutional guarantees of full freedom of religion, especially for their children, because "If a citizen does not demand his rights, he is no longer a citizen. He becomes a slave."

To understand why the Cardinal was arrested and forcibly prevented from carrying out his pastoral duties, it helps to recall that Poland—the first nation to resist the Nazi aggression—suffered defeat in victory. The Nazis were defeated but Polish Communists, aided by the Soviet Union, using the formula of infiltration and rigged elections, gained a stranglehold on the Polish people. For two years the Poles resisted the take-over. Gomułka admitted that over 20,000 Communists and several thousand militia and army personnel had been killed. But the Communists, using the organs of government, the militia, and the army led by Soviet Marshal Konstantin Rokossovsky quelled the resistance.

Having consolidated their totalitarian control, the Communists ruthlessly promoted the "Sovietization" of Poland, including the repression and control of religion. In their bitter anti-Church campaign, the Communists tried to infiltrate and create discord by means of the so-called Patriotic Priests. On February 16, 1950, Cardinal Sapieha wrote on behalf of the Polish bishops to President Boles-ław Bierut that the Church would not be intimidated by threats and would not yield on truths of doctrine and, if necessary, was ready to suffer persecution. As a result, an agreement safeguarding the rights and freedom of the Church and the people was reached and was signed on April 14, 1950, by the Church and the State. This is what Cardinal Wyszyński refers to as the Joint Commission's Mutual Understanding.

Despite the agreement, Bishop Czesław Kaczmarek of Kielce was sentenced to twenty years imprisonment for alleged treason. Eight bishops, including Archbishop Baziak, the administrator of Kraków, and one thousand priests were jailed. Over one thousand nuns were taken into custody after raids on convents. The State made it impossible for Catholic charity organizations to operate effectively. Priests were denied the right to hold religious services in hospitals, prisons, and military installations.

To discourage children from attending church, the most exciting excursions for children were held on Sundays and Holy Days. Crucial tests were scheduled for older students on Sundays with the warning that church attendance would minimize their opportunities of admission to institutes of higher learning. Records were kept of persons who attended church services, and churchgoers were excluded from advancement to certain positions. To neutralize the influence of the Church, a Pax organization of Catholics who favored accommodations with the regime was set up and financed by the government. Another organization of Catholic intellectuals called Znak was also set up to be independent of the Church and State. One segment of Znak aligned itself with the Archbishop of Kraków, while another segment, with little support from the people, aligned itself with the State. This was an effort to divide and conquer.

The Bishops of Poland, under the leadership of Cardinal Wyszyński, in a letter of May 5, 1953, demanded that the regime abide by the 1950 agreement, and cease its efforts to destroy the Church by terrorist tactics, and to deprive the nation and its people of its religious and cultural heritage.

Cardinal Wyszyński was the strong opponent of the effort to impose atheism on the people of Poland. In Budapest, Prague, and the Ukraine, the Communist Party arrested Church leaders and prevented them from exercising their pastoral offices. The Polish Communists arrested Cardinal Wyszyński, too. However, Cardinal Wyszyński would not yield or compromise. He protested that the regime had violated his constitutional rights, and breached their 1950 agreement, and was attempting to usurp the jurisdiction of the Holy See, which had appointed him to the Primatial See and which alone had the authority to remove him from office. His refusal to compromise the freedom of religion and independence of the Church was the reason for his imprisonment and internal exile for more than three years.

The regime was also ruthless in its efforts to subjugate all segments of society. When in June 1956 the Polish workers in Poznań demonstrated for better living conditions and greater economic and political freedom, an elite internal security brigade from Warsaw ended the demonstration with such bloody brutality that even greater dissension spread throughout Poland. The pressure forced a change in leadership.

The first Communist Party leader in Poland had been Władysław Gomułka. He had lost favor with the Soviets and been purged and imprisoned for being too nationalistic. Now the situation in Poland had become so critical that, in the judgment of some, the party could retain control only if Gomułka was returned to power as first secretary of the Communist Party. To indicate the Soviets' displeasure at such a move, Khrushchev made an unexpected and uninvited visit to Warsaw and Soviet troops stationed in Poland were moved closer to the capital. But the critically explosive situation called for Gomułka's return to power. To restore calm, Gomułka asked Cardinal Wyszyński to resume his office and functions as Primate of Poland.

In power again, Gomułka pursued the Communist objectives, not by ruthless force but by intimidation and severe restrictions. He made it clear that the Holy Father and Bishops from other countries were not welcome at the celebration for the Millennium of Poland's birth and baptism as a nation. I was among more than thirty Bishops of the United States whose plans were thus abruptly canceled. Gomułka restricted permissions to build churches, cut down on supplies of paper and ink for Catholic publications. He used crude devices to discourage processions and pilgrimages. Time and again Cardinal Wyszyński and the Bishops protested these tactics. Treading the thin line between resistance and compromise, the Cardinal in 1966 told the authorities: "After ten centuries of Catholicism, we have the right to be a Catholic nation, and we do not resign that right."

The repressive policies of the regime, the shortage of housing, and the lack of freedom generated an antiregime feeling, which late in 1970 exploded in violence by the Gdańsk shipyard workers. The internal security forces killed an estimated seventy protesters. As a result, Gomułka was deposed in December 1970 and replaced as first secretary by Edward Gierek.

Gierek promised to improve the social and economic conditions and to engage in "dialogue" with all sectors, including the Church, for the good of the nation. As Bierut had tried ruthless suppressions of the Church and Gomułka had tried severe circumscription to limit the Church's influence, Gierek now tried conciliation, to enlist the Church's support for his efforts to improve the social-economic conditions of the nation and its people.

Gierek encountered strong opposition when, in 1975, he introduced an amendment to the Constitution that would have institutionalized the predominant role of the Communist Party and made ties with the Soviet Union unbreakable. The amendment would deny the citizens the right to change the totalitarian dictatorship of the party and diminish the sovereign rights of the Polish nation. Cardinal Wyszyński and the Bishops were forceful in leading the protests against the amendment.

Gierek's promise to improve the economic situation was not actualized. On the contrary, the situation deteriorated. The nonviolent strikes at Gdańsk, and the August 31, 1980, agreement with the independent union, Solidarity, led to the departure of Gierek for reasons of "ill health" and his replacement as first secretary by Stanisław Kania in September 1980.

The Cardinal's interest and influence on the labor movement dates back to his postgraduate studies in Christian socioeconomic principles. He studied Christian labor movements in Austria, Italy, France, Belgium, Holland, and Germany. Between 1931 and 1939 he was in charge of the Christian University for Workers, worked with Christian trade unions, organized a Catholic Union for Trade Workers, authored 106 publications on Christian social principles, and in 1946 published his lectures under the title *Duch Pracy Ludzkiej* ("The Spirit of Human Labor").

The Cardinal's efforts of fifty years came to fruition in the organization of free trade unions for industrial and farm workers and in their recognition by the government. In 1981 he delivered a number of messages, oral and written, to Solidarity. Lech Wałęsa was no stranger in the Cardinal's home. I met him there more than once. The Cardinal supported the demand of the workers to organize self-governing unions. At the same time, he cautioned the workers not to resort to violence, and even to avoid general strikes which would bring harm to the country and its people. In his 1983 visit to Poland, Pope John Paul II quoted Cardinal Wyszyński's words that the right of workers to associate freely in self-governing unions is God-given, and the State is obligated to protect it.

On May 28, 1981, death silenced the outspoken voice of Cardinal Wyszyński—the voice of faith, hope, and love; the voice of moderation and conciliation; the voice of patience and realism; the courageous voice of truth. He survived the Communist leaders Bierut, Ochab, Gomułka, Gierek, and Kania. In the process, he helped to evince to all the world that the Communist Polish United Workers Party placed its own survival above the welfare of the workers, and the self-styled Communist Polish People's Republic did in fact declare a "state of war" against the people.

Cardinal Wyszyński was a specialist in sociology and communism. He was deeply aware of the unchanging goals and the changing tactics of atheistic communism. He once told me that the Communists did not want to coexist with the Church. They wanted to destroy it. Even if they were willing to settle for coexistence, it would be impossible, because just as fire and water cannot coexist, so militant atheism and Christianity cannot coexist. He knew also that Communists insisted on totalitarian control, which places the welfare of the party and state over the welfare of the citizens.

Cardinal Wyszyński's name will be inscribed among the great men in the Polish nation and in the Church. His prudent leadership prevented the subjugation of the people and the nation of Poland to the Communist way of life. As in no other Communist-dominated nation, Poland has resisted the collectivization of farms; it has not only resisted the intensive campaigns to impose atheism on the people, but in fact the Church has increased its strength and numbers. The spirit of freedom still prevails, and the aspiration of the people for human rights seems to increase with attempts at repression.

Cardinal Wyszyński has led the Church in Poland along the path of authentic renewal in the spirit of the Second Vatican Council. Where in other countries the efforts at renewal resulted in a weakening and loss of strength, the Church in Poland is thriving and today is sending out missionaries—priests, nuns, and brothers—to the Church in various parts of the world.

By any standards, Cardinal Wyszyński was a great churchman and a great Pole. His *Prison Notes*, which is here offered to the English-reading public, provides a valuable insight into the thinking, into the character, and into the deep spirituality of a great man of our times.

John Cardinal Krol
Archbishop of Philadelphia

February 1, 1984

Baltic
Sea

U. S. S. R.

Gdansk ●

■ STOCZEK
October 12, 1953
to October 6, 1954

RYWAŁD ■
September 25, 1953 to
October 12, 1953

⊙ WARSAW

POLAND

GERMANY

PRUDNIK ŚLĄSKI
October 6, 1954 to October 27, 1955

■

Krakow ●

CZECHOSLOVAKIA

KOMAŃCZA
October 27, 1955
to October 28, 1956

U. S. S. R.

Miles
0   50   100
0   50   100
Kms.

© 1983 A. Karl/J. Kemp

PRISON CALENDAR ✿✿✿

September 25, 1953
Stefan Cardinal Wyszyński, the Primate of Poland, Archbishop of Gniezno and Warsaw, is arrested late at night and taken to prison.

September 26, 1953
Cardinal Wyszyński is driven during the night to his first place of imprisonment—Rywałd.

October 12, 1953
In the evening, the Primate of Poland is taken to a new place of imprisonment—Stoczek koło Lidzbarka Warmińskiego.

December 8, 1953
On the feast of the Immaculate Conception the imprisoned Primate dedicates himself spiritually to the Blessed Virgin Mary, placing his total fate in her hands. By this act he committed himself to accept every expression of God's will.

July 2, 1954
Impelled by his feeling of responsibility for the Church, the Primate dispatches a memorandum to the government from his prison in Stoczek, summarizing all of the efforts of the Episcopate to achieve an understanding with the government.

August 6, 1954
The Cardinal receives some periodicals for the first time, a sign of diminished isolation.

October 6, 1954
The Primate is flown to his third place of imprisonment, Prudnik Śląski. He again writes to the government and does so once more during the illness of his father, but his letters go unanswered. He decides to abandon his efforts to contact the government.

Late 1954
The authorities allow the Cardinal to undergo a physical examination in a clinic, because of his deteriorating health.

August 7, 1955
Cardinal Wyszyński rejects the authorities' proposal that he continue his isolation in a monastery in exchange for resigning his Church responsibilities.

October 27, 1955
The government issues a decree directing the Primate to be moved to Komańcza, where he is less isolated, but the authorities continue to prohibit the Cardinal, in accordance with the decree of September 24, 1953, from performing any of his Church functions.

November 2, 1955
The Primate receives his first visit from Bishops Klepacz and Choromański and learns about the events since his arrest.

May 16, 1956
In Komańcza, the Primate drafts the text of the Vows of Jasna Góra, which present a spiritual program to prepare the country for the Millennium of Poland's conversion to Christianity.

August 1956
The imprisoned Primate develops the idea of a Great Novena for the Millennium (to last nine years), the next step in the preparation for Poland's Millennium of Christianity.

August 26, 1956
In Częstochowa, on the feast of Our Lady of Jasna Góra, Bishop Klepacz, acting head of the Polish Bishops' Conference, presents the Primate's draft of the National Vows of the Polish Millennium.

October 28, 1956
After representatives of the government promise to restore basic rights to the Church and to redress wrongs, the Primate returns to Warsaw at the request of the authorities and resumes all his Church functions.

A FREEDOM WITHIN

I

THE
ARREST

September 25, 1953, Friday

Warsaw. Today is the feast of the Patron of our Capital, Blessed Władysław (Ladislaus) of Gielniów. At seven in the morning I was in the chapel of the Archdiocesan (Metropolitan) Seminary with the seminarians who are about to inaugurate the new academic year officially. I offered Mass and remained at the altar to address them. I spoke about the pedagogical value of truth in life. After breakfast, in the company of the priest-professors, I went to attend the inauguration ceremonies. The rector, Bishop Antoni Pawłowski, spoke. My own speech concluded the convocation. Immediately following the inauguration, another meeting—that of the delegates of the Department for Priestly Vocations—took place. I listened to their annual report, indicated the general outline of work for the coming year, and bade farewell to all present in order to get home early.

For two hours after lunch I worked on my sermon for that evening in honor of Blessed Władysław, the Patron of our Capital. There is so little historical material available about him. The theme of the sermon was "the interior truth of a person of God." I wanted to condemn the pompous and officious kind of religiosity that renders such great harm to the glory of God, to the good of our neighbors, and to the good of souls. This modest monk, whose life was so little known, may seem to the active and carefree people of Warsaw quite unappealing as a patron of our Capital—it's like a competition between a saint and a mermaid. And yet the life of this saintly man is more relevant than the Mermaid.* Life is superior to legend. Because in life there is truth. My reflections went along these lines, and these were the thoughts I expressed in my sermon at St. Anne's.†

A large crowd of the faithful gathered; the church had never been quite this full. Nor had it ever been quite as hot at St. Anne's as today. But the people of Warsaw know how to listen. The silence was exemplary. After Mass I blessed the people with the Patron's relics.

At the stairway leading to the rector's quarters I was stopped by a group of scholars and devotedly pious women.‡ I asked them to pray: "Say the rosary. You know Michelangelo's 'Last Judgment'? God's Angel pulls man out of the abyss on a rosary. Say the rosary for my intention." With these words I bade the little group farewell.

This time I remained somewhat longer with the group of priests who had gathered upstairs for a modest supper with the rector, Father Zbigniew Kaminski. At 9:30 P.M. I left the church compound. A rather large group of people still waited next to the car. Someone started cheering, another quieted him down, warning against some type of provocation. Since I had often asked the faithful not to cheer me, the request was heeded as an expression of fear of provocation. The people still remember the sad experience of Father Padacz§ after similar cheering.

---

*The sword-wielding Mermaid has been the official emblem of Poland's capital, Warsaw, for almost four hundred years. The original is located near the Place of Victory, across from the Great Theater, in downtown Warsaw.
†St. Anne's Church is located at the southeastern fringe of downtown Warsaw, near the Column of Zygmunt and the Warsaw Cathedral, and is famous for its spiritual service to the academic community.
‡Literally, "women of the Gospels"—a Polish allusion to the women who are mentioned in Saint John's Gospel as waiting on Christ.
§Fr. Władysław Padacz, student chaplain at St. Anne's, who once delivered an especially inspiring sermon after which he received a tumultuous ovation outside the church. He was arrested and detained for extensive interrogations. The matter eventually was dropped.

Soon we were home on Miodowa Street.* I gave Antoni† his instructions for tomorrow. I met no one at the entrance to the house. I went upstairs and immediately went to bed.

About half an hour later I heard footsteps coming toward my rooms. It was Father Goździewicz.‡ He reported that some gentlemen had arrived with a letter from Minister Bida§ to Bishop Baraniak,‖ and they asked that the gate be opened.

I expressed surprise: "At this hour?" And I added, "Besides, please tell them that any letters from Minister Bida are forwarded to the secretary of the Episcopate, Bishop Choromański.¶ This visit puzzles me because Minister Bida knows perfectly well to whom the letters are to be directed." With some apprehension, I got up and dressed.

Indeed, several people stood at the gate rattling the handle. Father Goździewicz returned after conveying my response to the belated delegation through Mr. Cabanek.**

Now I knew very well who was paying us a visit. I went downstairs and told [the residence staff] to open the gate. Precisely at that moment Bishop Baraniak entered from the garden, led in by a group of people who poured into the Hall of Popes.*** "These gentlemen," said the bishop, "were about to fire."

"That's too bad," I replied. "If they had, we would have known

---

*In Poland the reference "Miodowa" is used to designate the Primate's residence, which is located at 17–19 Miodowa Street. Thus, in the memoirs "Miodowa" always refers to his residence.
†Antoni refers to Chauffeur Antoni Jędrzejczak.
‡Fr. Hieronim (Jerome) Goździewicz was chief secretary of the Primate's staff.
§Minister Antoni Bida was in charge of internal security in Poland. Polish police responsibilities belong to the Ministry of Internal Affairs—Ministerstwo Spraw Wewnętrznych. One section of this Ministry is Urząd Bezpieczeństwa or UB— Security Police—with national headquarters in Warsaw and a local headquarters in each voivodship. The UB is politically oriented and is interested in ideological adversaries. Its agents are usually not uniformed. Milicja Obywatelska or MO— Citizens Police—are uniformed police for nonideological affairs.
‖Bishop Antoni Baraniak was the Primate's personal secretary.
¶Bishop Zygmunt Choromański was auxiliary bishop of Warsaw and secretary of the Polish Episcopate.
**Mr. Jan Cabanek, porter on Miodowa Street.
***So called because of the portraits of Popes that hung there.

that they were housebreakers; as it is, we do not know what to think of this nighttime intrusion." One of the gentlemen explained that they had come on official business and that they were surprised that no one would unlock the gate. I answered, "Our official hours of duty are during the day, and then both the gates and the doors are open. The residence is not open now."

"But the government has a right," retorted the gentleman, "to confer with its citizens whenever it wants." I explained that the government also has the responsibility of acting properly toward its citizens, especially those who are known to be always available.

I went outside to find Mr. Cabanek, because none of the priests was around. But our dog Baca* attacked one of the men who was walking behind me and injured him. So I returned to the foyer to tend to his wound. Sister Maksencja† brought iodine. I assured the wounded man that the dog was not rabid. Bishop Baraniak came in; three men entered through the front gate, and we all went to the Hall of Popes. One of the new arrivals complained officially that the gates had not been opened promptly for the government authorities. I explained that at this point I still did not know whether I was dealing with government officials or with housebreakers. "We are living here in this desolation," I said, "amid ruins and rubble, and therefore we do not let anybody in at night."‡ All the more so since our visitors at the gate tonight opened the proceedings with a lie.

Finally, it all became clear. One of the gentlemen took off his coat, took a letter out of his briefcase, and handed me the document containing yesterday's decision of the government.§ As a result of this decision, I am to be removed immediately from this city. I will not be allowed to perform any duties connected with any of my current positions. He asked me to acknowledge this and sign the document. I stated that I could not acknowledge it, because I saw no

---

*A mongrel house dog that the Primate had once picked up on the street and brought home.
†A nurse and member of the house staff.
‡The cardinal here alludes to the destruction of Warsaw during the Second World War, the effects of which were still evident in 1953.
§The warrant to arrest Cardinal Wyszynki for "anti-government" activities.

legal basis for the decision. And I added that I could not obey the decision because of the way in which the matter was being handled. Representatives of the government—Mr. Mazur* as well as President Bierut†—have had many, many conversations with me. If they were dissatisfied with my conduct, they knew the proper way to tell me about it. The government's decision was most detrimental to Poland's image abroad, for it would open the way for attacks by foreign propaganda. "I cannot go along with this decision," I said, "and I will not leave the residence voluntarily."

The official asked me to append my signature to a statement that I had read the letter. With his pen I wrote at the bottom of the page, "I have read the above," and I initialed it.

I walked upstairs; several of the men followed. The house was full of people, downstairs as well as in front of the chapel. In my private quarters I was told to take with me whatever I needed. I said I had no intention of taking anything. One of the officials started to explain that life has its needs. To this I replied, "Such needs are met by everyone in his own home."

I tried again to protest against the invasion of my home in the middle of the night. The official continued to insist that I collect my things. Sister Maksencja arrived and joined in these attempts at persuasion. I replied, "Sister, I'm taking nothing. I was poor when I came to this house, and I shall leave it poor. You too have taken the vow of poverty, so you should know what it means."

The men grew fidgety. One of them took the suitcases and went into the bedroom.

They brought Bishop Baraniak. They asked me, "Who is in charge here?" I answered, "I don't know whom you are taking away. In my absence Bishop Baraniak is always in charge."

I attested to the bishop that what he was witnessing I considered a violation. I requested that no one take up my defense. In case there

---

*Marshal Franciszek Mazur was head of the government delegation to the Joint Commission (a group of representatives of the government and the Church) and responsible for Church-State affairs.
†Bolesław Bierut, President of Poland from 1945 to 1953.

was a trial, I did not want any lawyers. I would conduct my own defense. Bishop Baraniak left. I remained in my study for quite some time, putting my books in order. Finally one of the men suggested that we move to the reception room.

We crossed over to the other side of the house. Here I was able to collect some papers and lay them inside the cabinet. I noticed several new ones, ready for my signature; I signed them and placed them in the customary place. From that moment on I did not see any of my household staff. I did not see either Father Goździewicz or Father Padacz.

The police brought me my hat and coat. I took my breviary and my rosary. They suggested that I go to my private quarters. I returned to my study. They asked me whether I had taken everything. Once again I protested against this violation, I was taking nothing, I had my breviary and my rosary. We entered the hall. I wanted to stop at the chapel, but the representative of the government imposed a condition: "As long as you don't put up any resistance. Why should we have to fight?" I did not accept this condition. I stopped for a moment in the chapel to glance at the tabernacle and at the Mother of God—in the stained glass window. We went downstairs. At the door I glanced again at the painting of Our Lady of Jasna Góra,* hanging over the entrance to the Hall of Popes.

I repeated my protest and walked to the car. Three men entered the car with me. I do not know exactly what time it was when we drove away from the gates of Miodowa Street. In any event, it was certainly after midnight.

The car turned into Długa Street; we were surrounded by six other ones. The whole caravan continued on by the Mostowski palace, the East-West Highway, over the Śląsko-Dąbrowski bridge and Zygmuntowska Street, in the direction of Jabłonna. The road led toward Nowy Dwór (Mazowiecki), Dobrzyń nad Drwęcą, and Grudziądz. Along the way I was unable to read any road signs. It

---

*A reference to the famous miraculous image of Our Lady of Częstochowa (the "Black Madonna"), housed in a monastery on Jasna Góra ("Bright Mountain") in the city of Częstochowa.

7

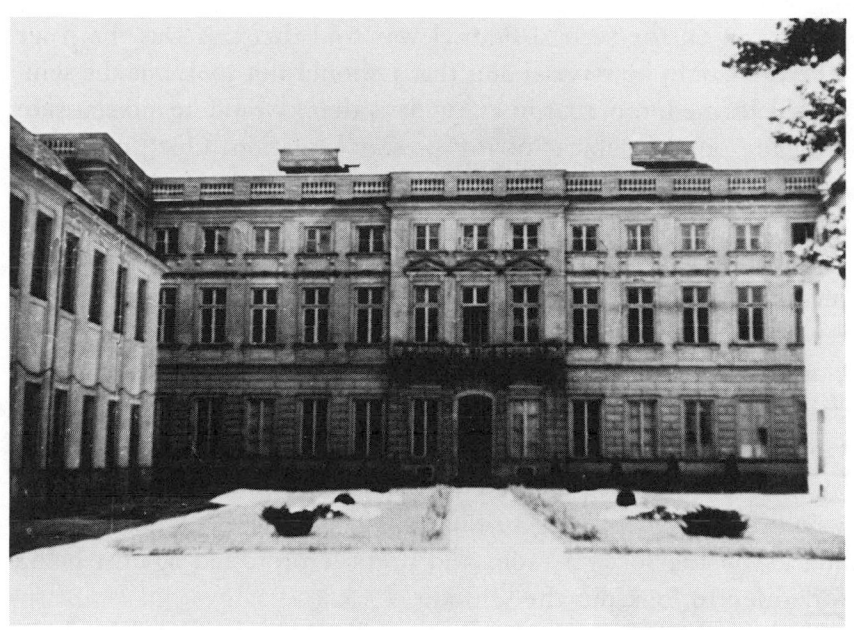

*Wyszyński's archiepiscopal residence on
Miodowa Street, Warsaw. It was from here
that the cardinal was taken to his first place of
internment, Rywałd, on September 25, 1953.*

was almost dawn when we stopped at the northern outskirts of
Grudziądz. After a short stop, we turned in the direction of
Jabłonowo. People were just going to work. We made our way back
to Rywałd, which we had passed earlier. This was my destination.
We drove into the empty farmyard of the Capuchin Fathers' friary.
I waited in the car for quite a long time before the "Man in the
Raincoat"* invited me to come inside the ugly building. I was led

---

*A derogatory metaphor for a member of the secret police, who always wore
raincoats and never identified themselves by name.

to a room on the second floor. I was told that this was the place where I would be staying and that I should not look out the window. I learned, too, that in a few days there would be a discussion with me on the subject of my present situation. Once more my escort heard my precisely formulated position relative to what had taken place.

I protested to him against the coercion that was used, against their methods of dealing with a citizen whom the government could have reached by other means, in accordance with the principles of the Constitution. I protested against rendering it impossible for me to direct the Gniezno and Warsaw dioceses.* I protested against the violation of the jurisdiction of the Holy See, which I was exercising by special authority. I pointed out that the action of the government would be very damaging to the country, because it would lead to attacks by the foreign radio and press. I protested against being forbidden to look out the window.

I glanced around my room, which showed signs of having been recently lived in by one of the Capuchin Fathers.

I was alone. On the wall over the bed hung a picture with the inscription: "Our Lady of Rywałd, comfort the distressed." This was the first friendly sign, and it brought me great joy. After all, what happened was that with which I had been so often threatened: *pro nomine Jesu contumelias pati* [to suffer abuse for the name of Jesus]. I had feared that I would never share this honor, which had befallen all my seminary colleagues. They had all experienced concentration camps and prisons. The majority of them had lost their

---

*Stefan Cardinal Wyszyński held the office of archbishop of Gniezno and Warsaw. "Cardinal" is simply a title (which is why the word appears in the middle of the name instead of at the beginning). Cardinals have certain special duties by virtue of holding that rank—they advise the Pope in council (the College of Cardinals, analogous to the House of Lords) and elect a new pontiff when the old one dies —but essentially elevating a churchman to the cardinalate is the ecclesiastical equivalent of granting a layman a patent of nobility. A "Primate" is a term for a cardinal with the honorary right of precedence over other cardinals in his country. Thus, though a prince of the Church and the foremost churchman of Poland, Wyszyński was actually responsible only for jurisdiction over his two archdioceses of Gniezno and Warsaw.

The abandoned friary of the Capuchin Fathers at Rywałd. Wyszyński's cell was the second window from the left on the second floor.

lives there; several returned as invalids, and one died after a term in a Polish prison.

Thus the prophecy given to us in the spring of 1920 by Father Antoni Bogdański, our professor of liturgy and the director of the Minor Seminary in Włocławek, was partially fulfilled. One day during a lecture in liturgy, this unforgettable man said to us, "There will come a time when you will endure sufferings the likes of which a man of our age cannot even imagine . Many priests will have nails hammered into their tonsures, many will suffer in prison. . . ." Not many of my colleagues remembered these words, but they penetrated deep into my soul. When in 1939 I visited Father Bogdański at his deathbed in Skulsk, I remembered these words. He told me then to prepare for the heavy and responsible road that awaited me in the priesthood. The eyes of the dying man blazed with a strange light. At our first seminary class reunion after the war, I reminded my colleagues about his words, but the survivors did not give the impression that they remembered.

My colleagues deserve at least a brief mention. They received Holy Orders from Bishop Stanisław Zdzitowiecki in the Cathedral Basilica in Włocławek on June 29, 1924. There were seventeen of us in the class, although not all were there to receive Holy Orders, since two had already gone to Lille to study, and I found myself in the hospital with a lung ailment. One of our colleagues, Father Konstanty Janic, had died of tuberculosis before the war. The following died at Dachau: Father Stanisław Michniewski, Father Julian Konieczny, Father Jan Mikusiński, Father Jan Fijałkowski, Father Zygmunt Lankiewicz, Father Bronisław Placek, and Father Stanisław Ogłaza.

Those who returned from the concentration camps: Father Józef Dunaj, our class leader, Father Stefan Kołodziejski, Father Wojciech Wolski, Father Marian Sawicki, Father Antoni Kardyński, and Father Antoni Samulski. I alone escaped the fate of the concentration camp, only because, at the order of Bishop Michał Kozal, I left Włocławek several days before the second roundup of the clergy. Those who did survive the concentration camps are practically invalids. Father Kardyński was used as a guinea pig, and long remained ill from inoculations given him there.* Father Antoni Samulski landed in a Polish prison for his work as the director of Caritast in the Wrocław diocese and came out in such poor health that it was impossible to save him.

---

*In concentration camps during World War II, prisoners were inoculated with pus and other purulent substances.

†After World War II, Caritas was the organization through which the Church supported and conducted its charitable work. In 1950, without the consent of the Episcopal Conference, the government confiscated all Caritas properties and assumed and funded its work independently of the Church.

"*On the wall over the bed hung a picture with the inscription: 'Our Lady of Rywałd, comfort the distressed.' This was the first friendly sign, and it brought me great joy.*"

And this is the story of just one class of Polish priests in the twentieth century. My brother Tadeusz had his share of camps and prisons: Soviet, German, and Polish. Most of the priests and bishops with whom I worked had experienced prisons. Something would have been wrong if I had not experienced imprisonment. What was happening to me was very appropriate.

Jesus called Judas "my friend." I could not harbor a grudge against these men who were my keepers and who had been rather polite to me, really. In a way, they had only facilitated the inevitable, which was obvious to everyone. I would have to appreciate all that was happening to me at their hands.

II

RYWAŁD

September 26, 1953, Saturday

I arrived here, I might say, directly from the pulpit of St. Anne's, under the banner of the Patron of Warsaw, Blessed Władysław.

Today is Saturday—a day when I customarily offer Mass in honor of Our Lady of Jasna Góra. This morning, for the first time in many, many years, Our Lady will not receive her Saturday Mass.

I looked at my desk in the cell. There was the *Merciful Christ*, a copy of a well-known painting, with the inscription "Jesus, I trust in Thee." I acknowledged this as the second blessing of this day. I placed myself under the protection of Him in Whose cause I find myself here. A picture of Saint Francis of Assisi listening to the music of an angel and a painting of a laughing musician in an open shirt were also on the desk. That was all.

I received my meal, said my breviary, put my room in order. The room to which they had brought me gave the impression of a place vacated in a hurry. The bed had not been made, and the personal belongings of the friar who had lived here were left behind. Among these belongings—a half-opened suitcase, with a recent copy of the publication *Kuźnica Kapłańska* [Priestly Forge], the subscriber's name on the cover. All the furniture was in a state of ruin: the desk "hanging on to the wall," the same with the bedside table; the washbasin still full of water; the wardrobe still containing garments and other personal belongings; on the floor a stack of books covered with a piece of paper. The floor was dirty, the corners full of dust balls. A typical monk's cell where the housekeeping is done by someone with more important matters on his mind. Two windows in the room faced the farmyard full of chickens, ducks, and turkeys, a barn with cows visible through the half-open gates. All deserted, not a living soul. In the hall young men in civilian clothes wandered about.

In the evening they brought me a suitcase with personal belongings, which had been taken from Miodowa Street on their own initiative, and some bedding. Inside were clothes and some minimal toiletries.

The friary at Rywałd had been converted to a prison. The first floor was entirely uninhabited. The X indicates Wyszyński's cell.

September 27, 1953, Sunday

I offered a *missa sicca* ["dry" Mass]* in my room. I asked the Man in the Raincoat if I would be able to go to church to offer Mass as I am obliged to do as the diocesan ordinary. I was told that it would be impossible. Today I was to conduct the visitation of the parish of the Holy Cross in Warsaw. I was concerned that one of the bishops should take my place. This was truly a "Holy Cross." Until now I had never missed a scheduled visit. I felt sorry for the Fathers of the Congregation of the Mission who had prepared themselves so diligently for this visitation.

I spent the entire day in my room. Many thoughts flooded my mind; they had to. I needed to accept them calmly and evaluate them honestly.

Was what had happened inevitable? Was it my fault? Was it to the detriment of the Church?

I reviewed the entire five years of my work as Primate of Poland and leader of church affairs. First, one *a priori*. From the outset everyone had prepared me to be a victim of circumstance. As I was entering the first parish church of my archdiocese en route to my installation as archbishop of Gniezno—the parish church in Toruń in Podgórze—the parishioners gave me a painting of Christ with hands bound, a soldier holding him by the shoulder. I hung this painting in my study in Gniezno. The picture became a symbol, although not my plan of action. In almost all of the installation addresses this was the transcending symbol.

From the very beginning everyone seemed to cry over me. My father was definitely concerned about my future destiny, and my sisters were as well. In my household, my impending arrest seemed so certain that even the chauffeur was on the lookout for a new job.

One day one of the young priests came to visit me and told me that before his death Father Korniłowicz† had told him to come. He told me about a dream that the father had had during the days of

*A term used to describe the recitation of the Mass prayers without the use of bread, wine, or water. The cardinal used this form because he had none of the elements required for the offering of the usual Mass.
†Fr. Władysław Korniłowicz had been the spiritual director of the Primate.

my consecration ceremonies. The dream foretold for me a fate similar to that of the bishop of Kraków.* Only the fear of my reaction had kept him from coming sooner. But on that day in 1949 he felt he could withhold the truth no longer. I listened calmly to his story about the dream; I thanked him, calmed him down, and told him I was ready for anything—and we parted.

The bishops, too, thought that I would end up in prison. One of

The friary at Rywałd from a distance.

*A reference to Saint Stanislaus, bishop and martyr, who was born in Szczepanów in Poland around the year 1030. He courageously rebuked King Bolesław (Boleslaus) for his immoralities and injustices and was put to death by the King's men while offering Mass in 1079. The King later repented.

the bishops presented me with the book Father Klimkiewicz had written about Cardinal Ledóchowski,* saying: "You would do well to read this book, it might come in handy." There were bishops who expected disaster at any moment.

The Holy See also seriously considered this possibility—and that rather sooner than later. I could sense this in every document that delineated my special powers.

Many of the priests were so convinced of the inevitability of such an eventuality that they requested a quick settlement of their affairs or a confirmation in writing of any verbal decisions of mine. The requests were clearly motivated by the fear that I might soon be unavailable. I encountered this attitude very often on all levels of the Church hierarchy.

Even the nation expected such a moment. Some people were obviously disappointed that it had not yet happened. Many rumors had been repeated with almost periodic regularity. Who was spreading them and for what reason I do not know. On numerous occasions, I entered a church to find the congregation crying.

There was universal agreement that I was predestined to go to prison, and it was in such an atmosphere that I had to do my pastoral work. Did I succumb to it? Subjectively, I was ready for anything. Objectively, however, I decided to work toward making such an occurrence—if it had to happen at all—come as late as possible.

Many a time government circles had accused me of wanting to become a martyr. The desire was far from my mind, although I did not exclude the possibility. From the very beginning of my work, I had taken the stand that the Church in Poland had already shed too much blood in German concentration camps to afford to squander the lives of its surviving priests. Martyrdom is undoubtedly an honorable thing, but God leads His Church not only along

---

*Klimkiewicz, Witold. *Kardynał Ledóchowski na Tle Swej Epoki: 1822–1902 (Cardinal Ledóchowski and His Times: 1822–1902)*. Mieczysław Ledóchowski, a count, archbishop of Poznań and Gniezno (1866–1886), who was imprisoned by the Prussians (1874–1876) for his opposition to the May laws during the Kulturkampf. He was named a cardinal in 1875 and served as the prefect of propaganda at the Vatican from 1892 to 1902.

an extraordinary way, that of martyrdom, but also along an ordinary one, that of apostolic work. Indeed, I was of the opinion that the modern world needed another kind of martyrdom—the martyrdom of work, not of blood. The extent to which I am convinced of this even today is proved by the fact that I communicated this message to the clergy at every opportunity. I had also presented this principle to the Pope* and to Monsignor Tardini† in Rome as the guiding thought for the Church in Poland.

I had arrived in Warsaw with an outline of a program, not fully completed and clarified. But I was not too far from beginning with a visit to the president of the country. The way in which I was treated from the very beginning—police harassment during the installation in Gniezno, the attitude of the press, and the like—led me to assume a vigilant attitude.

Nevertheless, from the very first weeks, I began to acquaint the bishops with the outline of my program. I wanted at all cost to create a permanent intermediary body between the Episcopate and the government. This later came into existence in the form of the Joint Commission. From this point the Joint Commission became a permanent element in my work. It met rather frequently. Before each meeting the bishops on the commission would meet with me for preliminary discussions; at the formal meetings of the commission, they would present matters already decided upon among us. After a Joint Commission meeting, there would be a reporting session from which would result dictated minutes. And so a huge portfolio of recorded minutes resulted—rich material for future historians.

In time, the Joint Commission assumed a special character and became involved with the text of the "Mutual Understanding." We had been working on it methodically since July of 1949—that is, just a few months after I had taken over the leadership of Church affairs.

Nothing discouraged us, not even the fact that the government, as if disregarding the opinions of its representatives in the Joint

---

*Pope Pius XII.
†Monsignor Dominici Tardini was Under-Secretary of State under Pius XII in 1953.

Commission, made many decisions without the knowledge of the commission, which was simply surprised with the accomplished facts. We protested, but did not suspend the work already in progress. The bishops had a general directive: we do not interrupt our dialogue with you. Very often, however, it would happen that the head of the Joint Commission, Mr. Mazur, would not call a meeting of the commission for months at a time, and there was no way to establish contact.

This day, after I had been pointedly accused of working against the Mutual Understanding, I must declare that—looking at it from the point of view of the Episcopate*—the Mutual Understanding would probably never have come into being if it had not been for the position that I took. Even Bishop Klepacz, the most consistent proponent of this line, sometimes departed from it. That's the way it was at the last moment, in Kraków, several weeks before the signing of the Mutual Understanding. So if the Episcopate should ever be accused of promoting the Mutual Understanding, truth demands that it be known I was the person responsible for the Mutual Understanding on the side of the Church.

Why did I work toward the Mutual Understanding? From the very beginning, I was and continued to be of the opinion that Poland, like the Church, had lost too much blood during the German occupation to be able to afford to shed any more. It was necessary at any and all cost to stop this process of spiritual bloodshed and return to a normal life so indispensable in the development of the country and the Church. To return to the simple, ordinary life—such a rarity in Poland.

The Church in Poland, after 150 years of bondage and limited activity,† had had less than twenty years of freedom. Hitler's occupation came as a terrible blow to work that had scarcely begun. We were still trying to cope with the backlog and had just started

---

*The Episcopate is the entire body of bishops of the country, collectively. Such terms as "Episcopal Conference" and "Episcopacy" also refer to various activities of the (Roman Catholic) bishops.
†That is, the years of Poland's partition among her powerful neighbors, Russia, Prussia, and Austria, 1772–1918.

mustering our forces. The religious seminaries had just acquired new, young professors; the departments of theology were starting to fill their faculty needs; Church publications had just finished training their personnel; Catholic periodicals had just been able to set up their workshops. Churches had just been rebuilt and restored, new parishes were organized, new Catholic schools were erected.

The clergy, even though it had clearly made progress in its working methods, still proceeded along its own old or borrowed patterns. Polish pastoral theology* had not yet been developed. In every aspect, we were still very young. And the war broke out just as we were preparing for a giant creative leap. All of our newly built strength was destroyed, seminaries were forced to interrupt their work, many dioceses stopped ordaining priests.

There was also daily the dismal news from concentration camps and prisons about the campaign to annihilate the clergy. We emerged from the war scarred—barely alive. It would have been unwise not to realize the gravity of the situation. We had no foreign models to look to either, because no nation—neither Czechoslovakia nor Hungary nor even Catholic Germany—had lost as many clergymen as Poland. To be sure, God has the right, always, to demand any sacrifice; the Polish clergy had proved that it was capable of answering God's new demands and would not refuse to sacrifice. Many of the priests who survived Hitler's camps found themselves in prisons again. It was up to the authorities in the Episcopate to conduct the affairs of the Church, in the context of the "Polish reality," in such a way as to spare the Church any new losses. All the more so because we could expect these to be merely the *initia dolorum* [the first of our sorrows]. The whole development of social change was certain to produce conflict: Christianity versus Godlessness. But to make certain that such a conflict would not find us unprepared, we had to gain time and build up strength to defend God's positions.

This is how reality appeared from the Church's point of view. From that of the government of the People's Republic of Poland,

---

*A branch of theology which is devoted to spiritual instruction of lay parishioners, sometimes called the science of the care of souls.

it seemed that, for reasons one could only try to surmise, the government *did* want a Mutual Understanding. This certainly would have been much easier to achieve had the government not broken the Concordat.* But after such a fit of Party demagoguery, there must have been certain considerations, perhaps strategic and tactical, that made it advisable to strive for a Mutual Understanding. We could surely mistrust them; the government, with its previously grim record in dealing with the Church, warranted such mistrust. This made things even more difficult for a Mutual Understanding, because if the Church mistrusted, so did the rest of society. Experience had shown, however, that the Church never said no whenever there existed even a possibility of peace or agreement. Even after the worst persecutions—in France or in Bismarck's Germany or in Mexico or Spain—an armistice followed. History gives us many excellent examples of Concordats and provides many possibilities and alternatives.

During the endless debates on the chances for reaching some kind of agreement, I was always mindful that this would not be an agreement between the government and the Church, because the Episcopate had no power to conclude such an agreement. So-called *causae maiores* [more important matters] are reserved to the Holy See. This was not, in fact, a question of a concordat or a mutual agreement *(accordo);* the term "mutual understanding" came up at the last moment. It was simply a question of finding a modus vivendi between the Episcopate and the government. It seemed to me possible, as well as indispensable, to establish several points in such a modus vivendi if the Church was to avoid a new—and perhaps accelerated and drastic—annihilation.

And so, the Mutual Understanding would be the buffer that could work to ease the growing conflict. Both yes and no! Such a decision was bound to be influenced by the method of reasoning,

---

*In 1925, the Polish government signed an agreement with the Vatican covering the jurisdiction of bishops, the rights of Church and State in carrying out religious education, division of authority between lay officers and clerics within the country, and other matters. Soon after coming to power, the Polish Communist government denounced this Concordat.

which flows from the spiritual makeup of the person taking on the responsibility. His reasoning process could be flawed, resulting in errors for which he would be held accountable. History will determine the degree of its imperfection. At any rate, when the decision had to be made and the Polish Episcopate stood undecided, I cast my own mental formulation, with its characteristics and deficiencies, onto the scale of discussion. And this formulation proved crucial—especially during the conference of the Episcopate in Kraków, in the presence of Cardinal Sapieha—to the decision that the Mutual Understanding had to be effected. Although an understanding of the realities was a deciding factor, the spiritual formation which the Church gives provided the proper atmosphere to the matter and was that additional, necessary ingredient.

It is a fact that the Church instructs us in the spirit of cooperation and social peace. The Gospel as well as Thomistic philosophy, the social philosophy and public law of the Church, Catholic teaching about government and authority, and finally general sociology or socioeconomic ethics, together with the social encyclicals—the collective weight of these disciplines, after many years of study, instills in each Church member an intellectual and moral foundation with a strong social consciousness. Such a foundation was undoubtedly my inheritance, too, and had to be an important factor in the efforts of searching for peaceful solutions. I was not opportunistic, I did not play politics, I did not play merely to survive. I believed that a compromise in the relationship was absolutely necessary, just as it was inevitable that this country with a Catholic viewpoint must coexist with its official materialism.

It could be seen that we were not standing on the same ground. While we negotiated from a position of principle, the other side was politicking, playing a tactical game, striving to compromise the Church—as was often said by our opponents in society. Even if one believed the assurances from government representatives to the Joint Commission discussing the Mutual Understanding—that they intended to live by their agreements—one still had to concede, as the more cautious maintained, that the positions of the two sides were not equal. But if one followed these basic teachings of the Church, one could not say: We do not want an agreement. Because the Church always wants to enter into an agreement, even when it is necessary to make concessions, as is evidenced by the history of Concordats. All the more because the text of the Mutual Understanding did not contain any legal privileges for the government; in Canon Law such privileges may be granted only by the Holy See. The Mutual Understanding was nothing more than a guarantee of mutual security in our coexistence. The Polish Episcopate could not have said no.

We did deliberate as to how the situation of the Church would appear if the Polish Episcopate said it wanted no Mutual Understanding. Since the government rejected the Concordat and did not recognize the Code of Canon Law or the Church Constitution, the resulting legal situation would have made it exceedingly difficult to avoid run-ins. The experience of several years of the Mutual Understanding proved to be useful, even though the agreement was not always effective, because it did tie the government's hands [to some extent] and restrained any programmed annihilation of the Church. Looking at it ex post, we could agree that as far as public opinion was concerned, the government had chained its own hands with regard to the Church. First, the government's program to destroy Church institutions did let up; and when the government had to speed up that program, it was obliged to cover up its actions as much as possible, so as not to appear in the eyes of public opinion as the violator of the Mutual Understanding.

In closely studying the historical development of the October Revolution,* I noticed that the tactical approach to religion underwent changes by exhibiting a certain flexibility. The original brutality of the trials,† the museums of atheism, the closing of Orthodox churches, the robbing of sacred art—these methods broke down and

---

*In the U.S.S.R., 1917.
†The Russian Orthodox Church had been disestablished by the Kerensky (provisional) government in early 1917. After the Bolsheviks took over, they inaugurated a campaign of direct suppression. Church property was confiscated or heavily taxed, religious education was prohibited, divine services were closely restricted, and prominent church leaders (lay and clerical) were exiled or put to death. Priests were often subjected to severe mistreatment—kicking, beating, and other physical abuse.

gave way to the Dimitrov method.* And when the Great National War† came, the government of the U.S.S.R. entered into a "secret agreement" with the Orthodox church. Of course, this "agreement" was made when it [the government] was in extremis; nevertheless, [it proved] that certain forces still existed in the country that could insist on such an agreement. This evolution shows that any form of government, no matter how ruthless, will slowly cool and wane as it runs up against difficulties that the bureaucrat cannot resolve without cooperation from the people. Somehow the people must be taken into account. It was possible, therefore, to expect that in our native experiment, which is not too original a copy of the Soviet model, such an evolution would be possible. In fact, even the very point of departure indicated this type of evolution. Societies in the West, who know the Bolshevik experiment in light of Archbishop Cieplak's‡ trial, are not aware of this evolution. Certainly in the trial of Cardinal Mindszenty,§ Europe was shown that everything was possible. But, after all, that was an experiment to test the atmosphere of Christian Europe.

---

*Gheorghi Dimitrov, first Secretary of the Communist Party in Bulgaria, whose method was especially duplicitous. He adapted Russian directives to situations in such a way that he was able to satisfy both the Russians and the Bulgarians.
†World War II.
‡Jan Chrzciciel Cieplak (1857–1926). After his consecration as bishop in 1908, he was appointed head of the Latin Rite diocese of Mogilev, the largest in the world, covering all of European and Asiatic Russia, and Catholic Primate of Russia. He visited Siberia in 1909, the first Latin Rite bishop ever to do so. On April 1, 1920, he was arrested by the Russian Communists for "antigovernment activities" (insisting on the rights of the Church); he was arrested again in 1922. After his third arrest in 1923, his trial lasted five days and ended in the death sentence. He remained in Butyrki prison (Russian prison for those sentenced to death) for eleven months. World protests resulted in a commutation of his death sentence to ten years in prison, and in 1924 he was set free. He returned to Poland, journeyed to Rome, and from there to the United States in November 1925. He died in Passaic, New Jersey, on February 17, 1926, of pneumonia and influenza.
§József Cardinal Mindszenty (1892–1975) was bishop of Veszprém in 1944 when he was imprisoned by the Fascists. He was archbishop of Esztergom and Primate of Hungary (1945) when he was arrested by the Communists and sentenced to life imprisonment. He was freed from custody by the Hungarian insurrectionists in 1956 and given asylum in the American Embassy in Budapest, where he remained a virtual prisoner for fifteen years. President Nixon persuaded him to leave, and he died in exile in Vienna in 1975.

This careful study of the development of methods of war against religion led me to believe that in Poland things could be different from those in the U.S.S.R., or in Hungary or in Czechoslovakia. At any rate, the constitutions of democratic countries in Eastern Europe,* especially that of East Germany, demonstrated that the legal aspect of these problems could look different from country to country. We know that the Catholic Church is in a much better position in Protestant East Germany than in Catholic Poland. Assuming, then, the unequal position of the two sides, assuming the atavistic nature of the lies with which the negotiating tactics of the other side are burdened, assuming the inconsistency of the behavioral patterns and the evolution of the methods applied, I was justified in expecting that the Polish experiment would turn out differently and could be approached boldly.

It was also a question of the restructuring of the entire program of socioeconomic changes, which we could not ignore before we made our decision. I was convinced that this program had a lengthy future before it and to some degree could be realized. Together with many others who long have fought for social justice in Poland, I came to consider that altering the socioeconomic structure was a must. I was not certain what kind of socioeconomic structure Poland needed. I did know that some kind of structure existed, that it could not last, and that social stability—that condition for internal freedom—required economic changes. A tremendous amount of energy of social forces had already been used to restructure the system, and in this effort there was no lack of encouragement and direction on the part of the Church. Indeed, it is not true that the Church did nothing in this respect, as is claimed by the "progressive social Catholics"; certainly, the Church did not become the patron of the revolution, but it achieved a tremendous liberation of conscience, providing people with the freedom to fight for a just social system. This was a psychological break, that drawing of fresh air into the lungs, for the beginning of a better future.

---

*The socialist countries of the Eastern bloc like to refer to themselves as democratic countries.

Poland had no shortage of social forces—among the clergy as well as among lay Catholics—that were spiritually prepared to rebuild the system. These forces were not altogether opposed to socialist aims, although the atheism that socialism spawned was here a harmful hindrance. Had it not been for this narrow atheism, which often carried it to the brink of religious war, Polish society, with its cultural, historically democratic tendencies, would be a most fertile field for a wise government to work with. Of course, this government would have to be free of demagoguery; it would need to be eminently social-minded and independent of outside pressures that would make it unpopular with the people who would have to make the sacrifices. I am not exaggerating the liabilities the government faced in rebuilding the socioeconomic system in Poland. It was obvious that these liabilities called for a wise course of action if the program was to produce the intended results. Unfortunately, observation proved how little talent in social work this government had; how very much it relied on political repression and force. This in itself negated a good part of the positive results, since the people, oppressed, stood up in opposition, even against many legitimate goals. If Marxism had come directly from the West, without Eastern intervention, it would undoubtedly have been accepted with greater trust, as prewar Marxism was received in the years 1905 to 1907.

The Polish government had allowed itself many mistakes: an exaggerated disregard for the values and economic achievements of prewar Poland; a lavish praise of Soviet economic achievements; the imposition of Soviet models and Soviet literature; the leaders' ignorance of political life; the wrong appraisal of Poland's socioeconomic reality; the ignorance of the psychological makeup of the nation; repression; the destruction of a richly developed social life; the liquidation of political parties and free labor unions; and many others. These were the irritating errors which impeded the start of socioeconomic reconstruction. In these circumstances, even the most moderate program could not have been realized without the use of force. Having committed so many blunders, the government understood that its only recourse was force. This "means of reconstruction" is least effective where the goodwill and the cooperation of all levels of society are sorely needed for the common good.

And the government did not refrain from using force. It was obvious that force would eventually become its *only* way of furthering socioeconomic reconstruction. And these blunders continued to accumulate; there were errors in the sphere of moral and religious life, abrogation of the Concordat, attacks on the Holy See, encouragement of loose morality among the young, attacks on the Church —all these must have displeased the people [of Poland], who never had battled with the Church. Even a society that is indifferent to religion is on guard and suspicious in the face of those who initiate religious strife.

Force and violence, used to bring about socioeconomic reconstruction, could make the Church's work impossible. A new work discipline, the proposed *nepreryvka,* * the substitution of a ten-day week for the seven-day week, would be enough to disorganize Church life. The new agricultural policy, the beginnings of which we saw in agricultural cooperatives, the PGRs,† could undermine religious and moral customs in the rural areas. There was danger of making all Church holdings communal property; after the Soviet experience, it was easy enough to predict the results. The Church in the rural districts would be dependent upon the PGRs and the agricultural cooperatives.

It's obvious the road from planning to execution is a long one, but if one has time and power, he can do it. One had to consider such a possibility when weighing an answer to the proposal for the Mutual Understanding. And the Mutual Understanding did ease the economic situation of individual parishes somewhat, and so far the Church had not suffered much in this area.

This was not the most important motive in the decision, but one further along the line.

All of this reasoning, presented at the Kraków Conference of the Episcopate (March 1950) in the presence of Cardinal Sapieha, led to

---

*A Russian word ("uninterrupted") used to designate a period of ten days of work without a break to substitute for the traditional seven-day week with Sunday off. It was modeled on an idea from the French Revolution.
†*Państwowe Gospodarstwa Rolne*—government farm collectives.

these decisions: (1) to work toward a Mutual Understanding; (2) to reedit the draft presented; (3) in any case, to continue the talks with the Joint Commission. On leaving Warsaw for Rome, Cardinal Sapieha was totally aware of this position of the Episcopate and shared its views. The Mutual Understanding, signed April 14, 1950, became from then on an argument on the side of the Episcopate in its struggle for the rights of the Church. It was in fact its only argument, for the government no longer honored the Constitution, broke the Concordat, and did not recognize the Code of Canon Law.

September 28, 1953, Monday
I was visited by the Man in the Raincoat, a tall, handsome man, still young, with an expressionless face. Once again I explained to him my position on the violence committed against me. For someone accustomed to law and order, it is absolutely amazing to think that a citizen's fate may be decided on the basis of a one-sided decision made in that citizen's absence—in violation of the Constitution and of the Mutual Understanding. In its decision, the government did not even make an elementary effort to follow the rules of primitive justice: *audiatur et altera pars* [let the other side be heard]. Since there were accusations, would it not have been simpler to tell me what they were? Maybe this could have avoided the type of action that would lay Poland open to attacks from the whole civilized world.

"You covered my windows with blotting paper so that people would not see the Primate of Poland. But no one will be able to shield these windows from the world; everyone is bound to know where you have imprisoned me."

"An exaggeration," remarked my visitor.

"It is not an exaggeration," I replied, "but a statement of fact that you do not know because you close your eyes to it. The office of the Primate of Poland means more than that of any other hierarch in Eastern Europe; this cannot be changed. The world is interested in the fate of every cardinal—this too cannot be changed. Whoever knows Europe, even a little, realizes that these are not dead issues. One has to be very blind, in dealing with a citizen, to use heavy artillery rather than normal, human speech. I still expect an explanation of this violation."

My visitor promised that in the next four days I would receive an explanation of the situation. He said I would be contacted by representatives of the government who would want to have a talk with me. I expressed my readiness.

After my *missa sicca*, I looked through the stack of books on the floor; among the many sermons and conferences of little value, there were a few which I selected for perusal.

Thus I begin the life of a prisoner. I should not use the word; circumstances around me protest that it is not a prison. And yet I am guarded by close to twenty people—"civilians." They never leave the corridor, day or night; I hear their creaky steps all day. The lighting is poor. One of the young men settles down for the night on a crooked stool by the door and, by the light of a smoking kerosene lamp or altar candles, reads books. In the courtyard there are always several young men who never take their eyes off my windows. Otherwise, they are polite and remain at a distance.

I ask about the possibility of offering Mass. I learn that I will not be able to go to church. In view of this I ask for the things I need to offer Mass in my cell. These can be brought from the neighboring church. I do not get them.

September 30, 1953, Wednesday

Today I received the Church furnishings and liturgical items to celebrate Mass from Miodowa Street. Some are missing: the altar stone, altar wine and hosts, cruets, and missal. They promised to get me some candles. When, before leaving my house, I had expressed the desire to stop at the chapel, the gentleman who had presented me with the government decree told me "there will be a chapel where you are going." He lied, just as did the men at the entrance gate who "had brought a letter from Minister Bida to Bishop Bara-

The corridor of the second floor at Rywałd, where the prisoners were kept.

niak." Obviously, they also lied to the staff at Miodowa Street, who did not know that I had no chapel and therefore sent me only the chalice and the chasuble. I was determined to offer Mass on the rickety desk, which until then had served me as a "dining room" and a "study."

Together with the items for Mass, I also received some books which will help me in my transition to the life of a "student." The list of things sent had been prepared by Father Goździewicz. When I learned this, I became concerned for the fate of Bishop Baraniak; this highly scrupulous and responsible man would certainly have prepared the list himself if he had still been at home.

Among the books brought to me from home I found *The History of the Church* by Seppelt; *The Story of Paul of Tarsus* by Father Dąbrowski; *The Resurrectionists and the Immaculate Conception Sisters* by Father Obertyński; *The Monarchy of Casimir the Great* by Z. Kaczmarczyk; and a little book about the devotion, *Three Hail Marys*, which some unknown priest had distributed in the bishops' quarters during the last retreat at Jasna Góra.

I made the decision to schedule my time in such a way as to avoid any questioning thoughts. And so after Mass (today it was still the *missa sicca*), I began reading several books alternately, so that the variety of subjects would prevent monotony. I found one book in French about Saint Francis—not a large book, but most worthwhile. And another in Italian—a collection of speeches. These two books will serve as my language exercises.

I generally interrupt my reading by saying the Little Hours;* in this way I combine work with prayer. I recite my breviary prayers† walking back and forth in my rather small room, so as to counterbalance the lack of air with exercise. In the evening, when it grows dark —and we have little light—I say the rosary pacing the room. I pray a lot to my patroness, Our Lady of Jasna Góra, for both my dioceses, for the bishops, and for the members of my household.

---

*Prime, Terce, Sext, and None.
†Book of prayers containing the Office or prescribed readings recited daily by every priest.

October 1, 1953, Thursday
This morning I received two tallow candles and two candlesticks
as well as a bottle of Riesling wine. I am able, therefore, to offer Mass
—the first since my abduction from Warsaw.

I am happy that I can begin the month of the rosary* with Mass.
I am grateful that Our Lady has smiled on me in this way. All of
my October Masses I will offer in honor of Our Lady of Jasna Góra.

Today my hands are full, and with them I offer the Father in
Heaven His priestly Son. A priest, after all, must have the Lord right
in his hands, so as to be able to stand before the Father in Heaven.
But he must also have the people with him. The loneliness that a
priest feels in offering the Holy Sacrifice alone is felt as sharply as
the absence of hands. A priest is, after all, intended *pro hominibus* [for
people]. And so, for my solitary Mass I invite all those whom memory can recall, especially those whom I had so often, at every opportunity, encouraged to say the rosary in honor of Our Lady of Jasna
Góra. I know that today I am their greatest trial. I must support
them, so they don't falter. It is so interesting, how close is fear to
unwavering faith. A person who believes very strongly expects to
receive everything from God quickly, and any delay makes him
anxious. It is not lack of faith, but rather surprise that there is
conflict—between the power of God and His goodness. I worry
about those who believe very strongly in the efficacy of prayer.
They should not want too speedy a result from their prayer, and
they should not give up if God's response is slow in coming. I knew
from the outset that my case needs to drag on. God requires it. And
it is not so much "my" case as the case of the Church. And such cases
take time.

October 4, 1953, Sunday
After Mass the Man in the Raincoat visited me. His eyes avoided
mine, his face was calm and had an impersonal look. The usual
questions. I reminded him of the "several men" who were to come
to talk to me. He replied, "This has been slightly delayed, because

---

*October.

new circumstances have arisen since then. But I am not authorized to make statements." I understood—it was the waiting game.

In the course of the day I accidentally happened upon a section of *Słowo Powszechne* [*Universal Word*],* in which I read that there had been a meeting of the Bishops' Conference headed by Bishop Klepacz, and that the conference had issued a statement. The statement was supposed to overcome all the current difficulties and to create new ways to carry out the Mutual Understanding, and it announced the [government's] granting of the requests that the Episcopate would present. In a word—*treuga Dei* [Truce of God]. I had to call upon all of my experience of the past years to know how to receive and how to read such news. So these were the "new circumstances" that had changed the attitude of the Man in the Raincoat and made him impolite.

My guardians read only the "Catholic" press; sections of *Słowo Powszechne* and the Wrocław weekly, the "repainted" *Tygodnik Powszechny* [*Universal Weekly*],† could be seen everywhere. One of the men guarding the corridor at night diligently studies *The Catholic Calendar*, published by ZBoWID‡ (Union of Fighters for Freedom and Democracy). Trash was carried out of the apartments wrapped in *Słowo Powszechne*.

Toward evening I happened to get hold of a September 26 section of *Trybuna Ludu (People's Tribune)* § with an article by Mr. Ochab‖ directed against the "current leadership of the Episcopate." The general accuses me of (1) interfering in carrying out the Mutual Understanding and (2) making it difficult to stabilize Church relations in the Western Territories.¶

---

*A daily published by Pax, a group of progressive Catholics.
†An independent Catholic weekly.
‡Związek Bojowników o Wolność i Demokrację—a government organization for groups of veterans.
§Daily newspaper of the Central Committee of the Communist Party.
‖General Edward Ochab, an important member of the government and later First Secretary of the Polish Communist Party. He resigned in 1956 and was succeeded by Władysław Gomułka.
¶Territories in present western Poland regained by Poland after the Yalta agreement in 1945.

34

*The evacuated friary at Rywałd
was surrounded by floodlights and
fences of barbed wire.*

It is a great comfort to me to read the book by Father Eugeniusz Dąbrowski, *The Story of Paul of Tarsus*. The book is extremely topical, answering whatever needs may arise in the soul of a man carrying *vincula Christi* [the chains of Christ]. The circumstances of our lives may be different, but the ideal is the same; the cause for which we suffer our denial of freedom endures.

But is there any comparison? One cannot compare himself with a man of the stature of Saint Paul. Nevertheless a joyful comparison comes to mind in considering the durability of Christ's cause. The cause of Christ has existed almost two thousand years, and people are still in prisons for it today. The cause has survived. It is alive, fresh, young, full of allure. How many guards have changed, prisons have fallen into ruin, keys have rusted, locks and chains been removed—yet the cause endures. So far it has been defended. The cause lives on! Paul's chains clank not only in historical recollections; their living current reaches all the way into my own prison cell. I thank God for the grace of this book.

Today I "erected" a Way of the Cross and marked the Stations with little crosses. The rest—*Ecclesia supplet* [the Church supplies powers in special situations].

Through the Man in the Raincoat, I asked Bishop Baraniak to send me a *Missale Romanum* [Roman Missal], the reliquary of Saint Stanislaus and Saint Julia that I had left in my bedroom, four wax candles for Mass, writing materials, and various personal items (razors, a toothbrush, thread and needles). I also asked for the following books: Dobraczyński's *The Letters of Nicodemus*; Manzoni's *Promessi sposi*; the two-volume set entitled *Maria*; the Russian edition of Tolstoy's *War and Peace*; Grabski's *200 Cities*; Thiels' *On the Priesthood*; and Saint Thomas à Kempis' *Imitation of Christ*.

October 7, 1953, Wednesday

There was a great celebration in my cell today—The feast of Our Lady of the Rosary. Mass was "crowded." I "brought together" all those whom I had encouraged to say the rosary. I wanted to arm them with patience. They might think that the time of grace for which they had been praying had come. But the graces for which we pray today, while we enjoy them in one form already, in a different form we will enjoy only later.

I see more and more clearly that the most appropriate place for me, given the current status of the Church, is in prison.

Time and again I heard it said, by those who studied the currents of social thought, that the people are not always sufficiently aware of the "political" tactics of the Episcopate. As early as the middle of May of this year, there was talk that the Church was attempting to protect itself "in any way that it can," that the bishops were not sufficiently protecting the priests. Obviously, the absence of a free press and opportunity for free expression made the dissemination of accurate information impossible. The public knew nothing about the many letters, memoranda, protests submitted by the Secretariat of the Episcopate and the indefatigable Bishop Choromański—as well as by me—to the government, in defense of the Church's rights. The memorandum of May 8 of this year never reached the wider circles of people. My sermon on the occasion of the Corpus Christi procession in the capital was merely a "dot over the i" in this difficult work of defending the rights of the Church against the new investiture.* The Polish people then were justified in voicing their doubts.

The trial of Bishop Kaczmarek was looked upon by the public with distrust; the directors [of such trials] had exaggerated again. They wanted to make a universal criminal out of the bishop. They did not know how to assess the likelihood of the Nation's accepting this. Poles, after all, are a people of great culture. To my mind the trial caused a lot of unrest; the people did not believe the accusations against the bishop. The intelligentsia was scandalized at the bishop's behavior during the trial. The simple folk resolved this "scandal" in their own way.

"This was not a bishop, this was an impostor," explained one workman to a priest in a suburban train. Yet [Kaczmarek] *was* a

*"New investiture" refers to a key violation of the Mutual Understanding by the government in issuing a decree in February 1953 that made all appointments to ecclesiastical administrative positions subject to government approval.

bishop. In addition, he "confessed" to deeds that he had never committed. He "confessed" that he was receiving instructions of a political nature from the Holy See, and that at conferences of the Episcopate he pushed his own political program, despite resistance from the bishops. All this was untrue. How could it have come to this? I had to protest against such insinuations attributed to the Bishops' Conference and the Holy See. And this is why, before my arrest, I dispatched a letter to the President in which I firmly stated that the Holy See never even attempted to give political instructions to us and that at the meetings of the Episcopate nobody ever pushed a political program of his own. I added that the only matter of any political nature was the Mutual Understanding. Perhaps this letter, which clearly undermined the value of the proof at the trial, angered the government. The letter had been sent as a result of a resolution of the Conference of the Episcopate at Jasna Góra.

But the nightmare of the case of Bishop Kaczmarek still weighed heavily upon me. I felt that it was not enough; that to sustain the moral authority of the Polish Episcopate, something more had to be done. And this is where the government itself came to my aid. Looking at this from the point of view of the political interest of the state, the government could not have made a more serious mistake than to allow these two events to occur in such quick succession: the trial of Bishop Kaczmarek and my abduction. The juxtaposition of these two actions speaks most eloquently.

October 10, 1953, Saturday
Gratiarum actio [giving of thanks]* for the victory at Chocim† was very solemn: one tallow candle, one-quarter of a host, and a few drops of wine. But the soul rejoices over the full chalice that the Church gives its servant, so that he may know how to thank the Lord for the blessings He bestows upon the Nation.

---

*Prayers of thanksgiving recited by a priest after he offers Mass.
†Battles of Chocim (modern Khotin, Ukraine) in 1621 and 1673 ended as two major military victories of Poles over the invading Turks. In the first battle, the Cossacks aided the Polish forces against the Turks; in the second, the Turks attacked in support of the Cossacks who had rebelled against Polish rule.

I spent much time today reading the biography of Aniela Salawa, the housemaid from Kraków. Although the book is poorly written, Aniela's personality comes across very clearly. The native intelligence of this simple highland maiden provided a natural basis for the working of grace. The more she was won over by the Lord, the more she surrendered herself in sacrifice and service to her fellowmen, assuming their suffering. She is an ideal patron for modern times. I resolve to make every effort to hasten her useful example of excellence to the altar as soon as possible.

The Man in the Raincoat visited me again. As always, he was "objective," courteous, with a stone heart—as good a candidate for an intellectual as for a political sadist. I presented my problem to him. I didn't know the situation on Miodowa Street, where construction was in progress. I didn't know whether Bishop Baraniak was there. If he was, then he could take funds from the Secretariat for the construction of the archbishop's house and the workmen would receive their pay. But if he was not there, the men would not be paid, because only I was authorized to sign the transfer checks. I considered this to be a more important matter than my personal problems.

My visitor was surprised: "More important than your personal problems?"

"Yes, because others are involved, not I, and my obligations to the working men are more important to me than my own imprisonment."

Raincoat replied, "We have allowed Bishop Baraniak to remain on Miodowa Street."

"And so, I don't need to worry?" I asked.

He answered, "Yes, but I shall mention the matter to my superiors."

October 11, 1953, Sunday
Today was the feast of the Motherhood of Mary. From a nearby church I could hear the singing of the people as the church (or maybe the choir) doors opened. The heart rejoices to know that Our Lady is receiving her homage.

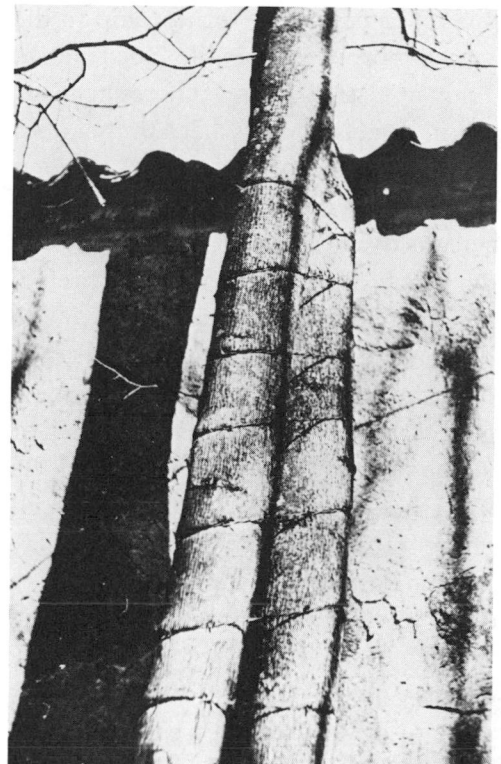

Rywałd: The trunks of the trees that were near the fence were covered with barbed wire to prevent escape.

Monitoring devices were installed throughout the grounds at Rywałd. This one is embedded in a tree trunk.

In my reading, my thoughts reflected on my relationship to the Mother of God. I had lost my own mother early in life. She had had a particular devotion to Our Lady of Ostra Brama,* where she made pilgrimages when we still lived in Zuzela.† My father, on the other hand, was always drawn to Jasna Góra. Devotion to Our Lady was very deep in our home; we would often say the rosary together in the evening. When my mother was dying in Andrzejowo (October 31, 1910), I heard her last words, which were directed to me: "Stefan, get dressed." I went out, put on my coat, and returned to the bedside. I did not understand what she meant. My father explained later what she had meant.‡ And after mother died, our housemaid, good-natured Ulisia, often spoke to us about our Heavenly Mother. I dearly loved the beautiful statue of Our Lady which stood in the church cemetery. Later, when I was in Warsaw at the Wojciech Górski school, I came to love the statue of Holy Mary Passawska§ in Krakowskie Przedmieście,‖ in front of the *Res Sacra Miser* [a Person in Distress Is a Sacred Matter]¶ church, where some of the students attended Mass.

During my stay at the seminary in Włocławek, two devotions complemented one another: one to the Sacred Heart of Jesus and the other to Our Lady of Jasna Góra, whose picture hung at the side altar. I celebrated all the feasts of Our Lady with great joy. I was ordained a priest in the chapel of Our Lady of Częstochowa in the Włocławek Basilica. I celebrated my first Mass at Jasna Góra, before the picture of Our Lady of Częstochowa. After that I always pre-

---

*A celebrated miraculous painting of the Virgin Mary that hangs over an old entrance gate called *Ostra Brama* in the city of Wilno (modern Vilnius, Lithuania).
†The village birthplace of Cardinal Wyszyński in central Poland in the diocese of Włocławek. He was born on August 3, 1901.
‡His mother probably referred to dressing in the sense of donning vestments or entering the service of the Church.
§This outdoor statue, possessing no particular artistic merits, enjoys great popularity with the residents of Warsaw, who are emotionally and religiously attached to it. It is famous for countless miracles of a personal nature.
‖The street that is referred to as "the royal way" and leads from Zamek Krolewski (the Royal Castle) to Belweder (the residence of the President).
¶A home for the aged where there is a chapel.

ferred an altar of Our Lady at which to offer my daily Sacrifice. Devotion to Mary became particularly important to me during the last war. I grew attached to the altar of Our Lady of Wrociszewo,* in front of which I spent long evening hours. In the course of my work in Laski† with the blind children, I used prayer to Our Lady primarily to keep up the spirit of those who were frightened by our proximity to the front lines. Interestingly, even though this institution suffered many a difficult moment during artillery fire and the encirclement of the Kampinos Forest,‡ we never missed our evening rosary.

I had intended to enter the Order of the Pauline Fathers and devote my life to work among pilgrims. Father Korniłowicz, my spiritual director, told me that it was not my vocation. But I never stopped believing that, however it was to develop, my life would have to follow Mary.

Since then, all the important events of my life have occurred on feasts of Our Lady. The "annunciation" of my being named bishop of Lublin was made in Poznań by His Eminence Cardinal Hlond§ on the feast of the Annunciation (1946). I immediately decided— when I expressed my canonical consent the next day—that on my episcopal coat of arms Our Lady of Jasna Góra would be dominant. That is why I chose her month for my consecration and installation and chose Jasna Góra as the site where it would be carried out.

That is also why all my important letters and episcopal decisions were issued on feast days of Our Lady. That is why I organized so many pilgrimages from the Lublin area to Częstochowa.

Later, when I received the news that I was appointed to the See of the *"Bogurodzica Dziewica"* [The Virgin Mother of God]‖ in

---

*A town twenty-four miles south of Warsaw.
†A town twelve miles from Warsaw, where the Institute of Blind Children is located.
‡The Kampinos Forest is fifteen miles from Warsaw. It was the site where the Nazi Germans shot many Poles.
§August Cardinal Hlond was Primate of Poland from 1926 to 1948.
‖Oldest Polish Marian hymn, dating from the tenth or eleventh century.

Gniezno, in a letter dated November 16, 1948—the day of Our Lady of Mercy—my devotion to Our Lady became the inspiration for all my work. I scheduled the formal installation in Gniezno for February 2, the Feast of the Purification of the Virgin Mary. Immediately after my installation in Warsaw, I went to Jasna Góra, where I made a week-long retreat as I had before my consecration as bishop. Then I was ready to begin my work.

And here also, all the dates of the major letters, announcements, and decisions bore the name of Our Lady. I organized many Marian congresses around Gniezno and Warsaw. I delivered over a thousand speeches about the Mother of God-made-Man. Every year I organized religious retreats for priests at Jasna Góra—one year for Gniezno, another for Warsaw. I always chose to organize bishops' conferences at Jasna Góra, and the bishops' religious retreats took place there. I visited Jasna Góra four or five times a year. Here I would meet the superiors of monasteries and convents. Often I celebrated pontifical Masses at Jasna Góra, and I preached the word of God to throngs of pilgrims. I would send newly ordained priests there to offer their first Masses. I asked Father General Markiewicz to accept me as an associate member of the Pauline Order, and I accepted this grace with great happiness.

I recall these important dates of my life today and place all my affairs in the maternal hands of Mary so that she, my Protectress, will carry on the work herself and will come to the defense of her soldier.

Rywałd: "The prison bars are crying," said Wyszyński, watching the rain drip from the metal.

III

STOCZEK WARMIŃSKI

October 12, 1953, Monday

After an unusually early supper, I sat down to read the book by
Father Bernard, K.B.* about Saint Joseph. My concentration was
interrupted by a knocking at the door, unusual for this time of day.
Without waiting to be invited, in walked the Man in the Raincoat,
hat in hand. "We'll be going on," he said to me.

I was not overly surprised. "How much time do I have to collect
my things?"

"Half an hour. We will help—we have suitcases."

"Thank you, I can manage alone."

My guest asked another man to join him, and they proceeded to
collect my belongings. I asked how far I would be traveling. With
some hesitation he answered, "About a hundred kilometers."

I reminded him that I never had had that talk he had promised.
The Man in the Raincoat didn't recall promising any such talk. I
realized then that the promise had simply been a police maneuver.

I packed my belongings rather quickly into the luggage the men
had brought from Miodowa Street. Down the dark stairway we

---

*Karmelita Bosy: a barefoot Carmelite.

went—the first time I had been downstairs in two weeks. Not a soul was around, not even a trace of the soldiers who usually made so much noise all night in the hallways.

I got into the car with the Man in the Raincoat. There were several other cars parked directly at a distance. We began to move. May the Lord guide us! I felt so much like a "thing" that I asked no questions. I commended myself to the protection of Our Lady and Saint Joseph, from whom I had been so suddenly separated.

The ride in the dark was most conducive to prayer and meditation. We headed in the direction of Jabłonowo Pomorskie.

They were careful to make certain that I saw no one. Along the way we passed Ostróda; for quite some time we stood in front of the voivodship building at Olsztyn. It was late—many people were returning from roads unknown to me. Finally, we continued on; we passed Dobre Miasto and Lidzbark [Warmiński].* Again, we were lost in the dark. We stopped on some road, waiting for another car. Soon it approached, was halted from afar, and turned around. We followed it. After driving a few minutes, we pulled up in front of a brightly lighted gateway; there were many lights; and the entrance had been freshly boarded up. Some unseen spirit opened the gate from the inside. We drove into a courtyard that in the dark looked jaillike to me. The thought crossed my mind that they had transferred me to a prison. The car stopped in front of an open door that led to a lighted corridor. They suggested that I get out. We stood in a bright and bare corridor, but this apparently was not our destination. Again, we found ourselves in the car, driving through a tall entrance made of fresh wooden boards and into a garden. Here, through a glass-enclosed veranda, we again entered the same corridor. Apparently the rite of installation in this new place required that I enter through the garden gate.

I was led up to the second floor, to a wide corridor aglow in white light. Fresh paint was obvious everywhere. I was now in a rather large room. My guide in the raincoat was no longer around, al-

*These are all towns in northern Poland. The cardinal was being driven first northeast and then north.

though I had asked him if we could talk, and he had assured me that he would come. He never came. Some tall, tough-looking individual in a big hat introduced himself to me as the Superintendent. He explained that the Commandant was out at the moment, but that he would return soon. And indeed, a stocky man who looked more like a maître d'hôtel soon arrived. Without introducing himself, he announced that this was my new place of residence; I had at my disposal two rooms, a chapel, a hallway, and the garden. Next door lived a priest, who was a chaplain, and a nun. They were asleep at the moment, but in the morning they would come and introduce themselves. I was not told the name of the place to which they had brought me; they did inform me, however, that the cost of my stay in this house would be covered by the government. Soon the Superintendent returned and informed me that the car with the luggage had broken down along the way and would be late in arriving; he offered me the house linen. I thanked him, saying I preferred to wait for my own.

After the two men left, in walked "Father Chaplain" Stanisław Skorodecki, a prisoner brought here the day before from Rawicz, where he had been serving a prison term. He was tall, handsome, and, although a young man, he was emaciated, pale, and stooped. He began by saying that he wanted to explain everything—wondering what I must be thinking of him? He really knew nothing, he said, although it might appear as if he were in the service of [government] intelligence.

"Indeed, it's a drastic situation for you, Father," I replied, "but let's leave that for later. I ask that you do not consider yourself as my chaplain. Only I can nominate my chaplain, not the security police. I want to see in you only a fellow brother, a prisoner like me. The rest the future will reveal. Now go to bed, tomorrow we shall begin with Mass, and later we will talk." He calmed down considerably, stopped crying, and left.

After a while a nun in the habit of the Sisters of the Family of Mary entered the room. She introduced herself as Sister Maria Leonia Graczyk, a prisoner, brought from Grudziądz. She had been told that the Primate was ill, was convalescing, and that she would be taking care of him. She was even more distraught than the priest. She wove her suspicions: Perhaps this was some kind of trick, maybe they would use her as provocation for some trial, etc. Now I tried to calm her down; I asked her not to succumb to conjectures. I was not in the habit of making judgments about anyone until I got to know him better. I asked her to get a good sleep, and tomorrow we would talk. The sister was even more emaciated than the priest— a tiny, thin, pale little thing, full of words and tears.

Finally I was alone. Once again the Superintendent in the big hat came in and repeated his offer about the linen because the car would be quite late. Soon they brought clean sheets and made the bed. I think it was two in the morning when I went to bed.

October 13, 1953, Tuesday

In the morning I became better acquainted with my companions and with their fate. Both were worn out by prison life. The priest much too thin; the sister skin and bones. We unpacked the Mass items and prepared an altar on top of the desk. We offered Mass without candles or a missal. Thus began our spiritual life—for the three of us.

After breakfast we inspected our residence. It was a large house, a former monastery building, recently vacated by unknown residents. Signs of recent renovation were all about—the corridor walls whitewashed, the floors refinished. The rooms bore signs they had been newly redone—and badly. Around the house were signs of spilled paint, scattered paint brushes, rubbish thrown into a trash can under the windows. The walls of the historic structure told us that trash had been discarded out of the windows. We found fragments of liturgical objects: broken candle holders, cracked fonts, remainders of the crosses and figurines of Our Lady. In the garden, the paths had been freshly spread with yellow sand. Many of the trees had been cut down. The trees next to the tall fence were almost completely wrapped with barbed wire as high as the fence. Many of the trees closer to the fences had been cut down; others had been chopped halfway down; some had been ancient, priceless specimens. Everywhere lay trash and neglect. The fruit trees bore no signs of fruit. Large fish ponds were full of trash, wiring, and mud. The entire interior of the fence had spotlights; and electrical wires and cables hung all over. We saw newly built high fences, still white, separating the garden from the workyard and from the northeast side of the building.

The building was obviously old; on the tower we noticed a little metal flag with the date 1675 (or perhaps 1645 or 1615). The structure looked like a Jesuit establishment, perhaps dating to the times of Hozjusz.* It was a tall, three-story house, facing north, with small windows, and a cloister garden within encircled by corridors. On the street side there was a little church with a rounded, domelike coping. The whole estate was hidden among trees through which little could be seen. One could only guess that there was a road along the northeast wall. Double rows of old and rotting trees provided a good place for walking. Very little else could be seen. At the end of the center road you could see the outline of the upper part of a one-story house; the top windows gazed toward the garden not only with their panes but also with the careful eye of a discreet guard. Another stood under a tree involuntarily reading a book.

The interior of the structure formed a square against which, from the side of the garden, leaned the main building and, along the road, the church. The outside walls were eroded by dampness up to the second floor, the inside corridors were wet, the air inside cold, the stone floors completely covered with water. Upstairs, on the second floor, the corridor and apartments were dry and clean, but the floors showed signs of wear and mold. We were assigned the corridor and the rooms on the second floor of the building next to the garden. I had two rooms. There was a chapel, a room for the priest, another for the sister, and several unoccupied rooms. All the rooms were furnished adequately with new furniture and carpeting.

---

*Stanisław Cardinal Hozjusz or Hosius (1504–1579), bishop of Chełmno (1549), and of Ermeland (1551), named a Cardinal in 1561. He had Jesuit sympathies and actively opposed the Protestant Reformation with his *Confessio Fidei Christianae Catholicae* (*A Profession of the Christian Catholic Faith*), which was adopted by the Synod of Piotrków in 1557.

At eleven the fellow alleged to be the Commandant of the institution came by. I was still not too clear about the nature of this place. All around I saw many men in civilian clothes milling about. I estimated there were about thirty of them, at least the ones I could see. The Commandant was a middle-aged man, stocky, wearing civilian clothes which fit rather oddly; his facial expression was guarded, slightly inquisitive. He informed me again that I might use the second floor with the corridor and the bathroom, as well as the garden. I might use the garden from early morning until eight at night.

Since this was a new situation for me, I again made my statement protesting this form of imprisonment. It is (1) a violation of a citizen's constitutional rights because it is based on a one-sided government order, (2) a violation of an elementary principle of justice, *audiatur et altera pars* [let the other side be heard], (3) a violation of the rights of the Church represented in my person as the ordinary of two archdioceses, the metropolitan of two church provinces,* and the Primate of Poland, (4) a violation of the rights of Catholics, who have a right to their shepherd, (5) a violation of the rights of the Holy See, in the name of which I served with a special jurisdiction granted me by the Holy Father, and (6) a violation of the Mutual Understanding, which recognizes the jurisdiction of the Holy See.

My visitor asked me what I thought of the trial of Bishop Kaczmarek and the rule of law in Poland. Without going into an evaluation of the trial, I stated that my views of the trial were expressed in my letter to the government sent a few days before my arrest, in the name of the Polish Episcopate. Bishop Kaczmarek "confessed" to things which he did not do. And so (1) he had confessed that he had received political instructions from the Holy See and passed them on to the bishops, and (2) that he had promoted his own political program at the Episcopal Conferences. How it could have

---

*A Church province is an archdiocese, usually centered in a large city, and including one or more dioceses in the area. The archbishop of such a province is called a metropolitan.

happened that the bishop confessed to deeds which he definitely did not commit, I could not understand. Certain facts about the bishop's trial were suggestive. There had been talk [at the trial] about my conversation with the Holy Father, which took place without witnesses. I spoke to no one about it and never divulged anything relative to Church affairs to the witness who testified about the conversation. The judge who heard the deposition of the bishop could have called as witnesses several participants in the Episcopal Conferences, which he did not do, thus providing the prosecutor opportunity for attacks on the Church.

"As to whether there is rule of law in Poland, surely you need no answer considering what you are doing to me."

October 14, 1953, Wednesday
Our lives begin to become normal. Slowly we become accustomed to one another. The sister and the priest once again bring up the matter of trust: "What do you think of me?"

The sister's fears seemed to be especially exotic. "I've heard," she said, "that they use women to discredit people. Maybe they counted on me to do that. Maybe they will want to find some accusations on moral grounds. . . ." etc.

"All these speculations," I explained to the sister, "are pointless. We know of what *we* are capable, but we don't know of what *they* are capable. So let's not waste time. Let us trust one another. We are children of God, and you, Sister, are a child of the Family of Mary. Not words but deeds will be our answer to any of their plans that are unknown to us. We shall pray, work, and await the Lord's mercy."

The frightened sister began to smile, probably for the first time. They had brought her here directly from Grudziądz, where she had been in prison for the past two years, sentenced to seven years. Her entire behavior revealed the mind-set of a prisoner: She spoke in a subdued voice, kept glancing at the door even when speaking on subjects of no interest to the authorities, she used substitute words, she was cautious and gingerly.

The priest had not known where he was being taken and why.

Removed after two years from the prison in Rawicz, where he was to have served a ten-year sentence, he was surprised and anxious. But a man can cope with anything more easily [than a woman], although he, too, showed signs of prison behavior. He paid attention to everything that happened around him. Everything could be useful to him; everything had significance. He studied the sister carefully. These two seem to observe each other in silence, as though they wanted to know about one another.

We are sentenced to a life together, a threesome. It will not be easy because it constitutes one world surrounded by another world. That other world carefully observes the first world. The sense of that vigilant eye looking through the window toward the corridor, from the windows onto the garden, measuring our every step, mistrusting—all this draws the three of us even closer together. We are "we," they are "they." Our "we" is a growing solidarity among us, regardless of occasional lurking doubts. There is no way that we can remain total strangers to each other. The priest is not only another fellow priest, the sister not only a sister. We have a common misfortune, a common fate; it is the closeness of people who pace the same floors. All of this provides material for a new bond, which is slowly beginning to become fruitful.

At eleven the Commandant comes to see me; he asks about my health and my needs. These two questions become the official ceremonial. "I forgot to tell you," he adds today, "that the place where we are is called Stoczek koło Lidzbarka. I apologize for not having told you sooner."

"It is good that you tell me the address; it seems more human. May I use it?"

"You may indeed," said the Commandant.

October 15, 1953, Thursday
Today the Commandant arrived accompanied by his first deputy, who is called Superintendent here, and he brought along another young man whom he introduced as the second deputy. I expressed surprise: "One more? So many men will be wasting their time around here?" The first deputy carried himself like a big shot. A tall,

simple peasant, obviously new to his formal suit of clothes, blond, reminiscent of a Nazi noncom.* He formed his sentences clumsily, his behavior was awkward. He carefully avoided looking at me and stared at the ceiling. His ceremonial questions about my health and my needs had a trace of discomfort. The impression he gave was rather pleasant. The second deputy introduced to me this morning left a different impression. He apparently wanted to appear to be an intellectual. A carefully pressed and spotless suit, perfectly combed hair and beard—the kind one sees in a barbershop window. His behavior was hygienic—a man cloaked in official indifference and objectivity.†It usually falls to his type to "represent policy." But we would see.

I asked whether I could write a letter to my father, who until now did not know about my fate. The Commandant replied that he would "present the question to his superiors."

I prepared a list of books I wanted from my library and handed it to the Commandant.

October 17, 1953, Saturday
Today I was told I could write a letter to my father. As a result, I prepared a short letter and gave it to the Commandant. The letter reads:

> My dearest father!
> Having just learned that I could send a letter to you, my dearest father, I am doing that which my heart tells me urgently to do. For I want your soul to shed all fears about me, I don't want you to waste your strength in sadness and doubts, but rather to fulfill the task which befits your ripe age—namely the task of praying for your son.
> The spirit of faith in which you live is for me a reassur-

---

*The cardinal later refers to this man by the nickname "Nazi," from the first two syllables of the Polish word *Nazista* [Nazi].
†This man is later nicknamed "Doctor" or "Aesculapius" (after the Greek god of medicine and healing), for his pretensions to medical expertise.

ance about your well-being. I know that in the spirit of faith you will understand everything; that with prayer you will extinguish sadness, and your heart will be gladdened by trust. But a man also needs human consolation.

Now a few words about me. I want to assure you, dear Father, with that inner truth which you always saw in me, that in the present circumstances of my life I am totally at peace and confident. I am unable today to serve the Church and my country as a priest in the house of God, but I can serve them with my prayers. And this I am doing almost all day. I have the joy of celebrating Mass every day in our house chapel. I have the companionship of a priest who serves as a "chaplain" and a sister who takes care of our daily needs. I fill my time with reading, prayer, and walks in a spacious park. My health is excellent. God does not deny me His pleasures and His abundantly good providence. I hope, also, that no one ever hears from my dear ones, either at home or outside the home, even the slightest complaint. I need your serenity, calm, and prayer. Do not lose faith in the goodness of God's providence, in the power, wisdom and charity of our dearest Lady of Jasna Góra. I kiss your hands, my dear father, with much gratitude, and send my blessings to the entire family and members of your household from the bottom of my heart.

Saturday, October 17, 1953
+ Stefan Cardinal Wyszyński

October 18, 1953, Sunday
Today I received from Miodowa Street the liturgical items we needed to set up our chapel and the altar: candle holders, a cross, a missal, candles, hosts, altar cloths, etc. We still need an altar stone. Father Stanisław improvised a tabernacle out of the chalice case. The table in the chapel is too low; they gave us four pegs of wood, which we placed under the table legs. Although it is very small and without

a predella,* it creates the impression of an altar. We covered our "tabernacle" with the chalice veil. Father Stanisław found a large wall cross and pictures of the Holy Family, the Sacred Heart of Jesus, and the Immaculate Heart of Mary in the neighboring room. All this gave the little room the appearance of a chapel. The sister was worried that she did not have vases and bowls for flowers; as it happened, you couldn't find a single flower in the garden anyway.

October 20, 1953, Tuesday
I renewed my request for an altar stone and the reliquary. I was assured that my request would be "presented to the superiors."

Our daily routine in Stoczek has come to be as follows:

A.M.

5:00	Rising
5:45	Morning prayers and meditation
6:15	Mass by Father Stanisław
7:00	My Mass
8:15	Breakfast and walk
9:00	*Horae minores* [Little Hours] and part of the rosary
9:30	Personal work

P.M.

1:00	Lunch and walk (second part of the rosary)
3:00	Vespers and Compline
3:30	Personal work
6:00	*Matutinum cum Laudibus* [Matins and Lauds]
7:00	Supper
8:00	Rosary devotion and evening prayers
8:45	Private reading
10:00	Rest

---

*Platform on which an altar is placed.

I began to plan work on a book, but we lacked adequate help. So for the time being, more time was devoted to reading the books that had been sent. Father S. and I tried to spend the time allotted to personal work privately. Our walks provided time for conversations. Father was teaching sister Latin. I read Italian and French books.

Our environment also determines the routine of supervision over us. They [the guards] constitute a separate world, right next to our own, their attention definitely directed at us. Near the glass doors leading to the corridor, beyond the frosted pane, there stands a small table—on top of it, a lamp with a green shade, by the lamp, a man with a book. Every movement of the door distracts his attention from the book. And this is how it goes for twenty-four hours a day. Only the people change, but "the work at the checkpoint" has the same quantity and value. True, there seem to be no true intellectuals among our guards, but a book is the only way of combating boredom.

Downstairs by the door, another man with a book stands guard. His diversion is having someone knock on the door to the courtyard, which it is his duty to open. Here, too, someone is on duty around the clock. What the duties of the many other people milling around the house are it is difficult to say. The house is illuminated all night long; sometimes the lights are left on during the day. It's the same in the courtyard and along the road. Military guards stand around the fences. You can hear their impatient tramping everywhere, even at night. The upper floor is always illuminated; even at night light shines from the upper windows onto the garden. Otherwise it is silent.

October 25, 1953, Sunday
Today I received my first letter from my father, sent from Zalesie Dolne* on October 21. So his reply to my letter arrived very quickly. The letter pleased me greatly, for it was written in the spirit I hoped for. It is a great grace from the Lord to have a father blessed with the gift of prayer. Because the stand which my father has assumed in this situation can only be a gift and fruit of prayer.

---

*A town six miles north of Warsaw.

Dearest Son,

With my whole soul I thank the Lord and thank you, my dearest son, for the news about you, the words of consolation and comfort which emanate from your letter. I want to assure you for myself as well as for the entire family, that in our prayers and thoughts we are with you, wishing, with our serenity, faith, and unswerving trust, to help you endure in the place where God at this moment has willed you to be. We fervently believe that God only desires our common good, and we submit to his will, trying as much as we can to maintain calm and serenity. In our ardent prayers to the Lord and to Our Lady of Jasna Góra, we commend our strength and you, dearest Son, begging for health, endurance, bravery for you, trusting that the Lord and His Mother will not desert you, will preserve you for us, and will allow us to see and embrace you soon.

I wish to let you know that I am well and strong as are the rest of your dear family and loved ones, your sisters and their families, Tadeusz with his family and the members of our household. We ask you, dearest Son, not to worry about us, because all is well with me and the rest of the family, and we lack for nothing. All we ask of you is news, as often as possible, especially about your health.

We commend you fervently to the Sacred Heart of Jesus and to Our Blessed Mother, assuring you once again that in our ardent prayers we shall support you with all our might. We also ask you earnestly to intercede for us with God.

I embrace you, my dearest son, most affectionately and hold you close to my heart. Many embraces also from Stasia and Julcia, who ask me to assure you that they are brave. Józio has been in Kazimierz for several weeks and returns today.

Zalesie, October 21, 1953
Your Father,
S. Wyszyński

October 30, 1953, Friday
Today I received the altar stone without the reliquary—an unconsecrated stone. I'm wondering where it came from, certainly not from Miodowa Street. Undoubtedly, my guardians, not wanting to reveal that there was no chapel on the premises, have attempted to provide an altar stone on their own. I decided to refrain from clarifying this matter.

October 31, 1953, Saturday
Today I sent a second letter to my father, in reply to his:

My dearest father!
Today, on the forty-third anniversary of my mother's death, I celebrated Mass for her intention, in remembrance and with filial gratitude, although for a long time I have been convinced that the fruits of the Holy Sacrifice now flow to others and are no longer necessary for the soul blessed with the vision of God.
I was very glad, Father, to receive your letter of October 21 which arrived on October 25. To the joy of the feast of Christ the King was added this human joy all the greater because your letter, dear Father, was written in the spirit I had expected and very much wanted from you and from my entire family.
I truly believed that you, dear Father, who received with concern and anxiety the news of my elevation to bishop of Lublin and later to Primate, have kept at all times that humility which is so very necessary in accepting God's plans. You knew that I never did anything in my life to gain this promotion. God acted on His own: He did the choosing, the expediting, the demanding. I see this very clearly. Seeing this truth today helps me very much to understand my present situation. God, who loves His creations infinitely, always acts according to His nature. Everything that befalls man in life must be seen to have signs of God's love. In this

realization, happiness fills the soul, and the soul can place total trust in God's direction and wisdom.

May this serene and trusting happiness be the dominating theme in my present life. I am truly joyful. I was afraid that I would not be honored in the same way that almost all of my schoolmates had been. Today that fear has left me. And that is why I am joyful in a way that you, my father, will understand. The Heavenly Father is as close to me with his goodness as never before, except perhaps the time during the war when I spent that first year in your hospitable home.

I am unable to describe all that I receive from Our Lady of Jasna Góra and my mother. Every Saturday is a festive holiday; each day a friendly support. I rejoice that under the cross Christ put us in the care of His Mother and made her the Mother of all her children. Christ was in His grave on a Saturday, but at the side of the *new* Infant, born on the cross—the Church—remained His Mother as once she had in Bethlehem. On that Saturday the newly born Church was under the command of the Mother of God. This is why Saturday is such an unusual joy.

And this Saturday is a double holiday: one of the mother who departed forty-three years ago, and the other of the Mother who watches over us to this day. This is why I am writing to you today, on Saturday, my father, so that you too may rejoice.

I am praying for you, dear Father, for my sisters, for my dearest friend, Bishop Baraniak, for whom I shall never cease to thank the Lord as the greatest gift during my five years of work in the See. I pray trustingly for my suffragan bishops, for the priests, and for both my flocks, because today I am able to help them only with prayer.

If I may, I wish to ask you, my dearest father, to take good care of your health, your eyes, not to tire yourself with too much reading, which is your passion. I worry about my brother, who forgets that he must use his strength prudently, for it has been abused in prisons and concentration camps. Please tell him so. And please ask especially that my sisters persist in confident and serene prayer. I pray to God that all of you should never waver or doubt in your use of prayer. At the earliest opportunity please give my greetings to all my dear friends in your household as well as the Sisters of St. Elizabeth.

I kiss your hands, dear Father, with all my heart. And I bless all of you.

Saturday, October 31, 1953
+ Stefan Cardinal Wyszyński

In handing this letter to the Commandant, I asked whether I could write a letter to the government of the Polish People's Republic asking them to clarify my situation. I felt it was my duty to do this, because my silence could be interpreted as relinquishing my rights or ignoring the accusations against me, especially by such influential representatives of the PZPR* as General Ochab, who in his article published in *Trybuna Ludu* (September 26, 1953) after my arrest, accused me of sabotaging the Mutual Understanding and hindering stabilization in the Western Territories. I had been planning the form of this letter for quite some time. I intended simply to enumerate my contributions to the Mutual Understanding and to stabilization in the Western Territories. I prepared a draft for such a letter.

The Commandant said that he would contact his superiors in this regard.

November 3, 1953, Tuesday
The Commandant, when asked again about my letter to the government, told me that I could write to Minister Bida [head of the UB]. To this I answered that I would not be able to take advantage of this permission for personal reasons. Minister Bida was one of the chief

---

*Polska Zjednoczona Partia Robotnicza, United Polish Workers' Party—that is, the Polish Communist Party.

organizers of the hate campaign against me. His office was instrumental in turning against me anyone visiting that office. Mr. Siemek, the director, formulated various complaints against me, even to priests who would come to his office from the Primatial Secretariat on official business. I had no guarantee that in such an atmosphere my letter would be received with discerning and serious consideration. I could, on the other hand, prepare a letter to Prime Minister Bierut or to the Vice-Marshal Mazur. The answer I received: "I shall present this matter to my superiors." I added that it was also my duty to inform Bishop Klepacz or Bishop Choromański about my circumstances. I wanted to write a few words to them. The answer was as before.

November 14, 1953, Saturday
Several times in the past few weeks I have requested an answer to the questions I posed. Each time I receive the same reply: "My superiors have not yet made a decision." I understand that they do not want to give me an answer and that I am to consider myself as having been denied those rights to which ordinary prisoners are entitled. In short, without trial I have been condemned to a "social isolation"* and reduced to the level of an outcast. It seems to me that I ought not to accept this position so easily and that I should do all I can to bring about an exchange of views. I asked the Commandant to notify his superiors about my attitude. He replied that he would.

November 17, 1953, Tuesday
Once again today the matter of the books which I had requested on October 15 came up. I still had not received them. The Commandant asked me to prepare the list of books once again, because the earlier list had "disappeared somewhere." And so I prepared a second copy of the list of October 15, which is as follows:
   (1) Newman's *Apologia pro vita sua;* (2) Saint Gregory's *Pastoral*

*Term used to describe one who has been deprived of all freedom, contacts, knowledge of accusations, and the like.

Rules; (3) two volumes by Cardinal Ledóchowski; (4) The Bible, complete, published by the Jesuit Fathers; (5) Bernardino of Siena *Opera omnia,* 2 volumes; (6) Dobraczyński's *The Holy Sword;* (7) Dobraczyński's *Those Chosen by the Stars;* (8) Makarenko's *Pedagogical Poem;* (9) *Pontificale Episcoporum* (abbreviated); (10) *Annuario Pontificio,* 1953; (11) Dąbrowski's *Jesus Christ;* (12) *Warsaw* (newest edition); (13) *Officium parvum BMV* (in Polish, for the sister); (14) my breviary, the other volumes (I have only that for autumn); (15) *Codex Iuris Canonici;* (16) *Rituale maius;* (17) *Caeremoniale Episcoporum;* (18) Vermeersch Creusen's *Epithome CJC;* (19) Le Hervé's *Summa Theologiae Dogmata* (6); (20) *Le Corps Mystique de J.Ch*—ecclesiology; (21) Prümmer's *Jus Canonicum;* (22) *Dottrina sociale cattolica*—a collection of Vatican documents; (23) Dictionaries: Italian, French, English, Russian; (24) Books by R. Plus; (25) Umiński's *History of the Church;* (26) Marmion's *Christ, Life of the Soul;* (27) Marmion's *Christ in His Mysteries;* (28) the New Testament, edited by Father Eugeniusz Dąbrowski; (29) writing materials.

November 29, 1953, Sunday

Since my questions had not been taken into consideration, I decided not to undertake any steps in my own defense. *Iacta cogitatum tuum in Dominum, et ipse te enutriet, et dabit Tibi petitiones cordis tui* [Cast your care upon the Lord, and He will sustain you, and He will grant you the petitions of your heart]. I shall also try to refrain from reflection about my present situation. One *"Ave Maris Stella"* [Hail, Star of the Sea]* provides more joy and freedom than the entire logic of a possible self-defense.

For some time now my soul has treasured the words of Cardinal Mercier, so often repeated by Father Korniłowicz: "I do not like to think of what used to be, nor foolishly dream of what will be—these things are up to God. The purpose of life comes down to the present moment." *In Te, Domine, speravi, non confundar in aeternum* [In Thee, Lord, I take refuge; let me never be put to shame].

---

*A Marian Hymn.

*December 8, 1953, Tuesday**

For the past three weeks I have been preparing my soul for this day. Following the directives of Blessed Louis Maria Grignion de Montfort, contained in the book *True Devotion to Mary,* I have given myself up today, through Our Lady, into total bondage to Our Lord Jesus Christ. In this I see the special grace of this day—that God Himself has provided me with the occasion to make this joyous commitment.

I have decided that the first parish I am able to establish will be honored with the title "The Divine Motherhood of Mary."

Act of Personal Dedication to Our Lady
(prepared in Stoczek)

Holy Mary, Virgin Mother of God, I take you today for my Lady, my Advocate, my Patron, my Guardian, and my Mother.

I resolve firmly and I promise that I shall never abandon you and shall never say or do anything against you. I shall never allow anyone else to commit any deeds which would belittle your honor.

I beseech you, accept me forever as your servant and your child. Be my help in all the needs of my soul and body as well as in my priestly work for others.

I surrender myself to you, Mary, into total slavery, and as your slave I dedicate to you my flesh, my soul, my internal and external possessions, even the merit of my good deeds, past as well as present and future ones, leaving you a complete and full right to dispose of me and all that is mine as you see fit—without exception—according to your wish for the greater glory of God, in time and in eternity.

I wish to become, through you, with you, in you, and for you, a total slave of your Son, to whom you, Holy Mother, offer me in slavery, as I have given myself into slavery to you.

*Feast of the Immaculate Conception.

All that I shall ever do, I shall give, by the means of your immaculate hands as the Holy Mediatrix of all grace, to the glory of the Holy Trinity—*Soli Deo!**

Mary of Jasna Góra, do not abandon me in my daily work and reveal to me your pure Image in the hour of my death. Amen.

Stoczek, December 8, 1953

December 17, 1953, Thursday
Today I was handed a package sent to me from home for Christmas. All the items had been unpacked and thoroughly searched; the baked goods and other food had also been examined, for they showed signs of being squeezed and broken. The sweets, removed from their boxes, were replaced quite carelessly and were crumbled and broken. I inquired about the letter. The Commandant answered that "apparently there was no letter, since it was not delivered."

I expressed my doubts: "My family know that I am more interested in letters from my father and news about what is happening at home than in food."

The Commandant repeated his "apparently." But he said it in a voice that lacked conviction, trying to avoid any discussion. I have still not received a reply to my letter of October 31. I feel certain the letter was never delivered to my father.

December 22, 1953, Tuesday
Since I have not yet received word from my father, I decided to try again. Today I handed the Commandant a third letter, with the following contents:

My dearest father!
I postponed writing this letter for the holidays until the very last moment, hoping that I would receive a reply to my letter written on October 31. Having received a Christmas

---

*This is the motto on the Primate's episcopal coat of arms: "Only for God."

package from home on December 17 with no letter inside, I have now lost hope. I would not want, my dearest father, this Holy Season to pass for you without a sign of my filial devotion and respect. And so, even in these short words, I wish to send to you, dear Father, and to the rest of the family, the members of your household, Bishop Antoni and Bishop Choromański, as well as the sisters, the expression of my deepest sentiments, Christian blessings, and the gifts of prayer. I trust that God's serenity, flowing from the Lord's birth, will be your privilege, that mutual prayer will become a blessed bond, that will never weaken.

I am grateful to you, dear Father, for the Christmas wafer* you sent me as well as for all the gifts, which show so much goodness and heart that it is difficult for me to accept them without feeling very moved. During my Mass on Christmas Eve, I shall in a particular way remember all those to whom I am bound by family love and grace and my priestly duty. I kiss your hands, my dear father, with deep reverence, and I bless you all.

December 22, 1953
+ Stefan Cardinal Wyszyński

The Commandant accepted my letter and declared that it would be given to the superiors.

December 24, 1953, Thursday
Christmas Eve. In my present "family"—serenity and jubilation. We fortify ourselves with prayer and try not to show our Heavenly Father and Our Lady any sadness on our faces. There is so much joy today in heaven and on earth; how could we muddle this harmony with our problems? Our guardians are proper, they behave

---

*It is a Polish tradition on Christmas Eve, before the evening meal—the *Wigilia* —to share an unleavened wafer with members of the family as a sign of reconciliation and forgiveness.

politely and with reserve. We had a short visit from the Commandant, who came with his questions: "Requests?"

"I have no new requests. The old ones you know."

Father Stanisław assumed the responsibility of preparing the crèche in the chapel. But how without the Baby Jesus? I work at the table, as usual. Around noon the Commandant appears again. This is most unusual in our circumstances. "Excuse me, a little package has come. It is from Miss Okońska."* He departs, leaving a small, unwrapped parcel on the table. I know what is inside: a crèche for our chapel. I have had a strange premonition that the Baby Jesus would somehow find His way to us. He did! There is much happiness and gratitude for this tender consolation.

The Baby Jesus didn't appear until the Christmas Eve supper, to which the three of us sat down at seven. What great joy beamed in the eyes of Father Stanisław—that unusually decent, noble young priest who had ended up here in prison because of his zeal for God in the souls of young children!

I received no Christmas letter from my father, although it was difficult to imagine him sending the package without a letter. But I forgave my guardians this need to demonstrate their power over me. They would never force me to hate them, no matter what they did.

December 31, 1953, Thursday

The last day of the year. The Church has prepared us for all our mundane problems with Advent prayer and with Christmas. A person who has Jesus can cope with all his daily problems.

We expressed three emotions: in the *Te Deum*,† a sense of gratitude for love, for life, for sanctifying grace; in the *Magnificat*,‡ a sense of happiness for Our Lady; in the *Miserere* § a sense of humility for unappreciated graces. With these three emotions I closed this

---

*Foundress of a religious group of women who served the needs of the Primate.
†A hymn of praise to God sung at the conclusion of solemn religious celebrations.
‡Mary's song to Elizabeth during the Visitation, Luke 1:46–55.
§Psalm 50 (Psalm 51, KJV).

year filled with labor and effort almost beyond the strength available to me—almost beyond it, until the very last moment before my arrest.

The evenings of the three days of the Christmas holidays we spent singing Christmas carols by our little Christmas tree, which Father Stanisław discovered in the garden. We recalled almost forty carols and sang two to three stanzas of each, one after the other. We would spend whole afternoons together, trying to find through our singing a bond with our rejoicing Church. We took our meals together. We tried to vary them with the gifts we had received from home. We seemed to be developing a unity in consuming our gifts of food—not in the sense, of course, of their nutritional value, but rather as an expression of communion with our loved ones.

This last day of the year it behooves me to prepare at least a brief examination of conscience concerning the most important virtue—love. I want to be clear. I feel a deep sense of injustice suffered at the hand of the government. I feel I was especially hurt by Mr. Mazur, who was aware of my sincere efforts to bring about an atmosphere of peace in working on the relationship between the Church and the government. I bear no grudge against President Bierut, although I think that he did not fulfill his duty to defend a citizen who was unlawfully denied his freedom. In spite of this, I have no feelings of animosity toward any of these people. I wouldn't even know how to hurt them in the least way. It seems to me that I have the truth on my side, that I am still filled with love, that I am a Christian and a child of my Church, which has taught me to love people, even those who wish to consider me their enemy, to change my feelings toward my neighbors.

Sic volo [That is my desire]! With this feeling I can bring to a close the year that is now about to die. Man lives on—before a God Who is ageless.

All the achievements that were good and wise during this dying year, I commit into your hands, Immaculate Virgin of Jasna Góra, to offer to the Holy Trinity—*Soli Deo in vinculis Christi*.

Stoczek koło Lidzbarka Warmińskiego, December 31, 8:00 P.M.

+ Stefan Cardinal Wyszyński
Metropolitan Archbishop of Gniezno
and Primate of Poland at Warsaw

Anno Domini [Year of Our Lord] 1954.
Soli Deo!
Maria duce [Mary, lead]!

January 1, 1954, Friday
In vinculis Christi—pro Ecclesia [In the chains of Christ—for the Church]. Although my [liturgical] year began on the first Sunday of Advent and all my inner experiences are associated with that date, still—because I live on this earth and reach God by means of it— I want all the temporalities that accompany me on this road to be sanctified in a special way. And this is why I begin this year, so blessed for me, in the name of the Lord. After all, in the Church the New Year feast [Circumcision] commemorates the bestowing on the Holy Infant of the name "Jesus."

From early morning I offer all that may befall me in this new year to my Mother, our Immaculate Lady of Jasna Góra. I want her to continue to lead me, as she has done since my childhood. I want her face, which I have on my Primatial coat of arms, never to lose its happy glow, always to receive proper homage through my deeds as well as my suffering and my prayers. I renew my act of dedication, devoting myself totally, through her immaculate hands, into slavery to her Son, whom I cradle in my arms. My Jesus is still tiny. But I want him to grow, just as I must make myself decrease.

I wish to maintain *treuga Dei* [a truce of God] with everyone. I wish to renew my most positive feelings toward all. Toward those who are now nearest me. And toward those farthest away, who are under the impression that they decide my fate—which, in fact, is totally in the hands of my Heavenly Father. I feel no malice in my heart toward anyone, nor hate nor a need for revenge. I wish to defend myself against such feelings with all my might and with the help of God's grace.

Only such an attitude and such feelings give me the right to live. Because only then will my life help build God's Kingdom on earth.

I extend my best wishes to my flock in Gniezno and in Warsaw, placed in my charge by Christ. I am unable to serve them directly, and that is why I commit them to the very special care of the Mother of God, asking her to watch over them and help them carry the cross of their orphanhood with dignity—even better than with my closest help.

But I am able to serve my flock through prayer and suffering, and this is what I intend to do. Thus I place in the hands of Mary all the prayers of the entire year, and I hope that the greatest share would benefit my suffragan bishops, all the canons,* members of the archdiocesan curias, the religious seminaries, all the clergy of both archdioceses—all the faithful placed under my care. My daily prayers are for them.

Today we experienced an unusual "visit." From the very edge of the garden, under the linden trees, there came sounds of music and singing. We recognized it as church music, although it seemed like a radio performance. Until now we had never encountered any sign of live religious activity from the church next to our prison. Slowly we recognized the words of the Christmas carol "Let Us Hasten to the Manger." The congregation was singing, accompanied by an organ. We listened very carefully and heard some of the words: "You were born this night to deliver us from the power of the devil." The singing was barely audible, far away. Never before had any church music reached our ears, although we had often heard the bell ringing, summoning people to Mass. We were both delighted. After all, we were churchmen. Our joy was to serve God, to pray with the people; that common prayer was the thing we missed most.

This present sign of common prayer was our greatest joy—our true Christmas.

---

*Members of the cathedral chapter (bishop's council and administrative aides), who live a semicommunal life in a cathedral community.

This is the jubilee year, the one hundredth anniversary of the proclamation of the dogma of the Immaculate Conception of the Blessed Virgin Mary.* We had already begun to prepare for this anniversary before my arrest. It is my strongest desire to add to the spiritual enrichment of these festivities by preparing my own archdiocese. I had intended to consecrate a new Church dedicated to the Immaculate Conception at Niepokalanów.† The date of the consecration has been set for September 8.‡ Would that I might receive this blessing.

January 6, 1954, Wednesday§

Herods are a strange lot. In hating too much, they become apostles of the cause they fight against. Herod was the first to believe in the King of the Jews. He created a good deal of publicity for Him all over Jerusalem. First he sent the Wise Men to Bethlehem. Then he assigned the scriptural experts to search the Books of the Prophets to find out where Christ was supposed to be born. They confirmed the news brought by the Wise Men. The world took notice. Jesus was only an infant, and already Herod's world trembled with fear. What would happen when Christ grew up?

But we should not reject these apostles of hate, who search for God with hatred in their hearts and publicly proclaim their hatred. In hatred there is faith, there is fear, there is the recognition of power, there is the dread of influence. There will come those who will cast aside hatred and will understand the hated God. The persecutors of God work for His Glory.

There is justification for a lack of faith. Not only does it reveal those with limited intelligence, who are incapable of comprehending God; but it also encourages mental effort, the uneasiness that causes men to search for truth and insight.

---

*Proclaimed by Pope Pius IX on December 8, 1854.
†A city north of Warsaw built as a Franciscan community by Saint Maksymilian Kolbe.
‡The feast of the Nativity of the Blessed Virgin Mary.
§The Feast of the Epiphany.

January 17, 1954, Sunday

A black crow sits on the top of a tall pine tree. It looks around proudly and lets out a cry of victory. The crow—that noisy apparition—truly believes that the pine owes everything to it—the tree's being, its tall beauty, its evergreen splendor, its power in battling the winds. What uncanny gall! The great benefactor of the serene pine tree. But the pine tree never stirs; it seems not even to notice the black crow. Lost in thought, it stretches the arms of its branches heavenward. It tolerates its noisy intruder calmly. Nothing can disturb its thoughts, its dignity, its serenity. So many clouds have floated past its brow, so many migrant birds have perched upon its branches.

They passed, as you will. This is not the place for you; you feel insecure, and that's why you compensate for your lack of courage with your screaming. I am the one who has grown from this soil— my roots endure in its heart. And you, meandering cloud, who cast the shadow of sorrow upon my golden brow, are nothing but a toy tossed by the winds. I must endure you calmly. You, crow, will caw your boring, empty, meaningless song—and then you will depart. What can you accomplish with your screaming? I shall remain to contemplate, to build with my patience, to survive gale winds and attacks, ever to climb so peacefully. You cannot hide the sun from me, nor thrill me with delight, nor change the course of my ascent. The forest stood long before you came—you will be gone, and the forest will remain.

A fairy tale? No fairy tale!

January 18, 1954, Monday

"Lest anyone think . . ." that You are a severe Father, that You are hasty in passing judgment, lest anyone wrong You with reproaches on my account—I declare that everything You have done, You have done justly. Who can know this better than You and I? For whom is it more difficult to admit that someone is in the right if not the one who has been tried by suffering? How intensely Job strained to justify himself against the reproaches of his friends! And yet of my own free will, consciously, I must concede that all Your ways are mercy and truth! Suffering is diluted in the experience of love. Punishment ceases to be retaliation, because it is a medicine administered with fatherly gentleness. Sadness that torments the soul becomes the plowing of fallow ground for new seed. Loneliness becomes the act of gazing at You more closely. The malice of men is an education in silence and humility. Separation from one's work brings an increase in one's diligence and dedication. The prison cell reveals the truth: we have no permanent dwelling here.... Let no one, then, think ill of You, Father; let no one assault You with accusations of severity—for You are good, for Your mercy is everlasting.

January 19, 1954, Tuesday
During the past few weeks my relationship to my guardians boiled down to a few concise words: my health is unchanged; my wishes are unchanged. My conversation today with the Commandant consisted of the same concise words. I have not had a letter from my father in three months; my second and third letters have not been answered. Today I decided to bring this up. The Commandant again passed the blame onto his superiors: "I have had no reply."

I began, "I have heard this so many times. Recently I read the *Chronicon* of Thietmar. It describes the case of Otto II, who met the man who had tried to assassinate him. After one simple plea he had the assassin set free. And he was one of those feudal lords of whom you gentlemen are so very critical. I am not an assassin, and I am unable to obtain even a simple request from you—an answer to my questions. This is supposed to be progress? After one thousand years? And you have the gall to disparage the feudal lords! You want to teach democracy by cruelties to your people? If that is what you need, you have me. But why are you so cruel to my father, an old man? What has he done to you? This is not human, this is not progress. And it is done by people who themselves have been in prisons, but who managed to learn nothing from them. Knowing this alone, one must realize that things must change in Poland. This is not persuasion."

The Commandant started to back away toward the door, repeating, "I will contact my superiors again."

We parted as usual. I made note of this conversation for the record, in case it was evaluated differently in the future.

73

January 25, 1954, Monday

When I read the words of Saint Paul—"It was to shame the wise that God chose what is foolish by human reckoning" (1 Cor. 1:27) —I feel that the Apostle's own life contradicted them. But when I think about myself, I tend to agree with him. God has the right to use inferior instruments in order to demonstrate the power of truth and of the mercy of God. I want to agree with everyone who sees me as a man of inadequacy and limitations, for I do not wish to contradict God. After all, those who think this about me also agree with the Holy Spirit, who inspired the words of Saint Paul. Thus they give testimony to the truth. This, after all, is what matters: that Christ be affirmed.

January 26, 1954, Tuesday

Quae utilitas [Of what use?] . . . There is at least one positive advantage, one sin less. All those who envied me my so-called career envy me no more—because careers usually take Joblike detours. Today they certainly would not like to be sitting at my right hand or my left, even though there are vacancies. A career in the Church demands you be prepared to follow Christ onto the cross as well as to prison. And even if this does not work, as in the case of Peter, you must go through that experience. . . . And so a number of the envious ones fall by the wayside. But not all, because the Church has always been rich in those prepared to suffer. These are the ones who continue to envy me, but their envy is no sin.

And there is this other great advantage, that my "brides"— Gniezno and Warsaw—will have a rest from their unfortunate groom, who loved himself more than those to whom he was wedded through the Church. How much anguish one can cause the Church when one is only learning to govern and to serve—that art one should have mastered long before. But who can predict the ways of the Lord? Who among us knows when he will be told, "Now I send you. . . ." When the time comes, all is not in readiness. And yet one does not refuse the Holy Father. So the poor condemned one goes into the Lord's vineyard, relying only on the grace of his office. If only one could remember that one must always look to the Lord with humility. Alas, it is easy to forget whence man came. Well, then, let them rest—the *Sponsa Gnesnensis et Sponsa Varsaviensis* [the Bride of Gniezno and the Bride of Warsaw]—so unfortunately wedded to a useless groom.

February 2, 1954, Tuesday

Today is the fifth anniversary of that day when, early in the morning, I started from Trzemeszno along the trail of Saint Wojciech* to assume the Primatial See at Gniezno. The day was cold and snowy like today. At the city gates the sun broke out. The memory of these five years of work dictates I thank Our Lord for the great honor bestowed upon me by the Giver of all work and mission. I was full of uncertainty then, as today I am full of shame that my work was so unworthy and inept. My zeal for the work and its burdensome responsibility often overshadowed the value of what I did. Whereas I was deeply devoted to the work, the pressures could be overwhelming, and I felt inept. Despite a sense of guilt, a sense of something incomplete, I think of the past with a sense of relief. It was very difficult indeed. It seems that only now, in my isolation, is there some relief, a chance to catch my breath—something I had been unable to do during those five years. As I conclude these five years of service here in prison, I trust that the Merciful Lord will look upon the time of my imprisonment as compensation for my having fallen short of His expectations. I continue to trust that the Supreme Shepherd of human souls will allow me to serve Him better "when lawlessness will cease." And this is why I spend this day in prayer for Gniezno, for the See of Wojciech, for the See of "The Virgin Mother of God, Mary, honored by God."† In her hands I place all my troubles and I ask her: *Dignare me laudare Te, Virgo sacrata* [Deem me worthy to praise you, Holy Virgin]. Allow me to build the Church of your Son, allow me to prepare your

---

*An allusion to the road traveled by Saint Wojciech (Adalbert), a tenth-century Slovak bishop, who labored among the Poles and Prussians; he is the Patron of Poland.

†The first words of the first Polish Marian hymn attributed to Saint Wojciech.

diocese and basilica for the great anniversary of our nation—for the one-thousand-year anniversary of the grace of Holy Baptism.

Today also we could hear a message from the nearby little church, such as we have not had since the first of January. Apparently they were celebrating a day of indulgence,* because yesterday we heard the bell ringing, as if for Vespers, and several times again today. From the distance we could discern the last words of the song, "Ave, Ave Maria," and nothing more. For the imprisoned, so much joy, so much happiness . . .

February 7, 1954, Sunday
Peter once asked, "We have left everything and followed you. What are we to have then?" Jesus said to him, "You will be repaid a hundred times over. . . ." (Matthew 19). Later Peter was in prison as well as in a circus arena and on the cross. . . . This was the beginning of the repayment. Michelangelo, in his frescoes in the Pauline Chapel, presented with his brush—as though writing the story of his life—how happy Peter was when he received God's payment in his rebirth. Since God is already starting to repay me today, it proves that He desires to see me in the rebirth. Therefore, I do not ask: What will be? It already is. I don't know how to be as joyful as Peter was on the cross, but this advance I accept—the rest will come more quickly since God has already begun His compensation.

February 22, 1954, Monday
The eighth sacrament in the life of the Church is martyrdom. Christ himself sanctified it when He said the blessed would be persecuted. And Christ's martyr-death, which theologians call the Great Sacrament, is it not the redeeming moment of the first experience of this Sacrament? The eighth? Should it not be the first?

---

*In Polish, *odpust*: an ancient custom that grants special indulgences (related to the doctrine of the remission of temporal punishment for good works and prayers) to those who visit a certain place or church and offer prayers on a certain designated day, for instance the feast day of the saint in whose honor the church is dedicated.

March 4, 1954, Thursday

The matter of the books which I had requested last October came up again. I still have not received them. I asked the guards if they had my breviary, because I needed the spring volume. The Commandant declared that everything they received had been delivered to me, they had nothing else. Although he added, "Maybe there are some things somewhere out there." Soon the so-called Superintendent [Nazi] came to Father S. and asked him to prepare a list of the books we had and those I had requested in October. Father S. explained that a copy of the list had already been submitted in November. The Superintendent said that apparently it had been lost somewhere. We therefore prepared a third copy of the list of books, which I had first requested on October 15, 1953, as well as a list of the books that had been delivered. Apparently they were storing my things and had confused the items—those received with those delivered. And since they betray very little skill in handling the printed word, they prefer to have everything black and white.

Father Stanisław submitted both lists to the Superintendent. Soon after, lo and behold, the Superintendent appeared at Father Stanisław's with the spring volume of my red-covered breviary, complete with the holy pictures that had been in it. What joy to have one's own breviary again!

I lived my priestly life wracked with misery, weakness, and wounds received along the way. Truly a worm, not a man. Everyone is entitled to gloat at my shortcomings. And yet, by living I fulfill my priestly vocation. My misery does not hinder me in serving the mercy of God by providing people with the benefits that the world regards as most valuable. This was how Christ himself lived—scorned by the mob, ragged, beaten, covered with street mud, spat upon. And yet it was He Who saved the world—and saved it even though the world sneered at its Saviour. How closely these two roads parallel each other. My inadequacy is supported by sacramental grace; the "inadequacy" of Jesus the Man is supported by His divinity . . . Let the world laugh, as long as the work of redemption is effected.

_____

March 10, 1954, Wednesday
Man, fortunately, does not have the power to eradicate totally and boundlessly the most essential of God's attributes—love. If man could bind in chains the love and forgiveness of the Almighty! Fortunately, God, in showing His mercy, relies only on Himself. His right to grace is a King's right and is irrevocable. He forgives because He wishes to forgive—for His own glory and because of His own goodness.

_____

March 18, 1954, Thursday
Today I received some of the books included in the list I made on March 4, as well as a cassock which I had not requested. Saint Joseph, in whose honor we concluded a novena today, sustained us with his kindness. The books will be most useful in helping to expand our intellectual efforts, within the modest limits of our existence.

_____

*March 19, 1954, Friday**
We follow the inspiration of the breviary. The *Responsory* after the first lesson of Matins reads: *Fuit Dominus cum Joseph, et dedit ei gratiam in conspectu principis carceris: Qui tradidit in manu illius universos vinctos* [The Lord was with Joseph and gave him favor with the warden, who put him in charge of all prisoners] (Gen. 39:21). Not without reason does the Joseph of Egypt provide a wonderful background against which we can clearly see Joseph of Nazareth. Although the Holy Carpenter never sat in prison, he protected the Son of God against Herod's torment. He was His guardian in Egypt, just as the holy patriarch, the prisoner, brought aid to his fellow prisoners: "Whatever happened [in prison] was in his care," states the inspired historian of Genesis. When we read these profound words, our hearts fill with hope, inspired by the

_____

*The feast of Saint Joseph.

Holy Spirit. This hope filled the hearts of the priestly brotherhood in Dachau; they prayed to Saint Joseph, and he came to their aid—at precisely the time of his feast day. So they hurried to the historic church of Kalisz to give thanks for their miraculous rescue and liberation. The effectiveness of Saint Joseph's help in battles against the bonds of the soul, in liberation from enslavement to sin, is well known to all who engage in pastoral, missionary, and retreat work. The Patron of the Church, who uses the key of David in his battles (*O Clavis David . . . qui aperis et nemo claudit . . . veni et educ vinctum de domo carceris* [O Key of David . . . who opens and no one closes . . . come and lead your captive from prison]), is the guardian of every soul that waits for the redeeming turn of that key.

March 24, 1954, Wednesday

A meeting of hearts . . . This crucial event took place in Nazareth, when Mary said, "Behold the handmaid of the Lord, be it done unto me according to thy word."* The Immortal Heart nestled beneath the Immaculate Heart, the purest Heart. God gave his own Heart, God experienced so much heart. The Divine Heart embraced the heart of man, man opened his heart and received God. The heart of hearts is an abyss even for the heart full of Grace. The coexistence of two hearts: of the Creator and the creature—God the graft, man the shoot. But this is a very special relationship: the Heart of Jesus, drawing from the Heart of the Word directly conveys the depth of love drawn from the Divine Being—for man. But that Heart of the God-Man, united with the life of Mary, is nourished by her blood. The Heart of Mary beats for the Heart of Jesus. The Heart of Mary, enriched in so unusual a way, brings to the Heart of Jesus all that an Immaculate Mother may draw from purest love to give to its Infant. As we identify most faithfully the likeness of a mother in the face of her child, so in Jesus we identify the spiritual characteristics of His Mother's

---

*Words spoken by Mary at the Annunciation (commemorated on March 25), when the angel Gabriel announced that she was to become the mother of Jesus (Luke 1:38).

heart. How ready and eager was Mary for every act of service: the response given to the angel, the visit to Elizabeth, Cana, Calvary—so swift in decision and in readiness to help and to serve. As Christ said: "I shall come and heal him." The young man from Naim, Lazarus, Zacchaeus, Peter's mother-in-law, the daughter of Jairus, the blind man from Jericho, the man with the withered hand—these are signs of Christ's readiness to serve men. The heart of Mary was mirrored in the Heart of Jesus. From then on the two Hearts, as one, would serve every man "who fell among thieves."

March 25, 1954, Thursday
Benigne fac Domine pro voluntate Tua [Deal kindly, O Lord, according to Thy will] (Psalm 50:20; 51:20 KJV). I know Your fatherly hands because they are the hands that have formed me. I can feel the imprint of Your Fingers on me. Nothing but goodness has flowed from Them onto me. And yet God's Finger disturbs me, even though its touch is usually through love. I humble myself before Your Finger, and I fear being consumed by the unquenchable fire that is You. There is still so much in me for burning. Oh, if only I were already a spirit! Your purifying fire would not consume it as it consumes everything else. *Benigne fac*—look how weak I am, how helpless, how I fear the power of Your gale. When You pass, the earth trembles. Is it surprising that the earth of my body is filled with fear? *Benigne fac*—like a father, who for the first time, takes the newborn baby into his arms. Is a mother not then fearful for her child when it is in the father's strong hands? At least you, Kindest Mother of the only begotten Son of God, keep watch over the Hands of the Heavenly Father when He holds me. Guard me and protect me. *Benigne fac*—I am a fragile vessel, and You a Giant who casts about entire constellations of stars as if they were mere toys. It is true, for Your hand a speck of dust and a planet have the same worth; You are Creator of one and the other. You have weighed everything in your hands. Why am I still afraid?

Benigne fac—I trust, but I seek your gentle touch. Best of all, give me to my Mother, as You have given her Your own only begotten Son. For all of her goodness stems from Yours.

April 8, 1954, Thursday

Today the Commandant started a conversation on the subject of my health. I explained that the symptoms which have been the source of my concern throughout the entire winter have not entirely disappeared. Apparently I caught cold in my kidneys while traveling from Rywałd to Stoczek; later, in the apartment, the condition worsened because of the humidity that seeped through the flooring from the apartment below. The Commandant took the position that there should be a medical commission. I asked whether I might be told who would be the members of the commission, as I could not agree to an anonymous one. The Commandant said he would not be able to give me a reply right away, but he would discuss this with his superiors. Then he brought up the question of responsibility for one's health; in the opinion of the Commandant, the responsibility for my state of health rested entirely with me. I protested against such an approach; if I were living in freedom and in control of the available means, that would be different, but if I am a prisoner deprived of all my rights, then the responsibility for the state of my health rests with the government. I further stated that it did not matter to me whether society placed the responsibility for my condition "on you." The Commandant did not share this view; he said that in the twentieth century man did have rights.

"I deplore the fact," I said, "that in the twentieth century there can be such lawlessness as that of which I am a victim. It is outrageous that a person can be treated as I have been: abducted in the middle of the night, practically from my bed, and denied any rights whatsoever. Because, really, what rights do I have?"

The Commandant declared that I have "the right to receive medical attention." Other matters, he said, he would be ready to discuss some other time, especially since he had already told me that I could write to Minister Bida and explain my situation. I reminded him that I had been denied the right to write letters, even to my father. I also mentioned that I wanted to write to Bishop Klepacz and Bishop Choromański. I had had no responses to the two letters I had sent to my father. I had no intention of writing to the archives. I regarded the attitude of the government as a violation of human rights. The

Commandant stated that the government had made no secret of what was happening to me, and that the entire country knew I was in a monastery.

Once again I expressed my regret at the behavior of the government. It was well known to the government, and especially to the bishops and Mr. Mazur, how much effort I had invested in making the Mutual Understanding possible between the government and the Church, from the very first moment after assuming the leadership of the Gniezno and Warsaw Sees. After so many efforts, I did not deserve to be treated as I was.

The Commandant returned to the subject of my responsibility for my health: "You are a doctor and an educated man, so you know. . . ."

"My doctorate is in a different field," I responded. I decided to agree to a medical commission under condition: "Please provide me with the names and I will decide myself whether they are agreeable to me or whether I will request that my own doctor be added."

The Commandant brought up another subject—that of my letter to the government. He would present the matter to his superiors and would be prepared to discuss it later.

I declared that before I could write a letter to the government, I needed a copy of the government's decision of last September, since I had not received one. Furthermore, there was still the matter of our relationship. "I am forced to regard you as a representative of the government that does me an injustice. It is not surprising, then, that my attitude toward you cannot be a friendly one, although I do not want you to see it as a personal animosity. I must fight for my rights, and you impede my contact with the government."

The Commandant indicated that "I was right."

April 9, 1954, Friday

A few remarks about our living conditions. Winter in Stoczek was indeed very severe. First, strong winds blew against our little windows almost constantly, helping us realize why such an imposing structure was constructed with such small windows. Snowstorms left huge drifts of snow around the house; very often in the morning we could not even get out into the garden. It became routine for us to sweep the snow from the steps of the veranda and from the paths under the windows. No one else followed our example. Only once did one of the guards drag a shovel over one of the walks. Another tried to sweep the steps from time to time. Still another improvised a shovel from such heavy wood that it could not be used. So we stuck to our own implements: an old garden rake and a plain board, which served for shoveling snow. We were able to maintain the garden area, because all the walks were clear for strolling. But this was very heavy work. I noticed that Father S. tired more quickly than I did. Perhaps it was because he had had no experience in such work. But for both of us this was a useful and healthy diversion.

Inside the house the situation was worse. The old building had a very antiquated heating system. The heaters were ruined and burned out; the pipes ran horizontally. Burning coal quickly clogged the pipes with soot. Quite often our guards had to play chimney sweeps. In this they exhibited considerable zeal. Especially Mo, an older man, who would take off his uniform and reach up to his armpits inside the ducts to remove piles of soot. This happened several times during the winter. The heaters smoked as a matter of course; the sister's room could not be heated at all, and she spent almost the entire winter in an unheated room. The priest's heater was also unusable. The heaters in my room were the best, but not sufficient to heat the room. They had to be lighted twice. Even so, the apartment was so cold that working at the table was virtually impossible; hands and feet would literally freeze. Even wrapping oneself in a shawl did not help. The problem was the same in the bathroom, where an old heater simply would not work; it would smoke up the entire house, no matter how many times it was cleaned. For a long time we had to wash ourselves in a cold bathroom. We were also plagued with water shortages; the old motor that pumped the water often refused to work. Very often we had no water at all and had to carry it up from downstairs. Finally the entire system froze solid. We were amazed by the blocks of ice carried out of the rooms below us. We were living over ice houses. The rooms downstairs were not heated and had become thoroughly mildewed. Nobody cared to heat them. The walls of all the hallways were layered with frost and ice. The poor guards had to sit in their sheepskin coats and heavy boots. They suffered even more than we. Their faces grew longer and longer.

In such conditions I began to experience a variety of ailments. I could not get my feet warm, even at night. My hands swelled as did my eyes. I experienced great pain in the region of my kidneys and throughout my abdomen. Every day I suffered headaches. The sister was constantly ill with the flu, pale and emaciated. Father S. seemed to suffer most. He sustained frequent liver attacks and other ailments. The doctors diagnosed it as a pancreatic disease. He spent several days in bed, very ill with the flu. The sister seemed to be the strongest of us, despite the heavy work which she had to carry out. Every day she had to light the heater in the bathroom and five other ones, which were very difficult to light. In addition, it was her duty to bring up the coal and carry down the ashes. The hardest of all was doing the laundry, which had to be done frequently because my companions had very little to wear. There was no place to dry it. Feminine fastidiousness drove the sister to polish the long corridor floors, the stairs, etc., frequently. Once in a while I managed to stop her from polishing the floors in my room, but the sister would find a moment when I was in the garden and would give vent to this need of her heart. Keeping the place clean was difficult, because the old floor boards were loose and sent up clouds of dust. But it is difficult to persuade a woman to listen. Such contretemps, stemming from our sister's "holy obstinacy," were very frequent. She could forgo eating, sleeping, praying—but she had to polish floors. Perhaps this work helped her escape from her thoughts.

———————

April 12, 1954, Monday
After my agreeing to the medical commission, the Commandant announced today that the government was sending its doctor, a Dr. Wesołowski, from Warsaw. In view of this, I submitted my own two names to choose from: Dr. Zero and Dr. Wąsowicz from Warsaw, according to addresses to be supplied by Miodowa Street. The Commandant stated that he would submit my wishes to his superiors.

The dilapidated monastery in Stoczek, Wyszyński's second place of internment. The building was in a state of ruin. The inside walls were wet, the floor was stone. During winter, water would run down the walls and freeze in sheets.

April 13, 14, 1954, Tuesday–Wednesday
Before Easter the three of us arranged a short retreat for ourselves in our little chapel. Our reflections centered around Thomas à Kempis' *Imitation of Christ.* The main theme was the ascetics of prison life as an unusual means provided by Providence, from the very beginnings of Christianity, to sanctify man. Christians embarked on careers as prisoners very early—since the time of the first sermons of Saint Peter the Apostle in Jerusalem. God's providence even allowed for a special period in the history of the Church—a three-century period of prisons, catacombs, and public executions. To this day that period is an inspiration to all whom God has privileged with suffering in His Name.

April 15, 1954, Holy Thursday
We spent Holy Thursday in our little chapel with almost basilica-like splendor. For the first time I sang Mass with a *schola cantorum* [choir] consisting of a priest and a sister. God will forgive our mistakes. In my heart and my thoughts I was in my archdiocesan cathedral, among the clergy and the faithful. I prayed that my substitute at the altar, while consecrating the oils and performing the *mandatum* [washing of the feet], would do it better than I, that he would bestow upon the priests the Body of Christ, instilling in them the spirit of diocesan unity, that he would kiss the feet of the poor as I did—with total devotion to the meaning of a gesture, which is so splendid but so difficult to achieve in the spirit of Christianity, because it must be the heart doing the kissing, not the lips.

Today I received the next installment of books from home, in accordance with the list of March 4. Among them was the winter volume of the breviary. I was still missing the summer volume.

Only God can appreciate in full truth all that befalls men on this earth. Human misfortune is often viewed through the prism of the friends of Job. They see in it either ineptitude and helplessness or a punishment—generally well deserved—or a social inevitability, a public good, or else the glory of God. This entire gallery of human spectators is generally in error, because its approach is one-sided. God and his Job generally reach an understanding of the whole truth. Because every Job sooner or later admits his guilt before God, often in what the gallery considers as Job's virtue: "Who among us is without sin?" "Who will understand the fault?" But on this score the understanding between God and Job comes rather quickly, even if Job has to work hard and long to overcome the effects of his transgressions. But personal suffering never remains locked in the heart and life of Job. Because that suffering, as seen through the eyes of the gallery, is often testimony to God and His intention. When the gallery does not know the cause of the sufferings, it replies: "God wills it." "It is for the glory of God." This is how one judges the suffering of the saints, of those persecuted for justice, idealists, Church heroes, and Church martyrs.

It is certain that in all that a man experiences there is a complex of causes. God purifies his servant, invites him to come and sit higher, makes him an instrument of warning for others, renders justice to persecutors, highlights the devotion of his servant to God, even in adversities, increases the glory of the Church, multiplies His blessings. Only God can settle many matters in just one act of suffering. That which in the eyes of man is only a fault in the eyes of God is glory. Only God in His goodness can administer punishment in such a way that the punished achieves glory *coram homini-bus* [before men]. The greatness of God's mercy is infinite.

April 17, 1954, Holy Saturday

After morning Mass the holiday spirit began to reign. We prepared ourselves yesterday, spending most of the time in the chapel in prayer. This evening at six the Commandant came in with two large packages from Miodowa Street as well as a letter from my father. The letter was dated April 3, 1954, and had been cut and repasted in three places. I asked the Commandant what that meant. He replied, "You are not permitted to know what was cut out." It is as if someone had surgically removed from a living human being a most precious and most desired organ. The rest of the letter is as follows:

My dearest son!

(cut out)

Our thoughts are always with you, our prayers flow constantly to our Lord for you and in your name. They soothe our hearts and our sorrow, but as time passes our concern increases and is more and more difficult to fight. But we do trust our God Almighty that He has you in His care; that He keeps you in good health and serenity, and on this day of the Resurrection of our Lord we wish with all our heart that you return. (cut out) All is well here, we are healthy and lead quiet lives. We send you our warmest greetings, and commend you to the care of our most Blessed Mother. (cut out) With all my heart, your faithful father.

Zalesie, April 3, 1954
S. Wyszyński

Included in the packages were, among other things, some medicines that had been confiscated: some iodine, adhesive tape, aspirin, penicillin tablets, coramine, cibalgine, bandages, cotton, petrolatum. More than once we had felt a lack of these simple medical aids. The few medical supplies I had received in the very beginning were almost gone. Our guards had nothing. It was difficult to get even a drop of iodine; it usually took days before they would bring some kind of pill for a headache. In spite of this, even though they were aware of their own shortages, they did not permit us to keep these simple medicines. Apparently they wanted to have control over even the slightest illness. All we could do was keep quiet. Especially since revealing any suffering did not always give the proper impression. The second deputy in particular—the one we called Doctor, because we suspected that he had something to do with medicine—would sometimes create hilarious situations. Whenever this man, perfectly indifferent to all human suffering, would hear a complaint from Father S. about pains in the liver or whatever, he would end his interview with a pat phrase, "very well then," and would leave the patient, showing no concern. It seemed that nothing impressed him at all except his own appearance, so carefully tended. One was often struck by the painful contrast when this official doll—suit carefully pressed, well shaven, preened, and smelling of perfume—would stand in the presence of this pale man in drab cassock and ice cold hands. Every time he left the room, I always felt deep relief, as though —despite his grooming—something dirty and suffocating had departed. I had to fight the instinctive desire to wash my hands. Interestingly, even though the Commandant, a typical old fox, had an unmistakably unprincipled personality, he did not leave such an unpleasant impression as this mannequin from a tailor's window. A man carries with him all that he is and all that he has; there is no ignoring it.

April 19, 1954, Monday
Strolling through the garden today, we found among some rotting leaves a letter from the Secretary of State of Vatican City numbered L.172634 and addressed to J. Gfoellner, bishop of Linz (Johanni Gfoellner, Episcopo Linciensi), expressing thanks for a copy of the *Linzer Prakt. Quartalschrift.* The letter was signed by E. Cardinal Pacelli* and dated November 23, 1938. We tried to guess how this type of letter could have landed with the trash in Stoczek. There is only one possibility: the recipient was brought here and took with him only his most important documents. The signature of Cardinal Pacelli was so clear and readable that there was no doubt as to its authenticity. I remembered now that the French press had mentioned Warmia as the place of deportation of many Austrian priests after the *Anschluss.*

We took it upon ourselves to clean up the garden; both of us began raking the leaves, which had been heaped up in huge piles in which entire colonies of mice were living. For weeks on end we burned pile after pile of leaves in order to free the garden from vermin. Our guards observed all of this indifferently with no desire to imitate. At

---

*Eugenio Pacelli, the Vatican's secretary of state between 1930 and 1939, became Pope Pius XII in 1939 and was still Pope at the time this letter was found.

The road on the monastery grounds in Stoczek. Here the cardinal was allowed to walk under guard.

the end of the hornbeam walk, in a group of linden trees, mostly half-sawed and wrapped in wire, we erected a cross made of two sticks tied with barbed wire. In this way we created a Calvary fenced with stones and bricks, and this became the object of our walks. Our work was made more difficult because of a lack of tools, especially a rake. Even though our difficulties were apparent, nobody offered us a rake. Indeed, they often borrowed the implements we had managed to make ourselves from the odds and ends found in the garden. In fact, our guardians expressed such indifference to maintaining order in general that we were frequently amused by the thought that we came off as the materialists while they came off as the idealists who scorned everything that required effort and maintenance of order. No one ever did anything on his own initiative; whenever they took our tools from our POM,* they would never put them back in their proper places. Usually they just dropped them someplace in the garden, so that we had to search for them again when they were needed. The listlessness and indolence of these people amazed us. The only person who would look for things to do was Mo; he would try to tinker with something, repair some toys, occasionally read a book, although sometimes he would become depressed and stand in the corridor in a stupor, or sit doing nothing for hours on end.

Looking at them, it was possible to predict the future of the system; if among this representative group for special tasks there were so many lazy and listless men, then what must their other people be like? These were obviously men in search of easy ways and a comfortable life. Who among them knew the Marxist doctrine well? And who believed in it? I was probably the only one in that house who had gone through *Das Kapital* three times, beginning while I was still in the seminary! And yet without knowledge and faith it is difficult to rebuild any system. Furthermore, the Church requires from us that we love the cause we serve. How can one even conceive of loving a cause which one is commanded to, dragging one's feet? All our guardians, even though they were officers, walk through the corridors dragging their feet. In the language they use, especially the younger ones, the most common word is "damn." When they speak of us they say "those ones."

April 20, 1954, Tuesday

There was not a single sin that I could find in myself today that did not irk me. I would prefer them not to exist at all. A sin, then, is only an illusion, since it tempts only before it exists, and immediately afterward ceases to give pleasure. There is not one illusive joy that I desire today; every one is a lie. Is not distaste for one's old sins the best caution against new ones?

Why should it be surprising, since even in those of my deeds that are considered good I find no satisfaction? I am unhappy with every

----

*POM—Państwowy Ośrodek Maszynowy—a government facility that supplied machinery, tractors, farm implements, etc. The cardinal is jokingly equating their "storage facility" with a government POM.

one of them. Each one of them I would do differently today. The most perfect of my deeds is full of imperfection. I must defend their objective value to myself.

Only God's deeds are perfect. Perhaps this is why I am so critical of my own deeds: I see them in the light of God's.

What would I not give to improve deeds already committed, make good ones better, add more love to the very best! I am not a master of the past. But I have a warning: every deed must be approached in the light of all past experiences.

A deed takes place once and does not change; it remains thus for eternity. But the evaluation of that deed changes with every decade. And this is terrible! How very perfect a deed must be in order to emerge victorious from the changing moods of history. This veteran climber continues to scale the rocky peaks of ages and from their heights looks down upon the lowly shelters of deeds. They seem to vanish from before our eyes. And yet they endure. There would be no history if there were no deeds, even miserable ones.

April 26, 1954, Monday
A bishop performs his duties not only in the pulpit and at the altar, but also in prison—*in vinculis Christi.* To give witness to Christ while in chains is the same kind of obligation as in the pulpit. It is therefore not a waste of time to remain in prison in the name of Christ. This is why God allowed so many servants of the Church to remain in prisons even when the crops in the fields were ripening, ready for the harvest. Saint Paul, during his most ardent missionary work, was abducted to prison, and he served terms in Jerusalem, in Caesarea, and in Rome. The history of the Church makes a substantial contribution to the history of prisons.

April 30, 1954, Friday
The Commandant asked about my health. Aside from my kidney complaints, I felt there were no other changes. I was waiting for the

doctor; the Commandant hoped that the doctor would appear "right after the holidays," as if I did not need a doctor during the Easter season. I reminded him of the letter to my father. I was prepared to give him another letter on condition that I received an assurance that my former letters had been delivered. The Commandant responded that since my father wrote to me, he must have received my letters. I retorted that this was only the Commandant's opinion and I had no assurance of the facts—an assurance to which I had a right. It was difficult for me to write into the unknown. I handed the Commandant a letter to my father, in which straight off (I read the letter aloud) I mention my doubts as to the delivery of my earlier letters.

I also brought up another matter, mentioned last April 8—the matter of the copy of the decree read to me on Miodowa Street by the representatives of the UB [Security Police] last September 25. The Commandant declared that he did have an answer: I could not receive a copy of the decree at this time because that would "be a polemic."

I replied: I had no intention to indulge in polemics, but it was essential that I have the decree, because for me it was my verdict and affected my legal status. In any case, all prisoners received copies of their verdicts, why couldn't I?

The Commandant suggested that the situation was different, since I was not here as a result of a verdict—I am only "temporarily isolated." When my isolation was over, I would be able to receive a copy of the decree.

I presented my point of view: it was generally accepted that documents addressed to citizens were the property of those citizens. The government decree was my property.

The Commandant believed that what was read to me was a "declaration." Anyway, he added, "You may write a letter to the government."

"In order to write a letter to the government, I must know the text of the decree which was read to me," I replied, "and today I do not remember it."

"But you know the charges against you—there were three of them."

"No," I answered, "the decree contained one complaint, relative to my sermons. The other charges were formulated in the press—primarily by General Ochab. They were (1) that I hindered the implementation of the Mutual Understanding, and (2) that I did not do all that I should have for the cause of the Western Territories. Not remembering the decree, it is difficult to write the letter because later there may be some inaccuracies."

The Commandant consented to inform the government that I did not remember the content of the decree read to me. I ended the conversation: (1) I expected the question of the delivery of the letters to be clarified, and (2) I expected a clarification on the matter of a copy of the government "declaration."

I handed the Commandant this letter to my father:

My dearest father:

Your letter of April 3 of this year arrived on Holy Saturday, in the evening. I awaited it as a visible sign, my dearest father, of your good health and well-being. Since I had no confirmation of the receipt of my letters of October 31 and December 22 of last year, I was forced to deny myself the pleasure of writing to my family at Easter time. But today, even though the letter I received is so short, it is a great joy to me, putting me in touch with you.

I thank you, Father, and I thank the family and all the members of the household for the gift of your prayers: they help me and they help you, because nothing can put one's thoughts and feelings in order as prayer can. Luckily, I have a lot of time for this in our modest little chapel where—in direct association—there abides the One Whom I have been serving for the past thirty years. I remember you, Father, in every Mass; each day I recite Terce for you so that you will never cease to be trusting and, despite everything, your thoughts will be filled with Christian sentiments toward everyone without exception. After all, the value of life is determined not by great deeds, but by love; one must, therefore, preserve this most precious good for oneself and for one's fellowmen who always have a right to our heart.

Also, dear Father, you must rid yourself quickly of sadness and worry—these are feelings that are contrary to Christian hope, that most conquering virtue that is capable of opening every door. During Easter week the Church has shown us the significance of its theological virtues. It devoted Holy Thursday to faith, the day when the Holy Eucharist was instituted, the day of the Apostles' first Holy Communion and their first Mass, the day of the first priestly ordinations, and the day Christ descended to his knees to wash men's feet. Good Friday—this is the day of love, even to the summit of the cross, the day of God's concession to human feelings and thus a day of sorrow; but there is only one such day in the year of the Church. Directly from the cross is born Hope, which reigns over the Saturday before Easter, the day of Hope, the brilliance of a new light—*Lumen Christi* [the Light of Christ] —and of that victorious optimism, which calls even Adam's sin "a happy fault"—*felix culpa*—for sin brought into being not only death but the Conqueror of death as well—the Commander of Life (Read in the Missal: *Victimae paschalis laudes* [Praises of the Paschal victim]). And so, when Faith and Hope and Love have been renewed in us—let us use these powers: daily to have faith, like the mustard seed, to trust almost in spite of hope, and not deny one's heart to anyone.

My dearest father—the Church repeats so often that everything helps those who love God toward good. And it is the same with me. I know that God has not turned away from me, He is closer to me today than ever before; I feel it all too clearly. And my God is not in the least severe, only serene, gentle, and most subtle. For a long time I wanted to find more time for my neglected reading; I set aside stacks of unread books—for later. Today I am able to read more —that is a plus. I have already read a great deal. Because I lack my scholarly source materials, I cannot do much writing, but I do not regret it, as I regret nothing that I am now experiencing.

You inquire, dear Father, about the state of my health. Let

me put it this way: it is no worse than it usually was. My health was always not the best, but I was accustomed to effort and work. I can't say that any of my ailments, so well known to the members of our household, stands apart from the others. I trust I can keep it this way. I consider it urgent and necessary to secure professional treatment for my kidneys.

I would like to remind you, Father, that the third of August will mark the thirtieth anniversary of my ordination to the priesthood in the Cathedral of Włocławek; May 12 is the eighth anniversary of my consecration as bishop at Jasna Góra. Both these days are as precious to me as the day of my birth, and therefore today I commend myself to you on these days and ask for your fatherly prayers.

I remember the day of your patron saint* and I am praying in your behalf, dear Father, to the Shepherd of Kraków.† Please accept my sincerest and best name day wishes which will be the intention of the Mass I will offer for you. Through your kindness I send my best wishes to Stasia, Stach, and little Staś, as well as to Monsignor. I remembered Naścia on her name day. Before our Lord I always remember your needs and pray to God that you never lack sincere trust in Him as well as love for your fellowmen.

The kindness of your hearts supplied us so generously for the Easter holidays! Definitely too generously; more than we need, since we have all that is necessary for life. But such gifts are more appreciated by our hearts than by our lips. And this is why they are dear to us as proof of your caring, love, and signs of our unity.

Dear Father, I kiss your hands with reverence, gratitude, and devotion, and I ask that you not be sad; I ask that you maintain your serenity, good cheer, and trust, believing that in everything that God provides for man there is more of His wisdom and goodness than may be expected.

*May 7.
†Saint Stanislaus, bishop and martyr.

To all the family and members of the household I send words of devotion, my sincere love, and my blessings.

April 29, 1954
+ Stefan Cardinal Wyszyński

April 30, 1954, Friday
If I were to see, in one glance, the effects of but one sin—even the most ineffectual sin in the history of a life—I would succeed in turning away from it. If I were to think how a forgiven sin can still be most irksome, how it can spring back into the memory, torture the imagination, how it insists on returning and taking its place in time, in thoughts, in struggle . . . If I could foresee the frontal attack that all forgiven sins stage on positions that were seemingly impregnable . . . If one sin is capable of unsettling a person, what is to be said about a whole lifetime of sin?

Conclusion: beware of sin, for one alone can start the avalanche.

May 3, 1954, Monday
I give birth in my soul to such heavy boulders that I may be unable to carry this fruit of my spiritual womb. So I drop them at your feet, Mother. Perhaps along the road of these stones you will lead me to your Son—the Way. Your Son refused to turn stones to bread. It is easier to reach your Son by a rocky road than by one paved with loaves of bread. Perhaps, then, the fruit of my womb, Mother, will also be blessed. Cast a smile upon my stones. This is all I can offer—the rest is up to you. I, too, do not want all of them to be turned to bread. But allow at least one of these stones to feed my hungry soul. Because *Petra autem erat Christus* [The rock was Christ] (1 Cor. 10:4).

May 5, 1954, Wednesday
Careless words are like empty boxes with illegible labels. Careless prayer is a stack of empty boxes. What use is a warehouse full of empty boxes? Who will find nourishment here?

You were present at Pentecost among the Apostles, as You were in Bethlehem among the shepherds. In the Upper Room was born the Church, Christ, as in Bethlehem was born Christ the Man. The infant Church desperately needed a Mother who would care for it. And this was why you were present in the Upper Room at Pentecost, in that Bethlehem of the Universal Church. What a marvelous grace for the Church was your Motherhood, from the very birth of the Church! How thoughtful of God never to leave us even for a moment without a Mother . . .

May 12, 1954, Wednesday
The doctor's visit began with a typical incident. We were taking our morning walk when in the distance we noticed the rocking figure of the Superintendent. "Some two men are here to see you, Father."

"*Some* men?" It sounded like something out of the normal. "You don't know who?"

"Probably the doctors," replied the Superintendent.

"So not '*some* men.'" I went back to the house.

After half an hour wait, two men entered the room. One was an old heavyset man, with the typical expression of a family doctor, the mien of a professor. The other was a young, short, thin man with a red necktie, who looked more like a UB functionary than a doctor. They did not introduce themselves nor did they explain the nature of their visit. I asked them, therefore, what it was they wanted. They explained that they were doctors and had been sent to examine me. I informed them that the Commandant of this house and I had agreed that the government would send Dr. Wesołowski, and at my request Dr. Zero or Dr. Wąsowicz would also come. The younger gentleman said that he was Doctor Wesołowski. What was happening today was not only a surprise to me, but clear evidence of the government's violation of our agreement. The choice of a doctor is above all a matter of confidence.

"I do not know you, gentlemen; what proof do I have that you are doctors?"

The older man, expressing his embarrassment in this situation, began to refer to me as "Sir."

I explained to him that I was a cardinal and that at the very least I had the right to be addressed as Father. The older man then began to call me Father. The younger man avoided calling me anything and remained gloomy and official throughout.

Faced with this unforeseen situation, I agreed to allow them to examine me, but only out of sympathy for the older gentleman, for whom it must have been an effort to come all the way out here. The older man performed the examination very carefully and conscientiously; the younger one rather superficially and formally. After the examinations, they consulted with each other and then announced their diagnosis. They found a possible condition of hyperacidity, an enlargement of the liver, small changes in bone, a soreness of the muscles, and some evidence of sclerosis—slightly more than what is normal for my age. They did not share my concern for my kidneys, and they attributed my headaches to the changes in bone and muscle.

After the consultation, I called the attention of the two gentlemen to the conditions in which we lived. I considered it my duty to make them aware of the responsibility they were taking in examining me —their responsibility to the people of Poland, who were not indifferent to my fate. I was of the opinion that it would now be more convenient for the government if I had my own doctor. For these two gentlemen as well. I also considered it essential to restate my basic position, assuming that the two gentlemen were not only doctors but also members of the Polish Nation. Since they were sent here officially, they must know the official side, but they should also know *my* side, so as to get the whole picture. They should know, therefore, that my health was also affected by the psychological circumstances of this place; they should know that I considered the way in which I have been treated to be injurious and offensive not only to me but to the Church. The realization that in Poland there were disguised concentration camps even ten years after independence was more painful than physical wounds and ailments. I had no way to contact the people, for I was separated from them by a cordon of guards.

"Whoever you are, gentlemen, if you are Poles, you have the right to know the thoughts of one of you whose rights have been savagely abused. Because what has happened to one Pole can happen to any of the other twenty-five million."

The doctors listened in silence. The older doctor then went down into the garden and looked at the house from the outside, at the nearby pond, and at the surrounding area.

During the entire consultation there was no sign of the Commandant, with whom the conditions of the examination had been established, or any sign of the supervising staff. What was more, both guards—the one at the "checkpoint" in our hallway as well as the one from downstairs—seemed to have disappeared. They obviously had wanted to create the impression of a prevailing atmosphere of freedom.

The Commandant, whom we had not seen the entire week, finally appeared today. I asked him pointblank why neither of my own doctors—neither Dr. Zero nor Dr. Wąsowicz—had come to the consultation as had been agreed. The Commandant said that he did not know, that "apparently that was what had been decided by his superiors, or perhaps the doctors were unable to come."

"These are only your suppositions," I retorted; "the fact still remains that you violated the conditions for the consultation that we established."

The Commandant disagreed. "The important thing is that the medicines help."

"It's possible that for many people this is the important thing but not for me. The important thing is to respect one's human rights and freedom of choice in the serious and delicate matter of putting one's health in the hands of those who will accept the responsibility. There is no such respect here. Only a slave can approach this matter the way you do. I am not a person with a slave mentality. Therefore, I want to register a protest against what took place on May twelfth."

May 20, 1954, Thursday

The first act of the New Covenant, willed by the Holy Trinity, was in you, Mary. The Father, your Creator, called you to be the Mother of His only begotten Son. The Son chose to live in your sanctuary. The Holy Spirit embraced you, his betrothed, with his love. The entire Holy Trinity was above you and in you. You are the most perfect creation of the Holy Trinity in the order of nature and grace. Is it not appropriate that this creation be forever reenacted in the work of the Church? Do you not stand at the threshold of every soul? It is toward you, therefore, that the eyes of the friends of the Betrothed, who invite the souls to the nuptials, must turn. Are you not the model and patron of spiritual shepherds? In your school we must learn the art of pastoral care.

June 1, 1954, Tuesday

The greatest enigma of man is his heart. It is so magnificent that God competes for it. So powerful that it can resist the love of the Almighty. So frail that many a weakness may snare it in its net. So wild that it may destroy all happiness and all order. So faithful that it cannot be subverted even by infidelity. So naive that it succumbs to every sweet temptation. Of such great capacity that it can contain every contradiction. And all this—almost—in every man, and all this—almost—in the wink of an eye. But man is a hundred times more grand, because he is capable of ruling it.

And God? He alone knows the routes into the most mysterious heart. That is why man opened the Heart of God on the cross to learn about His plans—*cogitationes.*

June 4, 1954, Friday

Verbum Caro [The Word (became) Flesh].

From the moment the Word became flesh in the womb of the Virgin, so that "Man could be born to this world," God became so enamored with this method that He returns to man, like a grain of wheat, in every Holy Communion, so that in this renewed incarnation every man can be born of God. From then on, Christ takes refuge within every person, so that His Christmas birth can be repeated in everyone. The Eucharistic Lord seeks endlessly for His Bethlehem, His crib. Often there is no room for Him at the inn, but whoever accepts Him, his stable is transformed into a temple, and he is made divine.

The Eucharist gives birth to a new species of mankind. It is the cradle of a new humanity—pregnant with God. A mankind that brings forth God to the world, carries God to all corners of the world, and brings God's Life to every grave. That is why the Eucharist is Resurrection, because it constantly germinates new life in the human soul, casting away and crushing the musty stones of a dying world. This is the joy of living, this is early spring, this is the rebellion of the young, the revolution of the infants, the Resurrection and Life everlasting.

June 5, 1954, Saturday
Ave verum Corpus, natum de Maria [Hail, true Flesh, born of Mary]. I know not how, O Mother, to honor properly the Guest of my soul. Allow me to use your own words. For you alone knew how to converse with your Son. . . . I salute Him with all your virginal Immaculateness, all your humble submissiveness, your living faith, ardent love, singular care, all your cooperation and cosuffering, all your faithful intimacy, all the holiness of your soul, every beat of your heart, every act of your mind, every gesture of your hands, every step of your virginal feet, every moment of your exceptional life, your consummate service to the Lord. . . .

When I feel Your presence in my soul, Christ, make me forget totally about myself, stop thinking about myself and telling You about myself. It is such an uninteresting and poor subject! I wish to think about You, to talk about You, and to praise You. I wish to thank You that You exist, that You are the Word, that You are the Son of the Father, that You wanted to take Your body from a Virgin, that You wanted to rest in the manger of Bethlehem, that you wanted to appear to the Shepherds and the Wise Men, that You wanted to walk the earth, that You wanted to be in the temple and in Cana, and on the shores of Lake Tiberias, and in Gerasa, and in Bethany, and in Jericho, and before Pilate, and on Calvary, and on the Mount of Olives. . . . I want to gaze at You, following You step by step. What a wonderful conversation it would be—about You! Protect me, that I may think only of You, when You enter my dwelling.

June 12, 1954, Saturday
Today I received a letter from my father, dated June 8, 1954; it contained no confirmation of the receipt of my letter of April 19, 1954. At the same time I was handed a package of clothes and the summer volume of the breviary, which I had requested two days ago. They told me then that they did not have that volume. Today it turned up. On this occasion the question of the books that I had requested in October of last year came up again. I was asked to check and see which books I had still not received and to prepare a copy of the list of the books received and the books missing. So Father Stanisław sat down to prepare what is now the fourth copy of the list of books which I had requested last October.

My dearest son!
I would like to express to you, at least in this way, the words of my ardent devotion and love as well as those of all your dear ones. My thoughts are with you constantly, and I wish my prayers, full of trust and confidence, which I never cease to direct to the Lord and to our Most Holy Mother in your name, to be a shield for you and help you suffer bravely all that God sends you. I believe that God's power is above everything and that His love directs the fate of mankind, turning temporary evil to our advantage and His glory.
We are all well and nothing new has happened to your dear ones and nothing has changed. The children are well, Staś will soon begin his first vacation. He is developing well and is becoming rather independent. Stefcio is making better progress than Zosia, and this year they are both doing well in school. Zocha has grown up and matured. Your

sisters, Tadeusz, and Zenia are working and healthy, and little Ania is healthy and developing very well. At Naścia's everyone is well. They all assure you that they are praying that you are well and strong.

I would like so much, my dear son, to see you as soon as possible, and, if it is allowed, at least to receive a few words from you telling us details about you, especially about your state of health, which worries us because we are familiar with certain of your illnesses.

I ask you, my dear son, for prayers in my name and for the entire family, as well as for all your other dear ones.

I close with these words of hope, trusting that the Good Lord will allow us to experience the happy moment when we can again embrace you and greet you among us.

We all send you our best wishes, words of respect, deepest devotion and love, asking for your blessing.

Zalesie, April 8, 1954
Your father S. Wyszyński

June 14, 1954, Monday
"Turn your merciful eyes upon me." . . . Allow your child to take advantage of his privilege and let him gaze into your eyes. . . . For a Mother does not turn her eyes away from her children. . . . Even through tears I shall see them. . . . Do not be offended that I may serve you only with my eyes, because I am allowed to look only upward and downward. . . . My lips have been sealed with a lock of silence . . . my hands and feet have been bound with garlands of wire. *Clausus sum neque egredi possum* [I am imprisoned and cannot depart]. But it does not matter, Mother! You have eyes and will observe the deep misery of your child. My soul longs for the altars of the Lord, for the prayer of a community, for the fragrance of incense, for the lights on the altars, for the singing of the people. . . . My lips want to profess faith in your Son to the people. . . . It is hard to retain the Word made Flesh—it wants to be born . . . even though there is no room at the inn. . . . You, Mother, know the pain

of bearing the burden of the Word for Whom there is no room.
Yours is a priestly soul so you know the woes of the Gospel writers.
Turn your merciful eyes—let your motherly heart sense the Mother
of Christ in us (Matt. 12:48–50). Help us give birth to the Word!

June 16, 1954, Wednesday

Christ spoke about whited sepulchers. It is strange how man likes
to conceal what is dirty by painting over it. After all, a whitewashed
wall does not cease to be dirty underneath. Is that perhaps why
people paint their faces, because they already see in them the decay
of the grave? Is that perhaps why they reach for perfume because
they realized that something within is rotting? Or perhaps why they
dress more and more meticulously, because they are beginning to
look worse and worse within? Do they want to vaunt their used
merchandise in new wrappings? The Egyptians painted mummies,
knowing that there was no longer any life in them. Is history also
to repeat itself here? And so, we should cry aloud, "Water!" But
Living Water, not the kind of water for which the Samaritan
woman went to Jacob's well. What is needed is the water with
which she returned to town. The Water of Christ. Because this
Water reaches *usque ad animam meam* [to my very soul].

June 20, 1954, Sunday

Love is the enemy of the laws of space. Only God, the Lord of all
laws, managed to violate this law when He became Nourishment and
penetrated the heart of man. And now He waits patiently until man
—aided by grace—manages to penetrate into the Heart of God.
Then the final obstacle will be destroyed: "I in them, and they in Us
. . ."

True friendship is a wall that unites and separates at the same time.
It can be maintained when both sides persist in scaling the wall.

June 24, 1954, Thursday

The Commandant appeared with the usual questions: my health and
my needs. I replied that my health gave no signs of any change for
the better. "Then perhaps a new medical commission?"

I expressed the fear that this would not result in much [improve-ment] if the circumstances were similar to those of the previous one. Although we had discussed [employing] my doctor, I was surprised by the members who actually comprised that commission. "What is more, you were not here, and I could not ask why this was so. If there is to be a new commission, one of my doctors will have to be a part of it."

The Commandant explained that it was not out of spite, but that "not everything could be arranged."

"I am really under the impression that you gentlemen like to play games with me. Example: my books, and especially my breviaries. Certainly, none of you gentlemen recite the breviary. So, why did you keep them? The same with the books. They have been coming since October."

The Commandant replied that it was hard to find them in the huge library.

I answered, "There is a librarian there who has catalogued every-thing himself; anyway, they are lying right on top. It is a question of four or five books. You've known about them for a long time. I would prefer our relationship not to develop into one of cat and mouse. I have no intention of being a subject for your malice and that is why I am making no new requests—why should I incite you to malice?"

The Commandant felt that there was no [question of] malice, that there were only difficulties that could not be resolved. "I still have a letter for you, Father."

He handed me a letter from my father. It was a letter of June 14, 1954, in answer to my letter of April 29. I glanced at it. In connection with this letter, the Commandant stated that the government wished me to write precisely about my health in my letters, since the last letter caused a great deal of trouble for the government.

I read the excerpt of my letter in which I referred to my state of health and explained that I could not write anything in detail be-cause I had not seen the medical commission for which I was wait-ing. "If my doctor had been included in the commission, it would now be much better for you."

The other request of the government was that my letters not contain "pastoral material," because that too created difficulties, which might result in prohibiting me from writing any letters at all. I answered that this was my usual way of writing to my father about spiritual matters. Since I sensed from my father's letter that he was worried about me, I wanted to cheer him up. Anyway, the things I wrote about to my father could not possibly be a threat to the state.

As for me, I still felt that the government was toying with me. The best proof of this was the fact that I had not received a response to my latest statement that it was impossible for me to write to the government since I was unable to remember the decree.

"You were to report to the government that I do not recall the text of the decree. I have had no response to this. Anyway, I have been convinced several times that you do not communicate the answers to me, even though you have them. You wait for me to bow and scrape. I tell you openly what I think of this method of dealing with a person, even though doing so might prove costly to me. I prefer a direct relationship."

The Commandant replied that occasionally he might not tell me something because he is uncertain about it. "And now I want to tell you officially that you may prepare a letter to the government and present your defense against censures or accusations regarding your antigovernment activities."

I answered, "This will be difficult for me to do, since I don't have the documents. I have had many conversations with representatives of the government, I have sent dozens of statements and letters. I don't even remember their dates, which are absolutely essential for such a letter, because I must respond to the accusations leveled against me. I had two conversations with President Bierut, and I must say that these exchanges were on a high level, within the bounds of loyalty. A long series of my conversations with Marshal Mazur were also on this high plane. These men did not present accusations to me. But other accusations were made after my arrest or—as you say— after I had been isolated in a monastery. A military man barraged me with accusations in *Trybuna Ludu,* even though he was well aware that I could not defend myself. I call that an unparalleled violation of military honor because a [decent] soldier never attacks the defenseless, as General Ochab did in this case. Under normal circumstances I would have responded to him by letter, because the principles of democracy demanded it. I did precisely that with those who attacked me, even Jacek Wołowski, who accused me in the press of a lack of love for country. I answered that charge. But now, without documentation, it would be difficult for me to do it; I had known this from the moment I arrived in Rywałd. The representative of the government who took me there heard me say that I was prepared to listen to the accusations against me. He explained to me then that in four days a representative of the government would come to me. Four days later, when questioned, he said that circumstances had changed and now he was not authorized to give me any information. When he came to move me to Stoczek, I asked him about it again; he answered that he did not recall any promise of a discussion. 'It is possible that *you* do not remember, sir, since this does not concern you, but I remember very well.' And so from the beginning I was convinced that some kind of clarification had to be made. And now I am ready to present my point of view objectively, even though it will be difficult without documentation."

The Commandant stated the position of the government: "I am authorized to inform you that you may write a letter to the government presenting your point of view. I do this now more clearly than before, even though I did speak about it previously, because now I have clear authority to do so. You may respond to the accusations made against you, Father, according to your understanding and point of view. Please explain everything."

Upon leaving, the Commandant said that he would like to talk with me again, since he had read several of my books when I was still in Włocławek. He would also have something to say about Jacek Wołowski.

We agreed as follows:

(1) As for the doctor, I would hold off for now, until I finished my medication, then I would present my request.

(2) I would think about the letter to the government.

(3)   I would write a letter to my father soon, although the restrictions made it difficult for me.

(4)   As for the conversation with the Commandant, I was at his service.

My dearest son!

I thank you very much for your letter of April 29, which was read to me on June 9. We were very pleased with the news about your life, even though there was nothing new. We were saddened and worried by the remark about your health; you write that your kidneys demand urgent treatment which means that they are in bad condition. You always took good care of yourself and never complained about anything, but your health always needed medical attention and constant care, so that in the present situation we worry about it constantly. You write very briefly about your ailments, and I would like to know about everything in great detail. Today I am also sending a notice to the government Presidium about your health, with a request for help from a specialist, if possible, and asking them for consultation with a physician who has known your illnesses. After such an examination, perhaps we could procure the necessary medications for you; we would like to help you as soon as possible. In the meantime I and the others are praying for you continuously and, full of confidence in God and in His Holiest Mother, I ask that you be granted health, protection, and a speedy return to us.

We remember about the anniversaries and will pray humbly to God. I thank you very much for your prayers for me and for your name day greetings. Stasia also asks me to thank you for thinking of her and assures you of her warm sisterly affection and of her prayers for you.

As I wrote in my last letter, everyone is well, except Tadek and Zenia who have a terrible problem: little Ania got sick with Heine Medina [infantile paralysis] last week and was taken to the hospital for more than forty days; the child must be quarantined and there is great fear about the aftereffects of this disease. Her condition is not critical, and the doctors assure her parents that the case is rather mild and that the illness should pass without trace, but the parents are filled with fear. I beseech you to pray for them. We send you our heartfelt best wishes and commend you to Our Lady of Jasna Góra, especially your health. Your sisters, Tadeusz and Zenia, and all your dear ones send their warmest greetings.

We all ask for prayers, blessings, and a speedy response.

Zalesie, June 14, 1954
S. Wyszyński

June 27, 1954, Sunday
I handed my fifth letter to my father to the Commandant today, in answer to his letters of June 8 and June 14. It reads as follows:

My dearest Father!

I hasten to confirm gratefully the receipt of your letters of June 8 and June 14. I am very pleased that the Good Lord has the whole family in His care and shields you from distress and illness. The ordeal visited on Tadzio and Zenia worries me very much. In my prayers, I commend little Ania to the motherly care of Mary, and I trust that she will protect her. Please assure her parents that I continue to pray for the little one's rapid recovery. I want to apologize to you most sincerely, dear Father, for the worry I have caused you in mentioning the state of my health. I was waiting for the doctors at the time, and not wishing to postpone my letter I briefly mentioned what worried me most: the symptoms I was experiencing. I suspected some sort of kidney disorder. Two doctors who examined me on May 12 declared that my kidneys are not in bad condition. They ascribe the pains I experience to "minor osteal and muscular changes." But they do suspect hyperacidity and confirm a slight enlargement of the liver. I report their diagnosis verbatim, dear Father, so that you won't be concerned. I am taking the medicines prescribed and hope that my frame of mind will improve. I have all the medications I need, so please do not worry about me. Together with your letter of June 8, I received the package containing clothes and edibles. Please thank Sister Maksencja for her thoughtfulness about my needs. I prayed for Janka and Julcia on their name days. Through you, dear Father, I send words of affection to all my sisters, my brother, and all of the household. Assuring you of my constant prayers for all of you, I kiss your hands with reverence, blessing you all.

June 26, 1954
+ Stefan Cardinal Wyszyński

June 29, 1954, Tuesday
You have filled my soul, Lord, with love for Your Church, for Your temples, for service at the altar, for the glory of Your House. You have infused me with apostolic zeal, with a need to profess publicly my faith in You; You have filled my house with an energy like that which drives bees from their hive. And when they swarm in one's throat, they choke a person suffering from a surfeit of gifts he cannot give away. How difficult it is to calm these industrious bees that struggle to bring honey to Your altars. Lift the latch, O Lord, and liberate Your servants so that they may go out into God's world and bring forth fruit. Not my will but Yours . . . You, the Master of a dormant hive.

July 1, 1954, Thursday
Every day I see evidence of Christ's truth in the words: "If they persecuted me, they will persecute you too. . . ." Christ foretold every aspect of the future of the Church: the cross, Peter's chains,

[martyrdom in] the arenas, to this very day. We all know how it is being fulfilled in us. Is this not a consolation, confirming the truth of Christ's words in our own lives? Should we not be happy with the revelation of this truth, even if it hurts . . . very much? And this truth liberates us ever so painfully. Christ never said anything that was not substantiated by history. Twenty centuries of the gospel is additional proof of its truth.

July 2, 1954, Friday
Today I wrote a letter to the Presidium of the government of the Polish People's Republic relative to the accusations leveled against me.

July 2, 1954, Friday
Non horruisti Virginis uterum [You did not disdain the womb of the Virgin]—and not only that. You have shown even greater courage. The hands of your purest Father—*Ens Purum* [Being Itself]—have prepared the womb of the Immaculate Virgin so that You could protect Your Godly purity in Him.

You were not frightened by the womb of my heart . . . barely concealing the stable dirt with a poor veneer of regret and shame. You chose a stable and dwelt within it, so that in the stable mud might rise the bread giving birth to virgins. This is truly Almighty Courage!

Mary, be vigilant that your Son, as often as He wishes to be born in the stable of my heart, may always be met by your immaculate arms; let them protect Him and guard Him from the impurities of my soul. You waited in Bethlehem to accept God—wait also in my soul, so that there may never be a Christmas in me without you.

July 10, 1954, Saturday
If sin is an expression of hatred toward God and the sinner is Your enemy, I wish not to wait until the Father "makes me a footstool under Your feet." I myself lay my hostile head under Your feet and

wish to be trampled upon by You. Fortunately, only an enemy has a chance to become a slave. I know now how to become one through love, so from an enemy let me change into a slave. It will be up to You, my Jesus, to conquer me for love.

It is much easier to become a prisoner of the Church defending its rights than a prisoner of Christ defending His rights to my soul.

July 12, 1954, Monday
The day before yesterday I asked the Commandant's first deputy [Nazi] when the Commandant would return. He answered that it would not be this month. Perhaps he would return at the beginning of August. "In light of this," I said, "I find myself in a difficult position, because the Commandant informed me that according to the government I may present my explanation. I prepared it; it was ready on July 2. I was not aware that the Commandant would be gone for such a long time." The deputy declared that both the first and second deputy knew what the Commandant knew and that I could give my letter to either the first or second deputy. I replied that I did not know what authority was vested in them, but it seemed to me that, since the Commandant had communicated this matter to me, its future course was in his hands. The first deputy explained that in this matter there were no distinctions.

Today I prepared the letter for delivery. The first deputy came, and I informed him of my willingness to submit the letter. There was a question regarding the date the letter was written and when submitted, but the deputy felt that this was a minor point. But when he took the manuscript in hand, he noted that it was not addressed properly, because the letter should have been directed to Minister Bida. I explained that this time the Commandant had not said anything about that.

"If he did not say it, he had it in mind," answered the deputy.

"At one time there was some discussion of this," I added, "but

I explained then that I could not address the letter to Minister Bida for reasons known to the Commandant."

"This is the official route," declared the deputy.

"For me," I answered, "the official route is the President or Deputy-Marshal Mazur, because I have talked with them, and they are familiar with these matters. And I have never discussed them with Mr. Bida. Anyway, I have suffered so much injury from Mr. Bida that I cannot look upon him as the appropriate party."

"Minister Bida," added the deputy, "will submit it to the Council of Ministers."

"That is not the way for me," I answered. "Even if I am to remain here for a hundred years, I will not do it, because it is contrary to my conscience. I believe it is better for the government to know that there are things I cannot do than for it to think I am capable of anything. I cannot act contrary to my conscience."

"In view of this," announced the deputy, "I cannot accept this letter, since the Commandant told me it is to be directed to Mr. Bida."

"So you two did talk about this? That was not my impression from my conversation with the Commandant, who previously had spoken about Minister Bida but had not mentioned him in this connection. He only presented the government's position, stating that I could present my case. My letter, therefore, will await the Commandant's return."

"I will report this to my superiors," returned the deputy.

July 30, 1954, Friday

I received a letter from my father today, dated July 27, confirming that my letter had been read to him on July 8. With the letter they handed me a name day package. I notice that this time the letter was delivered to me very promptly. But the package was in a very sorry state. The crackers were in dirty bags, crumbled and crushed. The whole thing looked rather sad, prompting the sister to describe it as something "out of a dog's throat." Apparently the inspection of the items required that they be damaged.

My beloved son!

In my name and in the name of your loved ones, I send you most affectionate greetings for the approaching feast day of your Patron Saint* and the thirtieth anniversary of your priestly ordination, wishing you all of God's graces, the fulfillment of all your wishes, and we pray especially that the Good Lord will be generous to you with strength, health, and perseverance.

We pray for this constantly and believe that our prayers will be answered. Our most fervent wishes, which undoubtedly are yours as well, we always commend to God and His most holy Mother, and we will do so especially on your name day. In our hearts and our thoughts we are always with you, especially on days when one feels more intensely and experiences more keenly.

I thank you wholeheartedly for your letter, which was read to me on July 8. The news about your health is extremely important to us and we beg you to give details whenever you can. Both ailments you mention demand not only medication but also the best of conditions for recuperation, and that is why we never cease worrying about your health.

The treatment for hyperacidity, as we learned from doctors, requires not only dietary attention but also meticulous and constant care, especially as far as food is concerned. You should eat little, but often. We would like to know more about your life and needs. Perhaps we could send you some things you need, or some books?

I conveyed your message to Sister Superior; she was very pleased and thanks you very much for remembering.

Little Hania has already returned from the hospital. She is still not well; serious aftereffects accompany this illness and a longer recuperation is called for, but we hope that the child will recover completely. Tadeusz and his wife thank

---

*Feast of Saint Stephen, Pope and martyr, is August 2.

you most sincerely for your words of encouragement and your prayers. Janka and Julcia asked me to thank you for remembering them in your prayers.

Everyone else is well. How I long for that happy day, my dear son, when I will be able to greet and embrace you. We all greet you most heartfully, and we ask for your prayers and blessing.

Zalesie, July 27, 1954
S. Wyszyński

August 1, 1954, Sunday
The Commandant appeared after a month's absence. He asked how things were; I told him there was nothing new, except for the pending matter of the letter to the President of the government. The deputy could not accept it, since he felt that it was misaddressed, and so the letter awaited his return. The Commandant explained that perhaps he had not expressed himself clearly—the deputy could accept the letter as addressed. I drew his attention to the fact that there were matters brought up in the letter that were known only to President Bierut and that for me it was a question of conscience whether a much larger circle of people should read it. The Commandant said that he felt he could accept the letter and took it with him, even though it was addressed to the Presidium of the government. Thus the matter that had been dragging on since the beginning of last October took a step forward today. Although I did not expect anything favorable to come of this turn of events, my conscience calmed down considerably with the knowledge that I had told the government what truth and the good of the Church demanded. If I had remained silent, I could always be accused of not having defended the truth vigorously enough, thus possibly of endangering the Church.

In this need to speak there was undoubtedly also the conviction that the truth once expressed must carry some weight. We do not always take into account the fact that the mentality of the other side may be radically different; if they seek the truth, it is not always because they want to know it, but only because they want to explore the very soul of the enemy. Catholics speaking the truth in court, the so-called whole truth, sometimes succumb to this notion that "the truth will set them free." Under normal conditions, that is the way it should be. Why this is not so under our conditions is the complicated problem of dialectics devoid of a dialectic.

August 1, 1954, Sunday
Arma lucis [Arms of Light]. We are, willy-nilly, a generation of heroes. In the course of the first half of the twentieth century, we spent many decades at war. We watched people man the trenches, armed to the teeth; cannons, bombs, and machine guns are our music. We have seen thousands of fallen soldiers, we have survived the deaths of giants, dictators, autocrats, and totalitarians. Governments changed before our eyes like leaves on trees. . . . Can anything impress us? We have ceased to fear the barrels of carbines and cannons. The man in armor invokes in us neither fear, nor . . . respect. What is more, to us the defenseless man seems more heroic than the armed one. To us an armed soldier looks ridiculous. The man whose profession is grounded on courage should enter the fray with his bare hands, like David. . . .

Now we wait for the giants of the mind, the will, the heart, and virtue . . . only these can we respect. Only these are worthy of enlisting in the struggle for something better. . . . *Abiciamini opera tenebrarum et induamini arma lucis* [Let us lay aside the works of darkness and put on the armor of light] (Rom. 13:12).

June 8, 1954, Friday
The measure of God's mercy is not so much the holiness and glory of His friends as the salvation of the greatest sinners. Only the sight of redeemed criminals whom the world has despised and whom God has still saved will open our eyes to the power of God's mercy. But this can only happen in the life to come, since at present we are incapable of comprehending it. First we must come to know fully at the Last Judgment our own worthlessness, in order to understand why God does not give up on sinners.

August 26, 1954, Thursday

"Those who love me I also love," says Mary to her servants, in the words of the Book of Proverbs (Proverbs 8:17). With fear I fight for this love. I am under the impression that I love, yet, I cannot spend one day without you, without your Name, without a Hail Mary, without the rosary, without my act of consecration to you. What would my life be if I were to forget about you? I cannot—even if I were weaker than I am, even if my conscience were to be over-grown with a forest of sins, even if I were to grow deaf from the suffering and agony of abandonment. But even then, in this valley of tears, I would still cry out: "Hail . . ." And so, I do love you! What a joyful conclusion, since He says to me that "Those who love me I also love." There is my answer! But I had no doubts of your love. In you there is love from the Father, who was the first to love. The Father gives birth to love. And the Mother follows His example. You love, because the Father loved. You loved before anyone loved you. And I love you because you brought me love from the Father.

September 15, 1954, Wednesday

I cannot recall exactly when the new Superintendent* appeared on the scene in Stoczek; he appeared in the garden one August day, stopped by every tree, carefully examined the windows, the fences, the wires in the trees. These walks were repeated every few days. We did not know the nature of his responsibility. Later, he directed his attention to the kitchen and asked if anything was needed there. Kitchen news seldom reached us; the sister was al-ways reticent to share her observations with us. When Nazi in-formed Father S. that he was leaving to take a new position, he revealed that a new deputy would be arriving. He had not visited me as yet, but he had visited my companion. Rather soon we no-ticed that the new Superintendent liked to walk down our corri-

---

*The cardinal later nicknames this man "Katz" (German for "cat"), from his habit of pussyfooting about the premises. Katz was a pejorative label used by Poles during the German occupation of Poland for SS (*Schutzstaffel*) guards, who patrolled the streets at night and were known for their excessive brutality.

dor in bedroom slippers and stop at the door. Once he was actually caught in the act. When Nazi told Father S. about the change, he urged him to present a petition for his own release: "You are not thinking about yourself, Father; you would like to send the Primate back home, but what about yourself . . . ?"

"Is it worth it?" Father S. asked doubtfully.

"It is always worth it," came the reply. "You have a sick mother, Father, you want to study. . . . Please write."

Father S. shared his doubts with me. I felt that he should write, even if Nazi's encouragement was only an exploratory remark. He did write, and when he handed the letter to Nazi, the deputy switched gears on him: "What, already? This won't go that fast." He went away shortly after that, taking the letter with him.

The new Superintendent kept his distance and did not come to me right away. One day, as usual, the doctor-deputy came: "Comments? Requests?"

"I make none known. You make these queries every day. Perhaps this answer would suffice for tomorrow as well?" A smile of acknowledgment ended this conversation. The next day he did not come. But the new Superintendent came. At first the situation was unclear, hanging by the thread of the unspoken question "Now who?" There was no explanation. My visitor did not clarify in what capacity he was coming to see me. For a few moments we looked at each other in silence. The new Superintendent kept his arms behind his back. He reminded me of someone. He could be the tall, slender functionary whom Baca had bitten on Miodowa Street. The ritual continued: "Requests? Comments?" and then the Superintendent left the room. This was repeated several times during the next few days.

Finally, one day, he became interested in the apartment, the heating, the books: "Perhaps you need some? We are ready to provide you with all the books you require, Father."

"From where will you get them?"

"We will bring them from libraries."

"I will think about it."

"I think we know each other," added the Superintendent.

"I don't remember you."

"Well, that's too bad. You should remember me. We saw each other often. We sat together at table during visitations."*

"I can't remember—and that is very understandable. So many people sat with me at table during visitations, for many years, someone different almost every day."

"And yet, we know one another very well! We talked together often!"

"I don't remember anything."

"That's a shame. You ought to remember."

"I don't like riddles! And anyway, my dear sir, it is a well-established courtesy to give one's name, and then one need not guess with whom he has the pleasure.' "

The man did not respond to the hint. He wished to remain anonymous. The conversation trailed off. "But we know each other very well," he added several times.

He tried to be polite and solicitous. He inspected the windows thoroughly, the creaking floor, and commiserated about the cold apartment. He was obviously waiting for something. I had the impression that the new Superintendent was introducing a new style of administration. He was clearly not in a hurry to leave.

Again he brought up the matter of books. I explained that I had no desire to ask for new ones, since I had not received the ones I had requested a long time ago. He wanted to know which ones I was missing. I reached for my lists. With the agility of a turkey, the Superintendent craned his neck to peer over my shoulder into my notes. Immediately I recognized a pro at snooping. I had to be brief. We bade farewell quickly.

He came back daily, always anxious to talk, always polite and inquisitive about problems, questions, wishes, requests. Both Father and I came to the conclusion that we should be brief with him. Sister, on the other hand, was clearly delighted with the new Super-

---

*In Poland every parish must be visited by a bishop for pastoral purposes at least once every five years to review every aspect of parish life, activity, instruction, and administration.

intendent, with his politeness and solicitude. He was exceedingly mobile—one saw him everywhere, at every time of day. He walked the corridor, the stairs, the garden; often I heard his steps on the floor above my apartment. He was a clear switch from officiousness to some kind of "humanity."

September 26, 1954, Sunday
The Commandant visited me after a long absence. I brought up the matter of books, which his deputy had touched upon in his absence, when he had expressed a willingness to supply the books. Four books had not yet been delivered: 1. *Annuario Pontificio;* 2. *Caere-moniale Episcoporum;* 3. *Dottrina sociale cattolica,* a collection of documents; 4. *Księga Henrykowska.* Today the Commandant declared, "My superiors have ordered me to tell you that for technical reasons these books will not be delivered." I remarked that these books were in my library; I saw no difficulties in delivering them to me. The Commandant repeated, "Well, nevertheless, my superiors have ordered me to tell you that for technical reasons these books cannot be delivered. Others, new ones, can be delivered." I answered that later I would prepare a new list of books.

It was hard for me to understand what these "technical considerations" could be. It was certainly not a matter of difficulty in finding these books or bringing them here. They were certainly in my library and plainly visible. Was this an effort to control the areas of my reading? But why? After all, they could not expect me to change my way of thinking?

October 5, 1954, Tuesday
After that longer absence, during which the new deputy of the former first deputy had visited us, Doctor—the second deputy to the Commandant whom we had not seen for a week—came to see us today. After some casual questions about health and requests, he heard my reply: "Nothing has changed, I am not making any requests."

Doctor. In that case, we have something to tell you. Since the climate here and the state of this house do not agree with you, Father, the government has decided to change the climatic conditions. In the course of this day you are to collect your belongings, the chaplain will help you, and tomorrow morning at ten o'clock we will fly you to your new quarters. The chaplain, the sister, and all of us will go together. The flight will take two hours.

Primate. I am surprised by this decision about my fate. I would at least like to know whether this place is far from here and whether the state of my lungs was taken into consideration.

Doctor. It is very far away, at the other end of Poland, and that is why the trip will be made by plane, so as not to be fatiguing. The climatic conditions will be better, and the house will be more conducive to health. We will go together.

Primate. I will be ready at ten o'clock tomorrow. But for me this is a very basic matter: I expected, rather, that I would be freed after one year in Stoczek and that I would be able to return to my work.

Doctor. This does not depend on me, but on higher authorities.

Primate. I am aware of that, but I have no way of reaching these higher authorities, who give no answers to my desiderata, so I must speak to the person I see before me. I have recently written a letter to the Presidium of the government with the approval of these authorities; it remains unanswered, even to the extent of acknowledging its receipt.

Doctor. Since the letter was submitted, it was certainly delivered.

Primate. Nevertheless, a citizen has the right to a confirmation that his letter was received. After all, the letter was written at the express wishes of the government authorities. I had the right to expect that the government would take my clarifications into account. Now I must describe my position explicitly: I feel wronged by the government, not only in my right as bishop of three million Catholics, but in my rights as a citizen. I am condemned to prison in absentia, without a document of indictment, without any opportunity to offer evidence, contrary to the principle of *audiatur et altera pars.* And so it has gone on for a year. I am treated like an internee of a concentration camp, despite the fact that the conscience of the whole world has condemned this method of treating citizens. I was kept in a house whose rot helped destroy my health and sap my strength. I was put in a place where the Nazis imprisoned Austrian bishops after the *Anschluss*. And this is happening before the very eyes of all of Europe, which carefully watches the fate of a man who—regardless of his personal merits—occupies a position to which the cultured world cannot be indifferent, especially the Catholic world. Does making a martyr out of me really help the government, and does it dispose society favorably toward it? After all, there is no shortage of Poles who find the Primate of Poland meaningful in their lives. It is difficult to act against public opinion because you cannot rule a country if you are at loggerheads with its citizens. After all, a state exists for its citizens and not the other way around.

Doctor. You are taking things too personally, Father, whereas this is a matter of the interest of the state.*

Primate. Am I really taking the matter personally? What is at stake here is a defense of my basic rights to freedom. In my letter of July 2 to the Presidium, I did not touch on personal matters at all. As for the idea of the "interest of the state," I am well aware of what this notion is comprised. If there is any other, please explain it to me. I have worked for so many years to establish coexistence between Church and State in Poland that I know very well the basic stipulations of the government. If, today, the government has new ones, would it not be simpler—instead of making a lot of noise that resounds through all of Europe—to express willingness to discuss those matters that concern the government? We have been able to have so many conversations, could we not have had this additional one? This is a more important matter than this or that climate for me. After all, if you change the climate by changing the place of my

---

Racja stanu, raison d'état [reason, interest, or good of the state]. Because Polish history involves so many attacks by its enemies, so many persecutions, partitions, and threats to existence, the term *racja stanu* has taken on a broader meaning in Poland to include its right to exist, to be independent, to defend itself, to be sovereign, and not to be threatened from without or within by anyone.

detention, if the matter is not resolved, the climate will really be the same. The thing that is fundamental to all interests of state is justice for its citizens. You cannot rule a country without respect for the rights of the citizens, because a state cannot exist without citizens. Whatever the interest of the state, its foundation must be justice for the people. Do you call this a personal approach?

Doctor. I will relay this conversation to the higher authorities. Well, then, tomorrow at ten. Perhaps there are some requests in connection with the trip?

Primate. I will be ready at ten. Has my companion been notified?

Doctor. He'll find out immediately.

Father S. came a little while later. The poor fellow was crushed by the news. He had rather expected to be released and returned to his sick parents. But soon he got himself in hand and interpreted the new experience as an act of God.

After dinner we began to collect our meager belongings. Our books and heavier things were to be put out into the corridor by ten o'clock that night, since they would be transported by a car traveling by night.

During our longer walk we bade farewell to our garden and assessed our pros and cons in Stoczek. We had suffered much here because of the harsh winter, the damp house, the mustiness of the ground floor that permeated the upstairs, the persistent winds from the sea that were almost constant during the summer months, the cold temperatures and shoddy heaters that smoked horribly; we had both been in a state of semi-illness all year long. The sister suffered with a chronic cold, Father had sciatica, and I rheumatism in my feet, which were cold because of the damp floor even in the summertime. Such were the health-sanitation conditions of our stay in Stoczek.

The spiritual side was much better. Our little chapel was alive. Jesus resided in the chalice case; we celebrated Mass without an altar stone. We sang joyfully. We spent the Christmas season singing carols in the evening for hours on end. We celebrated High Masses* often. We kept our spirits high with novenas: to Saint Joseph, to the Annunciation of the Virgin Mary, to the Patronage of Saint Joseph, to Our Lady of Perpetual Help, to Mary the Mediatrix of All Graces, to Saint Peter in Chains, to the Transfiguration, to the Assumption of Our Lady, to Our Lady of Jasna Góra, to the Nativity of Mary, to the Holy Name of Mary, to Our Lady of Ransom. The move found us in the middle of a novena to the Maternity of Our Lady. In short, we lived in a spirit of constant prayer, which overcame all of our pains, sorrows, and disappointments. But these sorrows, in some strange way, passed very quickly. Even though our hopes for a speedy release were postponed, at the end of every novena we were somehow mysteriously serene, peaceful, and happy. It must be said that serenity and gaiety prevailed. We did not treat profound sorrows tragically; they passed quickly, even when they came. Even though our personalities were so different, our prayer in common, our morning meditations which I conducted aloud following the Benedictine missal, our evening rosary—these united and drew us together. We prayed a lot for our guardians, whom we did not look upon as enemies.

One observation about our guards. Their behavior was above reproach. They were all polite, save one who always waited to be greeted. But all were laconic, terse, and avoided all but official contacts. Together with us, they suffered from the cold and dampness of the decaying house. They did all their work themselves. They had a most difficult time with the heaters, which smoked and cracked during the winter; the pipes had to be cleaned—a task performed with exemplary devotion by an old gentleman we called Grandpa. We felt sincerely sorry for these people, when they had to spend long nights on guard by the "checkpoint." If they had

---

*Before the Second Vatican Council reforms, a Mass could be Low—in which all parts of the Mass were recited—or High—in which some of the parts were sung or chanted.

trusted us, they could have gone peacefully to sleep. But they "could not," despite my assurance to the Commandant that I would not leave the house without express permission, even if all the doors stood open. And so they wasted their time and health in this mindless lingering, guarding people who had no intention of escaping. The sight was both sad and amusing. We were also amused by the thickets of wires and cables entwined around the posts of the high fence. I often thought: Either I am so dangerous or such a heinous criminal that I cannot comprehend it, or else, fear overmagnifies everything.

The garden was our great delight. All winter long the two of us were a brigade battling the snow that blocked the paths. This work consumed much of our energy. We fed the birds in "cafeterias" in the cedars and on the roof of the porch. Spring was delightful: the snowdrops amazed us with their power as they broke through the hard, icy surfaces; next, liverworts and periwinkles adorned the lawn that had looked like a rubbish heap in the fall. When the yellow sow thistle and the fruit trees blossomed, the sight was unforgettable. We fell in love with the starlings, whose motherly concerns and community lessons, but most especially the gluttony of the young, amazed us. All this enthusiasm for eating, so much pleading in the little gaping beaks, such great effort in providing can all serve as subject for meditation for many hours. How much one can see in a detached segment of the world, when one is forced to look only short range—I first realized this in Stoczek. If such a tiny piece of ground is so rich in life, what can be said of the whole earth?

A new second deputy visited us in the evening, to make sure that our things were ready for the overnight transport. They were taking almost everything in the house, including carpets and draperies. We were a little surprised at all this effort: "To live in decent conditions even for a few weeks," answered the deputy, "that is worth something too." During this whole process, the Commandant did not show his face at all so that the new Superintendent assumed the whole burden of the move. He was very solicitous and busy.

In the evening in our little chapel we thanked our Heavenly Mother and her Son for all the graces bestowed upon us here of which there had been so many.

The greatest shortcoming of an apostle is fear, because it inspires doubt in the power of the Master, cramps the heart, and strangles the voice. The apostle no longer professes. Is he still an apostle? The disciples who abandoned the Master no longer professed faith in Him. They encouraged the executioners. Anyone who remains silent before his enemies emboldens them. An apostle's fear is the primary ally of an enemy's cause. In a strategy toward godlessness, the terror that is practiced by all dictatorships draws its effectiveness from the timidity of the apostles. The first goal is to force one into silence through fear. Silence has its apostolic significance only when I do not shrink from my oppressors. This is what the silent Christ did. And by this sign He revealed His courage. Christ did not allow Himself to be terrorized. When He went forth to meet the rabble, He said openly, "It is I."

October 6, 1954, Wednesday
Stoczek Warmiński—Prudnik Śląski. My last Mass was offered in honor of Our Lady of Jasna Góra. Father S. offered the Mass in honor of Our Lady of Perpetual Help. The temporary altar remained without the *Sanctissimum* [Blessed Sacrament]. Such a conclusion is always painful. Breakfast, then a last walk in the garden, after we had handed over our things. They were taken to the plane at ten in the morning. At 12:15 P.M. we set out in the direction of Bartoszyce and Kętrzyn. The plane stood near Kętrzyn, on a field near the woods where Hitler's headquarters had once been. The plane took off at 1:00 P.M., our steady direction southwest. We were flying into the unknown. We recognized the Mazovian Lakes and the Vistula River as we crossed it. Then we rose above the cloud cover and could see nothing more, until the Oder River. At 3:00 P.M. we landed in a field near a town I could not recognize. I knew that

we were somewhere in the Opole region. Later we learned that we had landed near the Neisse River; from there we traveled by car by way of Głuchołazy to Prudnik Śląski. But we had to wait in the airplane until 6:00 P.M. We did not leave the plane until darkness fell; only then did we get into the cars. The trip took about forty-five minutes. We stopped by a house in the woods that had been designated as our new home. It was the Franciscan friary near Prudnik, now transformed into our new isolation camp.

IV

PRUDNIK
ŚLĄSKI

October 7, 1954, Thursday

So many thoughts go back to Stoczek. The most important impressions of the past are always related to people. We had met people about whom we had the right to think: these are communists, materialists, atheists, the chosen and well-matched, certainly typical of their kind, perhaps a peculiar elite of some kind, whose job it was not only to guard us closely but certainly also to "rehabilitate" us, to give us a new example of "progressive" life. Maybe these were an exceptional type of idealistic communists and thus people deserving of special attention and understanding, or perhaps they were only ordinary people frightened and obedient for the sake of a comfortable living—although it is doubtful whether people filled with a false enthusiasm would have managed to get these jobs. Or maybe they are spies, provocateurs who are working either for the government or for foreign intelligence—an internal diversion that is so common in the administration of "countries in revolution." Maybe, maybe . . . a hundred conjectures, a hundred suppositions. . . . And in addition to it all—keen attention to everything. I am not used to this, I remain in the world of my thoughts which do not permit me to become too interested in my surroundings.

Father S. has about him the mind and the attitude of an experienced prisoner: he knows how to look at everything through the eyes of a prisoner, he sees everything, it all has special importance for him. Such a talent is acquired slowly, at the cost of many painful experiences. There were many things [at Stoczek] I didn't notice: Father S. saw under which tree X stood, which window opened when we went out, at what time of the night the floorboards in the corridor creaked, at which door the carpet-hushed steps of the cat stopped, what scrap of paper lay in the bathroom, what disappeared from the corridor, what sounds came from the third floor. Such close attention to such things always rather surprised me, especially in the beginning; later I also became interested in these signs of life from the other side. But it was never a very deep interest. I was still a very "open" person, one for whom it was important to do things openly and publicly. It was very difficult to adjust to this other life.

The perspective for viewing this other side is certainly narrow. We had the opportunity to see one of these men for a minute and a half during a given visit—a short exchange of casual words, carried on in a telegraphic style that wearies me. We had a chance to see part of one man by the "checkpoint" and the back of another on the ground floor as we went down to the garden. Very seldom did we see anyone in the garden; this happened occasionally, once or twice a week—and then the phantom would disappear completely. There was, for instance, the sun bathing phantom who vanished abruptly. There was another—the Sunday morning excursions of the guards into the garden, their using of the benches not occupied by us. This too stopped suddenly. Next, there were the phantoms of the harvest, gathering fruit (this lasted the longest); they all came suddenly and left suddenly, breaking off in a mysterious way. There was the phenomenon of the stranger who appeared in the garden, strolled from tree to tree, stopped, looked to the right, to the left, studied the bird feeders and . . . disappeared. There was the phantom who had exercise sessions at night, and did odd jobs around the fences —that too stopped suddenly.

These were our limited opportunities to observe the new man— the man of the future, the progressive man to whom willy-nilly we compared ourselves, wondering what he would bring to Poland and how he would shape it. Obviously, this did not give us the right to draw conclusions and to pass judgment. But neither is this something of no value.

The composition of the group. Everyone is nameless, difficult to describe. Where do they recruit these people? What did they do before? Why did they choose work that brings so little satisfaction to any normal person with ambition? Because to sit around in a corridor night and day for months on end—everyone will admit—is not an occupation for a person nurturing materialistic-idealistic ambitions. Service for the cause? This would probably be the only plausible argument.

In their secret circles the Commandant was called the colonel. A man of blank expression, I never saw him in uniform at Stoczek, although I knew that on occasion he wore military dress. He was of medium height, stocky, with a tendency to weight problems—something we all noticed. He made clumsy use of trite propaganda slogans and seemed incapable of uttering a longer sentence correctly. Would he be able to act out a role or to carry out an assignment? Probably not. In situations that required action, he always disappeared. Then his deputy the Superintendent would come to the force.

The Commandant could be looked upon as polite. Mostly he lied, although he did so on behalf of his "superiors," whom he often called upon for authority. He was brief and concise, and avoided conversations. When they occurred, he was obviously uneasy and would hastily head for the door. One had the distinct impression that he preferred to hear less, to know less. It was obviously bothersome to him to encounter something that required him to write a report. He tried to make a friendly impression; in time he learned to smile. He could be rude, I understand, but I never experienced it. Occasionally, he would be overcome by impulses for social action. Then he would grab a rake and work in the garden with the others, but this never lasted very long. Usually, he stood by idle as the others worked. He gave the impression of an invalid, walking like a cripple; perhaps he suffered from a hernia or some old leg fracture. He always arrived clean shaven and "civilized"—that is, in civilian clothes that were well pressed, heavily scented, leaving behind a lingering fragrance. He was the kind of man of whom you could say "he knows not what he does." You could also forgive him a lot.

The second in command—the first Superintendent [Nazi]—was a man with a simpleton's face and the manners of a farmhand freshly dressed in business clothes, bereft of any intelligence, clumsy and awkward in conversation as in all of his behavior. We were given to understand that he was "the most important person here and everything depended on him." He was active, bustling, endlessly moving about the building, killing conversations whenever he drew near a group, clearly disconcerting everyone by his presence. He wore an emblem of a "Defender of Freedom," as he himself described it. He hailed from somewhere in south-central Poland, was attached to the mountains and talked about them eagerly. He knew the parts with which Father S. was familiar. This man we preferred not to see. When we learned that he had gone away, we were relieved. Immediately, we could sense an air of freedom throughout the house; the guards were also relieved and became more cheerful and cordial. He was responsible for the household, the kitchen, the sister; he looked upon himself as a person to whom a priest should be subservient in a special way. He came to me very seldom and rarely engaged in any conversations. Whenever Father S. went to the doctor or to see his father in Barczewo, *magna pars fuit* [it was a big thing!], the Superintendent went with him. Usually, during such trips, he created an opportunity to speak to Father S., to put pressure on him or to get him to express his opinions, displeasures, threats, and observations—more on this later. This gentleman never smiled. He always looked very worried when he came to see me; he would look to the ceiling, didn't know what to do with his hands, and never offered a handshake.

When we learned that the Superintendent was leaving us, probably at the beginning of September, we were all relieved. He went on to another position—to the satisfaction of his colleagues and the Commandant. After his departure, the Commandant himself felt more in the saddle, and it was clear to us that he was at last in charge, and had taken on some meaning. We called this first Superintendent Nazi, since both his appearance and manners were reminiscent of a Gestapo noncom; this annoyed him greatly, and he took every opportunity to throw this up to Father S., in his own name and that of his colleagues.

The third man in line in this house administration was the [second] deputy [Doctor], a slim young fellow, meticulously dressed, combed, and shaved. He was introduced to me by the Commandant in the presence of the Superintendent. I expressed surprise: "One more deputy?" He took this calmly; in any case, he remained completely composed until the very end. He was the one man who most closely approached the ideal of the progressive representative of the new style: an expressionless face, fixed, alien, distant, present here only physically. It seemed that nothing could possibly move this man, nothing could interest him. He was always impeccable, not the slightest imperfection in his clothing or shoes, well-pressed, as if he had stepped out of a fashion shop window, obviously a prewar one. This man would shake hands. From time to time he deigned to give a slight smile when someone remarked to him after his return from vacation: "What a nice tan you have." Anyway, he tried to maintain a tan. This was much more important to him than a conversation. We looked upon him as a physician and called him Aesculapius, although he never displayed any particular interest in Father S. when he was sick, even if he found him in bed, nor did he ever reveal any profound medical skill. A completely mysterious man. As I recall, he appeared in the house only for brief periodic visits every six days. He was seen at the military hospital, in unusual circumstances that are better left unmentioned. Once I saw him in military uniform, and this displeased him. He took care of no one, neither Father S. nor Sister. He appeared to be more intelligent than the Commandant; he only brought up opinions once, to which he received a concise reply. Otherwise, he remained a complete enigma.

Of the other persons appearing on the Stoczek scene, one who deserves attention is the Old Gentleman [Grandpa] of Semitic features and manners, and whose accent was also clearly Semitic, although it was said that he was not a Jew but rather an old railway worker from the Skierniewice region.* At least that is what the Superintendent told Father when he indignantly accused us of referring to him as Moishe von Schwinau (after the commander of the Teutonic Knights mentioned by Grabski in *Two Hundred Cities*). Perhaps this man was not a Jew; if he were, he could have been a credit to his race. It could be said of him that for a "new man" he displayed a great amount of humanity and some real values. It seems that he was a doctrinaire communist. He was the only one in whose hands I saw Marx's *Das Kapital,* a thick volume which lay on a table in our boarding house for a few days. This man was also the only one who sometimes could be seen writing or reading something more carefully or trying to busy himself with something during his tour of duty. At first he turned his back to us when we went down to the garden; from this we deduced that he was an "informed" believer waging battle against the "enemies of the people." Today we can understand that this is the way in which he represented and expressed the party line, since it was not yet time for coexistence. Later he turned to us halfway and finally with full face. But he was a man worthy of respect. He was the only one who did anything, who sought out work—he whittled, sculpted, painted, read. In a word, he did not let himself be swallowed up by the stupid, vapid existence at Stoczek. He was the only one who could fix the electricity, modernize the kitchen, repair the bathroom heater, or dig out the soot from the pipes with his bare hands. He would get terribly dirty doing this. Slowly he became more civil and capable of revealing his human qualities. We even began to like him as a representative of normal people.

The housekeeper, a permanent member of the group, also fit into this category. She was with me from Warsaw to Rywałd; I saw her in another car, carefully hiding behind the driver during a stop near Grudziądz. In Rywałd, where she brought meals to my cell, she was the first voice from that other world. These voices were very limited as to their subjects: "You must eat" she would say, "because that's

---

*About thirty miles southwest of Warsaw.

the most important thing." An oldish, sixty-year-old woman, stout, ailing, she always referred to me as Father. She was a problem for the group, because occasionally she would start fights, which we could hear even in our quarters. She would dress down the whole administration and all members of the group. We never knew what these fights were all about. It seems that the main sore point was the supply of foodstuffs for the kitchen; these were very hard to come by in Stoczek. After some time she began to drive to the market by car and then went regularly to Warsaw every month. Others did the same thing. Then Sister would go to the kitchen to cook. When Sister was absent, the housekeeper brought our meals up to us; she would stop at the door of the chapel and gaze momentarily at the altar "with faith." It seemed to me that she could be counted among the normal people.

It is difficult to say anything about the rest of the group. They were all anonymous, reluctant to work, most of them young, most either sick or sickly, ordinary, simple boys in civilian dress carefully concealing their uniforms. It was only when they traveled with Father S. to Olsztyn or Barczewo that they donned uniforms and carried handguns in their pockets. They led a carefree life, shuffling down the corridor, spending hours on end staring out the window. When on duty, they usually slept or dozed. They appeared rather forlorn and bored, and this would amuse us. Here we the prisoners were content, and they the rulers were despondent. They usually kept their distance. Whenever we met, which happened twice a day when we went for our walks, they reacted in various ways. Some rose from the table in military fashion and extended a greeting; others remained seated, but managed to mumble some sort of response to our greeting. Some did this very politely, others indifferently and gruffly. In the course of time their manners improved, especially after we had been together for a year. One of them tried to be especially courteous and talkative. This was during May and June. Then he suddenly disappeared. We nicknamed him Chatterbox. But he never ventured beyond the limits of weather, sun, and rain. He never asked any questions; and we never had a conversation with him.

One general behavior pattern observed by all of them was to be more polite when we met them alone; in a group they were stiff and formal. All were carefully perfumed, although some were dressed more poorly. All of them languished in boredom and idleness. If they read anything, it was trash. None of them seemed inclined to work. If sometimes they began a task, they did not persevere long. Their greatest achievement was mowing the lawn; they all mowed expertly, which indicated that they were first generation peasants. Most of them were masters at cursing. When their conversations could be heard, they were usually extremely coarse.

Their attitude toward work, with the exception of the railroad man from Skierniewice [the Old Gentleman], was highly indifferent. They could watch the garden grow full of weeds without doing anything about it. When the grass was finally mowed, no one removed the cuttings, so that in time they rotted. When the putrid stench of rotting grass filled the air, a military vehicle appeared one morning to haul it away. Beyond the fence cows grazed on a parched pasture. The rest of the grass was burned in the garden, revealing to the whole world a highly progressive method of drying hay. We were amazed by such a simple idea of expedience in agriculture—that it took people so long to hit on this idea, and that it happened here, in Stoczek, before the eyes of backward people, enemies of the new order!

The subject of the education of the progressive citizen provided much food for thought. If these were the results it brought among the elite, with whom we were always surrounded, what could we expect from the others? These people were not capable of promoting material prosperity in Poland. Often they borrowed tools from our storehouse, where we had stored some gardening tools we had found in the field; they never replaced them, but left them wherever they used them. How many times we had to gather up these tools and return them to our little storehouse under the porch! It turned out that we idealists respected these tools more than they, the materialists. We were also more adept at working in the garden, even though the work was very limited (we always maintained the paths ourselves and cleared them of snow).

Were there any attempts to pervade our community life? It appears there were, even if it was not done directly. Let me cite a few observations and remarks against the background of various facts we exchanged.

Above all, the question of surveillance: eavesdropping is so common under the present system that it would be hard to believe that there was none in our case. One could not present any technical evidence or indications of technical preparations. Yet, there is no doubt that they knew about many matters one would consider unimportant to those around us. From the conversations the Superintendent had with Father S., we concluded that our friends took a lively interest in our life and coexistence, and that even those things we considered ordinary and meaningless did not escape their attention. After Christmas, we began, as much as possible, to spend the holidays together: mornings in the chapel, afternoons in my room, which doubled as a dining and reception area. Our afternoon meetings were of great interest to our friends; they asked pointblank what we talked about. Actually, there was nothing to disturb them: we had presentations and discussions on Church history, ecclesiastical art, liturgy, choral works, tourism in Catholic countries. Sometimes we limited ourselves to reading aloud from a book. We left ourselves no time for *de quolibet* [regarding anything] conversations. During the Christmas season, we devoted nearly all of our time to the singing of carols. Thus our life was politically superpure. However, our pattern of life was not completely to the liking of our friends; we feared that perhaps they would forbid us to hold our meetings without the permission of their "superiors." But it never came to that. It is almost certain that the Superintendent stole his way to the door of my room, leaving the prints of the wide soles of his shoes on the waxed floor. A lot of what was said during these conversations, usually calm and cheerful, came out inaccurately— no doubt by eavesdropping at the door, which was rather flimsy and loose. We made this easier by not subduing our voices. No doubt this eavesdropping by our Defender of Freedom was the source of the reproaches he made to Father S. during a conference in Olsztyn. He accused us outright of being ill-disposed to our surroundings, of criticizing them, and wanted to hear an apology.

There was a time when Father and I began to speak Latin at meals to keep in practice. Apparently this came to the attention of the Superintendent rather quickly, since he expressed his displeasure during the next conference with Father S. He even accused us of trying to hide something from the sister, who was supposedly hurt by our behavior and took to crying in the kitchen. We never tried to confront the sister with these accusations. Rather, we tried to show Sister our full confidence in her, that we had nothing to hide from her. We never noticed indications that she was uncomfortable with us. She was rather talkative, cheerful, given to joking; she also accepted our teasing jokes and never took offense. Because we lived so closely together, having been condemned to each other's company, it was imperative to maintain both remoteness and proximity in precise degrees. A remoteness existed between us and the sister to the extent that we could not talk with her about everything and avoided excessive familiarity. But we also had to be close, because Sister had to know about our personal needs, which she took care of, using familial discretion and confidence. Our common fate drew us closer together. Often I had to listen to the sorrows and complaints of my companions; I had to identify with them in order to help them shed these depressing feelings. Sister was always discreet, well mannered, retaining the proper dignity and decorum of a nun who valued her call to serve God. As for us, we treated her like family, with affection and friendly informality. We did not exclude her from our spiritual life, conducting our meditations and retreats together. Sister appreciated and respected this. Nevertheless, there was obviously an attempt to wedge a feeling of distrust between us, since appeals on behalf of the sister continued, addressed to Father, particularly by the Superintendent.

On several occasions Father S. was questioned about me—how I felt and what I thought. They were told it would be best to ask the Primate himself. Let me add, by the way, that my visitors always addressed me as Reverend Father. In speaking to Father about me they respectfully referred to me as *Ksiądz Prymas*

[Priest-Primate], and in speaking to the sister they called me *Ojciec* [Father.]* This pattern, with slight deviations, was followed by them all. As the first anniversary of my imprisonment approached, the Superintendent asked Father what were my thoughts on this anniversary, whether I would not try to obtain my release. Father could not give an answer to this question, because he did not know my plans.

One incident was of greater interest to us. After some medical tests in Olsztyn, Father was waiting for his medicines in the garden with Chatterbox. Chatterbox flauntingly read a newspaper in which Father noticed a statement by the Episcopate regarding the international situation. After his return from Olsztyn he informed me about this incident. I then ventured the opinion that it seemed our guards had wanted me to know about the statement of the Episcopate; and I felt that we should not say anything more about it. But that was not the end of it. On his next visit to the doctor in Olsztyn, Father had a talk with the Superintendent [Nazi], who angrily accused him of informing the Primate about what was written in the newspapers and that he, the Superintendent, had proof of this. Supposedly, he had found some scraps of marked newspapers in the ashes taken out by the sister from Father's stove. This was the "material proof" on which he based his accusations. He reminded Father that he was a prisoner, that he could be returned to prison, that he was not supposed to tell the Primate everything he had seen along the way, that they had no need for such a chaplain and would look for another. Father defended himself against this fury by saying that he was my confessor and as such could not speak about the Primate, because this would trouble his conscience. The Superintendent, of course, claimed that he did not want to know anything about my [sacramental] confession, but it took him a long time to calm down. By this

---

*Each title used carries a different connotation: *księdz* can mean either "priest" or "Father"; *Prymas* [Primate] is the title given the ordinary of the oldest diocese in Poland (Gniezno); *Ojciec* literally means "father" and is used for religious-order priests; here it is used as a term of respect in the sense of "father of a family" or "head."

outburst, he revealed many things that could serve as a good orientation for the tactics used by our friends. He shouted with a stentorian voice that they would not give in on anything, that they knew everything anyway, knew our thoughts, and that he, the Superintendent, was ready to plunge his own hands into the pits of the garbage bins to search for scraps of newspapers, and so on. After this storm, Father returned most upset, but the next day the Superintendent was very polite, pretending that he knew nothing of what had happened the day before. We considered the whole incident an attempt to provoke us, using Chatterbox as the instrument. There were many similar incidents.

One other deserves to be mentioned. The Superintendent was transferred. He considered it his duty to inform Father about this. He waxed polite, urging him to renew his request for release: "I am leaving, but someone else will come in my place, and he also will know everything, like me, and through him I will know everything too." Was this a threat, or a justification for his behavior? In any event, we received the news of the departure of Nazi with great relief. During his last days, the Superintendent was most cordial to both Father and Sister. He did not come to see me before he left. His successor arrived before Nazi's departure, but he [the successor] did not come to see me for quite a while, even though he administered the kitchen and the garden, and soon began to "administer" outside my door. Because he wore bedroom slippers and had something butlerlike about him, we dubbed him "Katz."

October 9, 1954, Saturday

After an interval of two days, the other deputy, whom we called Doctor, arrived with the usual questions about our health and needs. I told him I felt well, much better than at Stoczek. In this house I did not freeze as I had at the Warmiński residence—the air was better for my lungs. As for other needs, I did not know precisely what I should say. Should I consider my stay in Prudnik a lasting period or an interim stay? If it was to be a long residence, I would think about the books I would need for my work. A prisoner knows how long he is to stay in prison. I did not know, even though I was not looked upon as a prisoner. This was the very least any thinking person would demand.

Doctor. The authorities know about our last conversation in Stoczek. The rest is up to them.

Primate. That is true, but this is precisely the situation that offers me no possibility for contact. I am usually told the same old thing: my conversation "has been reported." And that's it, period —because the other side never answers. It was with the express permission of the authorities, as communicated to me by the Commandant in Stoczek, that I forwarded my defense against the accusations made against me. Two months have passed since I submitted this letter, and I still do not see the slightest sign of any desire on the part of the authorities to discuss the matter. Does not such a silence create new difficulties for a dialogue? Am I supposed to write again? This is a serious problem for me.

Doctor. If I may say so, I would be of another opinion—that you should write again.

Primate. But that is the crux of the matter. In my first letter of July 2, submitted on August 1, I gave a definitive response on the subjects that could create difficulties. Despite the fact that my reply was exhaustive, I received no indication of any desire for a discussion. If the government has any objections to my interpretations of the matters I brought up, let them tell me so. Let the government give me an opportunity to hear its objections and to explain my understanding of the matter. Apparently what I covered in my previous letter was not everything. In the past you have said that I present things in "too personal a manner," "reasons of state" are at stake here. I would be happy to hear what these "reasons of state" might be, because since I am not aware of them, I must perforce discuss the matter from a personal point of view. And I would like to understand them.

Doctor. Everything depends on you, Father. In any case, our previous conversation has been reported to the government, and this one will be too. Are there any other needs?

Primate. I could speak about my needs only if I understood my present situation. Is it temporary and for how long? Based on that, I could request books from home, and I would like to write my father, to whom I have not written in a long time.

October 10, 1954, Sunday

The manner in which we were moved from Stoczek to Prudnik deserves attention—as a police maneuver involving much energy and caution. A few days before our departure we saw a plane searching for a place to land; shortly thereafter the plane disappeared behind the trees. On the day we left, Father S. and Sister were taken away first. I was to go in another car. I went out into the garden; there stood a car with the chauffeur whom I already knew. The windows were smeared with a dirty rag. I had to go back to the driveway. Then the inner gate was closed, and I was allowed to enter the car. One of the young men stood by the gate; the Superintendent [Katz] and his deputy concentrated on me. The Commandant was nowhere to be seen during those days. It seemed to us that the deputy was in charge of the operation, although the Superintendent was very busy and involved with preparations for the trip.

The new Superintendent deserves a few lines. The first time he came to see me, he did not say in what capacity he was visiting me. He began with the usual questions about my health and needs as well as requests. He implied that we already knew each other, that we had sat together during visitations at many rectories. I had no intention of guessing, although it seemed to me that we had certainly met at least once—on Miodowa Street, when Baca bit him. But I had no desire to remind him of this incident. The Superintendent returned to the subject once again, pressing me "to recall where we had met before." I did not take him up on it. He was a slender man, with strong Hungarian features and most unpleasant eyes. He showed a great deal of concern that the move should go well. He wanted to take the religious pictures from Stoczek, but we explained to him that they were "local" property and that it would not be right to carry them off without the knowledge of their owners. He did not agree but did not touch the pictures. As we left the outer gate into the square in front of the church, some interested children crouched to see who was in the car. I had a feeling these children knew something. The ride to the airport took three-quarters of an hour; my escorts were visibly nervous. From a distance I saw the plane in a vacant field and not a living soul around it. But at a distance, at the edge of the woods, there were silhouettes of men guarding access to the airstrip. When I entered the plane, I saw that Father S. and Sister were visibly upset; maybe they were afraid that I would not come, and they would have to make the trip alone. The takeoff was perfect. The Superintendent and his deputy were in the cabin with us. We practically never saw the crew. The rest of the journey was uneventful. As we landed at the airport near Nysa, it was the same thing—not a soul in sight. We were not allowed to leave the plane; we had to wait half an hour until the car delivered our things and returned. In fact we waited for several hours, until it grew dark. It was probably the dark that they were really waiting for, so that it would be safe to pass through the villages and towns. We thought we saw the Commandant in the distance in a military vehicle, as he raced around the airport. As we left, we saw the whole flight crew, composed of about seven persons, standing by the propellers. With great interest they watched this developing spectacle —a group of civilians leading two priests and a nun to a car. My companions entered the first car and I the second. The trip to Prudnik was made in complete darkness.

October 11, 1954, Monday
The most obvious arguments with which we try to win God to our side do not bring us inner peace. Is this not because they are full of human discernment that cannot see everything, that cannot see in its integrity what only God can see? Does not this absence of peace lead us to seek new arguments? When man tires of this futile effort he falls silent, like a child weary of crying, when it buries its tear-streaked face in the folds of its mother's dress. Then he experiences relief. When I fall silent, my weary brain rests, peace returns. One thing remains for me to say like Peter: Lord, You know, You know everything. . . . There remains my humble sigh: Father, Father . . . Mother, Mother . . . When all the presumption of my arguments and

attempts to persuade God leaves me, I remain but a child—a child who understands nothing, who becomes submissive, quiet, humble. Humility restores my peace of mind, my peace of heart, and my trust . . . God has persuaded me. . . . Cast your troubles on the Lord . . . trust. . . .

October 12, 1954, Tuesday

The Superintendent came to see me today with the usual questions. He wanted to know if I was satisfied with the new place. During our conversation he mentioned that I had been in isolation for a year, and that it was time to think over my position relative to the present government and the prewar one—my work before the war and now. I answered that the government knew my attitude, since I had personally stated it clearly in many conversations, and most recently in my letter of July 2, submitted on August 1. I considered it inappropriate to delve into my prewar work, of which I was not ashamed. Not upset by this answer, the Superintendent expressed the conviction that the whole Catholic and religious community was pleased that I had been removed from my position, and so far no protests had been received by the government. I answered that I considered this statement an attempt to insult me. I had not been removed from my position, since no one had the authority to do this. But it has been made impossible for me to carry out my duties—a fact I had always protested and continue to protest now. Locating me here I consider harmful not only to me but also to the government, and guarding me in a style used in concentration camps runs contrary to all basic rights of prisoners. He denied I was a prisoner: "This is not a prison, it is a monastery." I explained to him what was meant by the term "putting someone in a monastery"—a term the Russians used to use with reference to their treatment of Catholic priests during the period of the partitions.* My situation could not be compared with that earlier one, since those priests had freedom of correspondence, press, and movement throughout their neighborhoods, of which I was deprived.

I summarized the conversation in the following points: (1) I asked

---

*1772–1918.

for a copy of the decree by virtue of which I found myself in the present situation. (2) I asked for the reason why my letters to my father were being held up and not delivered promptly and, when delivered, then only read to him. (3) I wanted to know how long I was to remain in this uncertain situation, worse than that of any common prisoner who knows for what he is sentenced and for how long. (4) I would be very happy to hear from someone delegated to convey the accusations made against me by the authorities, so that I could understand them clearly and concretely.

I also touched on the fact that I had received no answer to my letter to the government written on July 2 and submitted on August 1.

October 13, 1954, Wednesday
We quickly managed to orient ourselves to the new lay of the land. We are on top of a hill, with a leafy forest around us, some 250 meters above sea level. Our home is a former friary building that was originally owned by but hastily appropriated from the Black Franciscans in Silesia. The building was adapted to suit the new requirements by installing a high fence with barbed wire. These new barricades, three and a half meters high, all secured with barbed wire, are painted green; next to them is a long, sparsely planted row of spruces. It is impossible to walk in the small, sloping garden when the ground is wet. There are many fruit trees still with their autumn fruit. The house is a three-story structure, with a high cellar and ground floor. It is dilapidated and shows signs of the war, of exploded bombs and artillery shells. Part of the roof is temporary. Next to the house stands a small church, its mortar walls pocked with artillery shells. It all leaves a rather gloomy impression.

Inside the building, they assigned us the second floor with windows facing the garden, to the north. Our friends occupied the third floor. The ground floor is for the kitchen and the guards. We share the stairwell, from which we enter the garden, and there is a veranda onto the outer courtyard. The designated area is totally surrounded by beautiful tall trees, which completely cut off the rest of the world. We see only a patch of sky—that is all. In the distance, on a long hill, stands the town of Prudnik, some two and a half kilometers as the crow flies; we are separated by fields and fish ponds that buffer the friary grounds. The place is full of mechanical contraptions for surveillance, in the house as well as in the garden. The house has running water although sporadically the pumps do not work. Electric lights, central heating—everything is in a state of great neglect. The house is whitewashed. Our floor has a long corridor separated from the stairwell by a wooden partition. The left side of the corridor is assigned to us; the sun rooms, locked and nailed shut, are on the right side. The entire complex has a greater sense of isolation than the one in Stoczek. From here we cannot see a living "normal" person; everyone around us either walks stealthily outside the fences or wanders up and down the corridors. Our corridor is out of bounds, the "checkpoint" is not within view as it was in Stoczek. To the right

Prudnik Śląski. The third prison. The building stood on a hill, totally isolated and surrounded by a twelve-foot fence of barbed wire. The windows in the corridors were boarded up.

of the entrance are the dining room and chapel, to the left our rooms. I was assigned two rooms—a bedroom and a study. Next to me is Father S. and further down the corridor Sister. At the end a bathroom; that is all.

In this new place we are even more condemned to one another's company than before, since no one comes to see us, and no one can control the traffic in the corridor. Everything has been hastily, poorly painted. Everywhere there are signs of recent renovation: abandoned paint brushes, cans of paint, piles of rusty nails, hand saws, hammers—about which no one seems to care.

As usual, we gathered everything onto the garden veranda, and from there it all slowly disappeared. We will have trouble taking walks here; the sloping, slippery terrain will make it very difficult. On the other hand, the house is more comfortable [than the one in Stoczek], dry, with spacious windows carefully screened with curtains and drapes. We were given an order not to look out of the windows, that we should draw the blinds before putting on the lights. In reality, there is nothing around us and no one to be seen, but it is our duty to conceal ourselves from the soldiers guarding us outside. Of course, only Father and Sister were told of this duty. I don't get such reminders.

October 23, 1954, Tuesday
I have asked for a medical commission. Because the symptoms that developed in Stoczek still worry me, I have decided to submit to a medical examination. My request was granted eagerly, as if they had been waiting for it. Since I did not get to see my own doctor the last time—despite the fact that the Commandant had agreed to it— I did not raise the issue this time. I did not want to be subjected to any new chicaneries, like the ones I had experienced with the Commandant last May.

October 24, 1954, Wednesday
Will I ever be in a more fortunate position in my life than I am now? One thought about how many people are praying for me lifts my spirits. And yet the intrinsic value of these prayers is a hundredfold

more meaningful than this feeling itself. Would they be praying for me so much if I were at home? And all the priests whose duty it is to pray *pro Antistite* [for the ordinary],* how often they don't even notice the name of their bishop in the Canon of the Holy Mass! Today we are drawn together by our common suffering, and it makes us more aware. When I return home from prison, I will surely lose the fruits of this intensified brotherly sensitivity. Truly, I will never know times more blessed in spiritual fruit, in the help of prayer. What more do I need for happiness?

October 26, 1954, Tuesday

Under these new conditions, our life has become stabilized. I returned with enthusiasm to the work begun in Stoczek, to the meditations on the Liturgical Year. Every day I conducted morning meditation for "my flock" in the chapel, and after breakfast I attempted to condense these thoughts into brief points. Thus grew the project which now in large part is completed. Although it was conducted in our circle, in editing it I directed my thoughts mainly to lay Catholics. I wrote both cycles at the same time: *Proprium de Tempore* [Proper of Time]† and *Proprium Sanctorum* [Proper of the Saints].‡ I lacked the proper materials necessary for this work: liturgical books, lives of saints, histories of the Church. I had at my disposal only my missal, breviary, the Bible, and—my head. The work was not easy. But writing is great preventive medicine against the dangers that threaten a brain not challenged by constant effort. Thanks to this work, the day passed very quickly. The pattern of our day did not change—it only grew more intense. We were all beginning to hurry. Father also started writing liturgical sketches, his for school-age children. We encouraged Sister to read the history of the Church and books by Rops.§ This was a little more difficult

---

*The prelate governing a specified territory, such as a diocese.
†Proper of Time or the Temporal Cycle of the Church calendar begins with the first Sunday of Advent and commemorates the events of the life of Christ.
‡Proper of the Saints or Sanctoral Cycle commemorates the feasts of the saints.
§Henry Jules Charles Petiot Daniel-Rops (1901–1965), a French spiritual writer.

for her, since her lively, womanly temperament distracted her to a variety of trivial details.

It could be said that during the morning hours the "entire colony" works very hard. After lunch, until 3:00 P.M., we are usually in the garden; it is hard to walk here, unusually stifling, with little air. Walking the steep area in either direction is very tiring. It is wet, the ground is damp and soggy, in spite of the slope. The garden is a minus in this new place, but the living quarters are a plus: dry, bright, heated. We are able to linger longer at the table, since our hands and feet do not freeze as they did in Stoczek.

Today I received a letter from my father together with a food parcel. The letter from my sister, Stanisława Jarosz, was a pleasant surprise. This was a broadening of contacts.

Our Commandant is still not here; either he has been transferred or he has met with some accident. It is mostly the deputy who pays us visits, coming every day. He is becoming increasingly humanitarian, and even manages to smile in a dignified and magnanimous manner, out of the left corner of his mouth. But he does so with great restraint and according to the "plan." Perhaps he too will become a human.

> My beloved son!
>
> I received your last letter of July 8, which I answered with my letter of July 27, accompanied by a package. We still have no answer and no news of you.
>
> A year has gone by since that painful moment, and I still do not know your fate or where you are, my son.
>
> I am an old man and unable to understand these present times and that, despite the dozens of requests I have made to see you, my requests have not been granted. It is my fatherly duty and my heart's desire to seek a way to see you —as long as I can I will continue trying. You asked in your first letter that no complaint should ever pass from the lips of your closest ones—your wish is our command and something we hold holy, but there is suffering that rends these complaints from us despite our resolve.

All of us trustingly turn to God for help and wait for our wishes to be granted. I especially pray that God will give me strength, that He will help me to understand everything and that He should make me worthy to share this suffering with you.

Please also pray, my beloved son, for your father. I would so like to live to see your return.

Everything in the family, thank the Lord, goes well: our health is good, and we try to keep calm.

The children are studying. Ania is feeling better, and her parents hope that the child will recover entirely. They ask you to pray for her.

Please reply as soon as possible with news about you. We would like to know everything about your health and about the problems you mentioned in your last letter. Are they improved? Do you have the opportunity for medical care? Do you need anything?

We send a package together with this letter.

I commend you, my dear son, to Our Lady of Jasna Góra. Your dear ones ask me to assure you that they are with you in spirit and in their thoughts and that they are praying fervently to God and to His Mother for your protection, health, and strength. I send you greetings and kiss you, my beloved son, asking again for your prayers and for your blessing.

Zalesie, October 18, 1954
Stanisław Wyszyński

My dearest brother!

I add some news to Father's letter—I hope that you receive them and are pleased. I ask you not to worry about the family. Our father is bearing up extremely well despite his years, and his fortitude serves as an example for us.

I am with you in my thoughts and my heart nearly every hour of the day. I commend you to God in my prayers and believe that there is meaning in our suffering and that it serves a purpose. We long for the day that we will be able to see you again, my beloved and special brother, to greet you and to embrace you.

I am keeping well, working, and until now I find the strength for what I have to do. Józef is painting, as he used to, most often by the river, although sometimes he slips a little farther away. He was just in Szczebrzeszyn near Lublin, where he painted a windmill that reminds me of a similar one from our childhood near Zuzela. It is strange how that first one has always stuck in my mind. Józef looks well, although his blood pressure is unpredictable; last month he had to go on a diet because his weight went above 260. I was afraid that it might end badly. As usual, he was not too concerned about it.

I often think of your health and fear that it might not be good. I ask you to take care of yourself and get medical attention if necessary. With arthritic changes one must avoid catching cold; sometimes complications set in after some triviality and they may be very hard to cure.

We wait for news of you; please tell us about your life in detail. Everything is important to us, and every word is a source of joy.

I send you affectionate greetings, dear brother. I commend all your affairs to the Blessed Mother and ask you to remember me in your prayers. Włodek asks for your prayers and your blessing. His grades last year were good, and he plans to continue to strive toward his goal. I also send greetings and best wishes from Sister Superior.

October 18, 1954
Your devoted sister,
Stanisława Jarosz

October 29, 1954, Friday
I prepared two letters yesterday, one for my father and one for my sister. I gave them to the deputy today, asking that they be delivered.

"The letters will be delivered," the Superintendent repeated. To the letters I added a list of requested books, in duplicate. The Superintendent assured me that all the books would be brought to me.

My best and beloved Father!

My deepest apologies for not thanking you for your letter of July 27 and for your package. I sensed that there were some difficulties resulting in the retention of my letter after it was read to you. I did not want to be the cause of new problems and that is why I delayed. The letters of October 18, delivered to me on the twenty-sixth of this month, so full of great anxiety about my fate, force me to thank you sincerely for both letters and the special gifts contained in the package delivered with them.

Please forgive me that my letter will not give you the answers to all your questions. My legal situation has not changed, although I have asked several times verbally for its clarification. On August 1 I sent a long letter to the Presidium for which I still have had no answer. I am so sorry, my dear father, that your attempts to see me have caused you so much suffering. Although you have a fatherly right to see me, your peace of mind, emotional state, and health are more important to me.

For a few weeks now, I have been in a new place where the living conditions and the climate are better for my health. During the past winter I developed a variety of disorders that have still not left me completely. I am writing about this, my dear father, only because you want to know everything. The present state of my health: besides continuing problems with hyperacidity, constant headaches, lower abdominal and leg pains, besides a growing sensitivity of the liver and a general weakness, nothing new is bothering me. The state of my lungs is satisfactory. I am very grateful for your advice, and try to follow it as much as I can. I beseech you, my dear father, not to worry about my health. I am confident that the Good Lord will not deny me His protection and will allow me to survive. I have been in poor health all my life, and now this condition has become an advantage.

You have expressed your willingness, my dear father, to send me new books and necessities. I enclose with this letter, in duplicate, a list of books that could be useful to me in further work. Some of them are in my private library or are lying on various tables in my apartment; others are in the house library on the third floor. Nearly all are cataloged, so there should be no trouble in finding them. I need some Italian books very badly; I would like to ask the bishop to lend me a few books from his library (law, literature: Papini, Dante, Ferrari—whatever he has on hand).

For a year I have been offering Mass without an altar stone, on an improvised altar. A year ago they sent me a stone, but not a consecrated one. If one of the priests could take the altar stone from the curia* and enclose it well-wrapped with the books, I would be most grateful.

Also, for a whole year I have not had the archdiocesan Ordo. I need it very much, since I am obligated to follow either the Gniezno or the Warsaw liturgical calendar. Therefore I ask you kindly to get for me an Ordo† from the bishop.

As for some little things, we need (1) two clerical collars with collar buttons, which we don't have, a mirror, and a comb, (2) for the approaching winter, a few pairs of long woolen socks, (3) a few pairs of warm underwear, which Sister Superior will easily find in my dressers, (4) we always welcome honey, lemons, coffee, bars of ordinary dessert chocolate, and homemade biscuits, which are very good for me. But please do not send tea or cigarettes.

My dear father! I kiss your workworn hands with filial respect, begging you not to lose faith in the wisdom, love, and goodness of our common Father, who is in heaven. I pray to God for your peace and faith, love and patience that

---

*The Archdiocesan Chancery offices.
†A printed calendar containing directives for daily Mass and for the breviary.

soothe all pain and make understandable even things that are unpleasant and unclear. At every Mass that I celebrate in the morning at 7:30, you have your part, as does my family and those close to me. I know that my protracted absence is a difficult test for many. But God has the right to demand everything from us, and we must give it with love and peace. Our suffering cannot make us worse or deprive us of love for mankind, because that would be a defeat.

Today is Tadeusz' name day. Please tell him that I am praying for his family and for little Ania. I send my special brotherly regards to my sisters, and to their families I promise my devotion. I thank all for their prayers and ask them particularly to commend me to the care of Our Lady of Jasna Góra. I remember the anniversary of Mother's death. I remember all the members of my household with gratitude and bless them all from the bottom of my heart.

Dear Father, I kiss your hands in gratitude and bless you with the fullness of my priesthood.

October 28, 1954
Stefan Wyszyński

enclosures: 1. list of books
            2. letter to sister Stanisława Jarosz

My very special sister!
I received the letter you enclosed with Father's letter; I am very grateful to you for your goodness, because your words make it easier for me to understand the family situation. I sensed from Father's last letter that my absence has exhausted him and that he is very worried about me. I am not able to write in such a way as to conceal the truth he seeks. Particularly, news of my health might upset him. His frustrated attempts to see me have caused him a great deal of sorrow. I would like to call upon your good sense and experience, my dear Stachna, to ask you to be a calming

influence on Father. I know that what he is going through is too much for his years, but you can persuade him to put his trust fully in the wisdom of God. I am a servant of the Church, and in my life there are more of God's ways and plans than man's. We must not complain about anyone or blame anyone, but rather we must pray more patiently that God allows us to perform our present duties.

You will learn the rest from my letter to Father; I trust that they will reach you. I was worried about how Janka was coping with her children, especially Stefanek. The news about Włodzio made me very happy, I bless him with all my heart; may the Good Lord guide him. Please give my regards to Naścia, Janka, their families and Józio. Also take care of yourself, since I know how you like to use up all your strength. Please give my warm regards to Sister Superior. I am with you in heart and mind, my very special sister, and I bless you with brotherly love.

October 28, 1954
+ Cardinal Stefan

October 30, 1954, Saturday
"Referring to our conversation of October 9, I have prepared a letter to the Presidium, which I am now ready to hand you with a request that it be forwarded." The man I addressed declared his readiness to accept the letter, expressing the opinion that its subsequent fate should be left to the government. The letter was dated October 26.

November 25, 1954, Thursday
How quickly. Today the doctors showed up, the same ones who had examined me in Stoczek. The older doctor conducted the examination, while the younger one spent his time looking out the window. In their opinion, the general state of my health has not degenerated in the past half year. They did confirm signs of serious exhaustion and weakness: "We are not delighted with the general state of your health," the older doctor declared. The questionable conditions must

be clarified by additional clinical tests, which should be conducted as soon as possible. I asked the doctors to examine Father S., who is more seriously ill than I. They were reluctant, explaining that they were rushing to catch a train, but finally they did go and hurriedly examine him. Apparently, I was supposed to have been their only "item."

November 26, 1954, Friday

I received a letter from my father with a note from my sister, Stanisława Jarosz, as well as a package of food. My father is feeling well; the letter was much calmer than the preceding one. My loved ones are gradually getting to know more about my life, even though I cannot write them much about it. I can tell this from the contents of the packages sent to me.

November 30, 1954, Tuesday

The joy of justice. God permits us to experience the great joy of justice, that He is just when He tries us, when He makes us aware of His power and His presence. In the rendering of justice I have experienced, I feel the presence of a just God. And this presence brings joy, even if justice is punishment. Joy at the realization that justice exists dwarfs the severity of the punishment. Indeed, the severity of the punishment enables us to see the justice all the more clearly. Who is able to compensate God for all his sins? I admit I am guilty, since God, present as I committed this act, has given me the grace to recognize my fault. Only God and I see my fault clearly. And I am also happy that all those who knew how to point out my faults, weaknesses, incompetence, clumsiness, and ineffectiveness can see the justice of God, who came to rescue the people from my weakness. This is a consolation for those people thirsting for justice, even if they see it differently from the way God and I see it. In the end, the measure of God's justice that I experience with joy brings advantages to everyone, even my accusers, when God in turn lets them experience His justice. . . . And if, in the meting out of this justice, God is so very delicate and merciful, this again is God's secret and mine. . . . My accusers, in acknowledging God's justice toward me, also acknowledge His justice toward them.

_____

December 3, 1954, Friday
Today I received the second shipment of the books I asked for on October 28 together with the medicines. Everything had been inspected but put back in better order than before. They tried to hide traces of the inspection.

_____

December 5, 1954, Sunday
Quia non iustificabitur apud Te omnis vivens [Because before You no living person will be justified] (Ps. 142:2; 143:2KJV). . . . Slowly, every armed word slips through our fingers, we lose our defenses when grace enlightens the interior of our soul. What can I hold against God? The purest man immersed in His light looks like dust in a ray of the sun. And what can I say when I see how my sin is always my enemy? Shall I challenge God, tell Him that He must be just? It is I forcing God to punish justly; it is I violating God, and God is defending himself against me with His mercy. I see this mercy even in the measure of His justice! Am I to accuse my brothers by saying that their prayers are not effective enough? Does it not rather attest to the magnitude of my guilt that the prayers of such good people are not enough to satisfy God? Is it not rather I who should ask their pardon that because of the magnitude of my faults God is forced to refuse them, to not answer their prayers? Should not I beg God— because of the magnitude of my faults—to spare pain and suffering for those who are saddened by my suffering, whom I cannot serve as is my duty? I am to blame for the suffering of my Betrothed deprived of their pastor. It is I who should beg their pardon that because of my transgressions they are left without leadership and protection. Shall I blame the instrument of God's justice? It is but an instrument, hard, passive, mechanical, unintelligent. Judas, whom Jesus called his friend, was such an instrument. Pontius Pilate was such an instrument, to whom Jesus explained, "You would have no power over me if it were not given to you from above." An instrument functions

today and tomorrow lies discarded under a bench: that is its fate. Far more inferior is a hammer than a bar of molten iron. Right here it is a question of this bar. It is rather I who should beg their pardon that they are gathering guilt while I am cleansing myself. Who is able to justify himself in Your eyes, O Lord?

December 6, 1954, Monday

I am running out of arguments; my power of speech is languishing for want of words. Beg for mercy? Is not God's first grace the very idea of begging? Beg Him to hear? He never ceases to hear, even when I am silent! Beg Him to show mercy? Why, every moment owes its existence to the mercy of God! Beg Him for forgiveness? He forgave before the offense was committed! Word falls silent, thought ceases, as in the soul of Peter: "Lord, You know! You know everything! You know that . . ."

My companion limps. I ask him not to bother to exert himself, I can manage alone at Mass. But my companion does not give up; I see how he is overextending himself. Is it not better to obey than to serve? His painful attempts become my suffering and . . . distraction. What would be more considerate: to obey or—despite pleas— to serve? Perhaps the most considerate thing to do is keep silent and allow the service to go on, even at the cost of suffering? Then my distraction becomes a struggle for concentration, and his suffering a merit!

December 8, 1954, Wednesday*

What praises shall I use? Shall I praise you with words? Mother of the Word Incarnate, what meaning has the dry whisper of the dried leaves of my words? Each one burdened with original sin, each uncouth, clumsy, every one hard, brusque, crude, sharp as hailstones on rose petals! My words debase your pristine freshness, maim the ideal beauty of integrity and harmony; they are stains on a master-piece. Am I to praise you with the feeling in my heart? With the very gaze of its soul, the defiled heart conceals the Woman clothed

*Feast of the Immaculate Conception.

with the sun! The best of feelings are but dim shadows beside the luminous purity of a perfect hue. Shall I praise you with a thought? This impudent bird tires too rapidly, folds its wings and falls. Shall I praise you with tears? Perhaps that is the one thing in me that is the purest and . . . without blemish!

I do not even dare to look at you, Immaculate One, so that my gaze should not distort the image of beauty that you radiate. The great master of color and mystic discovered you in the heavens and revealed you to the world in his masterpiece of the Immaculate Lady. Murillo saw you the way little Bernadette Soubirous did. But I prefer to gaze upon you without the help of paintbrush and chisel. When I see you that way, I wish to see nothing else, all falls silent.

O *Purissima* [O Purest One] . . .
O *Integra* [O Chaste One] . . .

December 9, 1954, Thursday
Immaculate One—*Niepokalana, Immaculata, Immacolata, Immaculée Unbefleckte, Sünderbare*—all these words carry a demeaning connotation. They all contain pejorative attributes, like bugs in a rose. Of what help is that negation, that meaningless no? We are so inept that we cannot find a word—pure, chaste, brilliant—to reveal what God wrought in the Conceived Being and in the Mother of God-made-Man.

We must seek words pure, clear, translucent, and brilliant; words that will embrace the unexpressed truth without eclipsing it.

December 14, 1954, Tuesday
For Christmas I sent the following letter to my father:

My dearest and best father!
I received your last letter (undated) on November 26, 1954, together with a package in which I found all the things

I asked for in my letter, as well as a cassock. I am grateful for everything. I feel deeply embarrassed by the goodness, thoughtfulness, and help given to me, since I have no way to show my gratitude. I am really living on the generosity of others, and this could even be humiliating if there were not so much care displayed in these gifts. I accept them all . . . as proof of love that I do not deserve. I want to repay you with love and prayer.

Of the books I requested on October 20, 1954, I have so far received (1) D. Rops, (2) A. Bruckner, four volumes, (3) J. Kitowicz, (4) three Italian textbooks, (5) *Vatican*, (6) Sienkiewicz's *The Deluge* without the first volume, and *The Teutonic Knights*, two volumes, (7) Gołubiew, complete, (8) S. Thomae, *Summa theologica*, volumes III and IV. It is difficult for me to express my gratitude for the two photographs sent to me: that of Our Lady of Jasna Góra and copies of the photographs of my late mother. I wanted them so much and had even considered asking for them. Kindness anticipates wishes.

On November 25 I was again examined by two doctors; although the tests necessary for a complete analysis have still not been made, the doctors did not find any deterioration in the symptoms they discovered six months ago. The doctors see a general weakening of my condition, and they advise more exercise and better nourishment within the limitations of my diet. I received the medications and am taking them. Despite these ailments, I am not depressed—I am cheerful and avoid staying in bed at all costs. Probably the best medicine at my disposal is to refuse to dwell on the past or the future. I arrange my time so as to fill it completely with reading, which—besides prayer—is my only occupation. Despite my forced inactivity, I am really busy, and have no time, even here.

My dear father! This is the second Christmas you will be spending without my Christmas wafer. But do not think that you will be neglected. We will both meet in prayer before the Heart of our Heavenly Father. I pray for you a great deal, more than ever before in my life. I always return to you in my thoughts, and every such thought ends in prayer that you—as you yourself wish—may find the strength to suffer in a Christian way. It is not easy to suffer with me, since God has to make demands on me in keeping with my priestly vocation. But if you subordinate your experiences to the plan that God wants to accomplish—in accordance with His needs—you can rest assured about the value of your suffering.

My companion and I are already praying for a Christmas gift for our parents: complete serenity and trust. I embrace you with all my heart, my dear father, together with all my brothers and sisters and all my loved ones, and wish to assure you of my most fervent prayers for you, to sweeten those sorrows of which I am the unwitting cause. Even without a Christmas wafer, I share my heart with all of you. On Christmas Eve, when we celebrate Mass in our tiny chapel, I will commend all of you to our Supreme Father and to the Holy Mother of God. Kissing your dear hands, my kindest father, and with all of my priestly powers I bless you, my brothers and sisters, and all my loved ones in Christ.

December 14, 1954
+ St. W.

P.S.: I thank Stachna for her kind note, for the picture of our late dear mother, and to you, Stachna, and Juleczka, I especially commend our father, so that his health may stoically withstand everything.

December 15, 1954, Wednesday
All week long during the octave of the Immaculate Conception, words and thoughts have centered on the Purest One. Are they not shadows on the sun? What is left for us? With blemished lips we can utter but one invocation: Refuge of sinners . . . But the

holy Catholic Church of the sinners is bold; it prefers that the shadows of our thoughts fall on the Immaculate One rather than be absorbed by the darkness and shadow of death. The sun shines equally on both the stable and the puddle next to it. The people, submerged in darkness, beheld a great Light. Thus, behind the curtain of the shadows of my thoughts and words, I pilfer rays from "the Woman clothed with the sun."* This "theft" needs no restitution. . . . Perhaps this is *occulta compensatio* † for a fallen but redeemed nature.

December 18, 1954, Saturday

In a few days Poland will begin an unusual Jubilee Year: Three hundred years since the defense of Jasna Góra. When in November 1655, the waves of the "deluge"‡ reached the ramparts of Jasna Góra, Father Augustyn Kordecki spoke these words at the initial meeting of monks and noblemen: "The enemy mocks us and holds us in disdain, asking what has remained of our old virtues. And I will answer: they have all vanished, but something has remained, because our faith has remained and our love for the Virgin Mary, and on this foundation the rest can be restored. . . ." (Henryk Sienkiewicz, *The Deluge*).

The Jubilee will begin on Saturday, the day dedicated to Mary, since in this particular year Mary gave birth to Her Son on a Saturday, and everything will take place under the sign of her day.

It would be worthwhile to reflect on the "defense of Jasna Góra" in the year 1955. It is a defense of the soul, the family, the Nation, the Church—before the deluge of a new "enchantment." My Jasna Góra presses in on me from all sides with ramparts of torment; missiles of superstition and reactionism attack my Chicken Coop.§

---

*Apocalypse 12:1.
†Occult compensation: a way of recovering one's property or of collecting what is owed from a debtor if ordinary means cannot be used.
‡In 1655, a group of monks and noblemen under the leadership of Father Augustyn Kordecki successfully defended themselves against a "deluge" of some 9,000 invading Swedes behind the fortifications of the Jasna Góra monastery in Częstochowa.
§During the siege of Jasna Góra, the Swedes disdainfully referred to the monastery as a chicken coop, indicating that they considered it easily subduable.

Three hundred years ago the Chicken Coop survived, and it stands to this day.

The defense of Jasna Góra today is a defense of the Christian spirit of the Nation, a defense of our native culture, a defense of the unity of human hearts within God's Heart; it is the defense of man's right to breathe freely, who wants to trust in God more than he wants to trust in people and to trust people in a godly way.

December 21–22, 1954, Tuesday–Wednesday
Additional medical tests were conducted during the last two days: X rays of my chest and abdominal cavity, a blood analysis, and a dental examination. The tests took place at the WUBP* in Opole, where I was driven during the evening hours (between six and nine o'clock). Today I was given the results: The condition of my blood was very good—my blood was excellent (to the surprise of the woman doctor who made the tests). My lungs were clear, nothing was found in my abdominal cavity. The overall report: "A completely healthy man." This report did not agree with the examination of the doctors who ordered the additional tests. The results were a bit too optimistic. I have never heard such a medical opinion about my health before. Dental X rays were taken; I received two new fillings, and one that had fallen out was replaced. The woman doctor declared that this should last for a few years. A general observation about the doctors: they were very polite, very professional, sensitive, and knowledgeable. They lacked only one thing that has great meaning for a patient: more than healers they were bureaucrats. The physician must be a friend to the patient and not to a third party on whom he betrays his dependence.

December 22, 1954, Wednesday
For two days I have been in the hands of the medical clinics in Opole. I use the term "clinics" rather than doctors, because they behave like automatons: efficiently, professionally, almost infallibly,

---

*Wojewódzki Urząd Bezpieczeństwa Publicznego—Provincial Office of the Security Police (UB).

but without the medical spirit. For the unfortunate patient, these people have no human side, something an ailing body needs more than a prescriptioh. We have here a bureaucrat for whom propaganda is more important than medicine. His conscientiousness, his politeness, his efforts are not for the patient but for an unknown third party, who orders him to make a good impression, to be polite and thorough. The presence of this third party is felt so strongly that the patient is reduced to the level of an object, a bureaucratic piece to be disposed of as instructed.

Poor people, with a distorted sense of conscience! They are also aware of this third party. For them it is critical that they make a good impression on this third party. The patient profits from this not because he needs help, but because he is in the hands of a third party, which has both the patient and the doctor in hand. Do medical ethics still exist? Do professional confidentiality and discretion still exist?

It is the third party that is given the doctor's report. The patient is informed only by the third party. But the third party is also more concerned with whether the doctors were polite, what impression they made, than with anything else—for them it is more an issue of propaganda than medicine. One can be cured and one can die on the orders of the third party. And everyone has to lie a little. The doctor must confirm the state of health that the third party wants. The patient does not want to harm the doctor, so he keeps quiet. And this third party passes the verdict: "a completely healthy man —amazingly so." Now, beware, "man," do not dare to fall ill.

Today I received a letter from my father and sister, as well as my brother. They sent me a large carton of Christmas gifts from home and some Christmas wafers.

December 24, 1954, Friday
A few thoughts and observations on my recent medical experiences. One thing must be emphasized: the great haste with which the doctors were summoned this time. In connection with the whole course of clinical examinations, I must note the increasing courtesy of those around me, as well as that of the medical personnel.

The whole apparatus of the UB continues to function with total and precise caution. The very way I was always taken to Opole attests to this fact. The departure was always announced for an earlier time, but it always took place well after dark. All precautions were taken during the trip. Entering the gates of the Voivodship Office, where the clinics were located, we were always aware that everything was well prepared: the gate was wide open (to the office of the Security Police, at that hour!), not a soul in the courtyard, even the police dogs were gone from their large cages, which stood empty. The car stopped directly in front of the side entrance. First, one of the men made sure that everything was all right in the corridor. Then we stepped out of the car and climbed one flight up empty staircases and through evacuated corridors. Emptiness everywhere, like in a haunted house, although traces of life were everywhere. It looked as if people had evacuated suddenly before some plague.

In an office, a doctor was already waiting by an X ray machine, and a woman dentist was standing by. They helped one another. The doctor, seriously crippled, moved with difficulty. Everything took place in total silence. My constant companion during the examinations was the Superintendent. The Old Gentleman who had accompanied us to Opole sat in the corridor, just outside the door. The laboratory technician, who took samples of my blood, was particularly clumsy; she smeared the blood all over her hands, as if it gave her pleasure. She was silent, although full of feminine pretensions. The woman dentist, on the other hand, worked with extreme efficiency, speed, and sensitivity.

Our departure was conducted with the same pattern of security precautions. The Old Gentleman went down the empty stairs first; the corridors were empty the whole time, as were the staircase and the courtyard. The silence was absolute, as if something peculiarly mysterious was taking place. I can safely say that no one saw me there. I certainly did not see anyone other than those authorized to be there.

A similar "ceremony" took place on the following day, adhering to the same pattern of discretion of the previous day. During the trip, complete silence prevailed again, with the exception of the statement the Superintendent made regarding my health: "The doctors are amazed—they have never seen such a healthy man." This was the first time in my life that I had heard such an opinion about me.

Today I received more of the books I had asked for on October 29: the writings of the Fathers of the Church, the works of Saint John of the Cross, Norwid *(Krakus)*, and Sienkiewicz *(The Deluge III, Pan Wołodyjowski, Quo Vadis)*.

Our Christmas Eve is similar to that of last year. But we did get a Christmas tree that Father decorated with his own ingenuity. The Christmas Eve supper also resembles more the usual family traditions. Perfect silence reigns through the house. We sent a Christmas wafer to the housekeeper. We lacked the courage to provoke the universal sentiments of our keepers by offering them a wafer. Maybe that was cowardly on our part, but I rather think that they would not have appreciated it. They are all sad and solemn. Upstairs in our quarters there is peace, serenity, and joy.

After supper we spent a long time at the table, talking. At eleven o'clock that night we began to sing Matins in the little chapel. Sister followed with text in hand. At midnight I began to offer Mass. The first was a High Mass, the following two Low Masses;* my flock sang carols. We were very happy in that poor little chapel, without a flower, with smoky cheap candles, in the presence of Christ, Who chose to be with us on this day, in this "inn outside of town." We decided to spend both holy days† together as a group, from morning till night. No one was to feel lonely. We tried to combat one another's nostalgia, every reverie, every excuse to be alone. God had willed us to be together, and we had to help one another. We also promised each other that we would pray for one another's parents and families, to dissipate the clouds of sadness that might enter their lives. We suspended all our usual work for tomorrow, agreed not to touch a pen or any of our books; we are allowed to talk about

---

*On Christmas Day every priest has the privilege of offering three Masses; each of these has different prayers and readings. The first is intended for midnight, the second early in the morning, the third later.
†In Poland the day after Christmas, the Feast of Saint Stephen the Martyr, is also a holy day. There are several Saint Stephens in the Calendar of the Saints.

everything, to censor nothing, even if it was not very smart. Complete freedom for the children of God.

The Holy Masses lasted until two o'clock in the morning; afterward, we continued to pray for quite a while for the Church, for the Holy Father, for the Polish bishops, for the religious orders, for our dioceses, for our own families. It seemed to us that through prayer we had come to such a frame of mind that the Good Lord had no reason to be sad as He gazed upon us. Our final prayer was for our guards, especially for those now sitting in the corridors, and for the soldiers standing around the grounds in the snow, in the woods, on guard. We knew that for these people it must be most painful and difficult.

By two-thirty in the morning our floor finally slipped into darkness. It was a sleep filled with joy. We trusted that God did not regret that He had kept us in prison for the holidays. And we too did not regret that He chose prison for us for these holy days that brought the Key of David into this world.

The shortest way to an internal reconciliation with those who wrong us is to remember the question posed by Christ to Judas: "My friend, for what purpose hast thou come?" Still "friend"! Christ always used a word that revealed the essence of the matter. The traitor a "friend" of the Saviour! Because the Saviour wishes to redeem the world and Judas helps Him by his treachery, he becomes an involuntary instrument in the plans of Christ, he cooperates with Him. A collaborator in the Redemption. All of our enemies, against their will, cooperate with us, and contribute to the release of divine power in us. Perhaps they do not even realize what a great favor they are doing for a person who knows how to take advantage of God's mercy, who wants to take advantage of the grace of suffering. What of it that they *want* to be my enemies, when in them I only see friends and collaborators in the work of my redemption?

The most effective way to fight sadness is to recall the wisdom, goodness, love, and perfection of God, all of whose creations are perfect—and so, including those that relate to me. In every one of God's acts there is only wisdom, only goodness, only love. Maybe I do not understand them perfectly, maybe I think only in tiny beams of light. But the fullness of light reveals itself when I comprehend the meaning of God's actions.

I cannot seem to get away from the thought—what would Saint Paul do today if he were walking down my corridor? Perhaps he would take the Christmas wafer and go downstairs to say to the jailer: "Brother!" Would he ask him about his personal philosophy? Would he be afraid to break the rules? And how one would wish to have the freedom at least to be able to say to everyone: "My brother!" This certainly could not be considered unlawful propaganda.

God began His first attempt at pleasing mankind by taking a man from whose rib He fashioned a woman. Everything was destroyed by sin.

He began the second time by taking a woman, from whom He drew a new Adam. This time He was successful. The first Adam failed because of a woman; the second Adam succeeded through a woman: Eve and Mary . . .

December 25, 1954, Saturday

Gaudium magnum [A great joy] reigned from early morning to late at night. Father Stanisław celebrated three Holy Masses in the morning; we sang carols and prayed for all those who were thinking of us: for the Church—the Mystical Body—of which we are a part, for our dear ones to whom we are bound by ties of blood, for those to whom we are bound by ties of friendship, love, and work. Breakfast, dinner, and supper were filled with a hearty cheer and good humor; luckily no one was ill. After dinner we read the description of the feast of Saint Stephen in *The Deluge*—this was the last day of the Swedish siege of Jasna Góra. Then we sang carols into the evening hours.

Father Stanisław was holding up well, even though his sick mother was much on his mind. After evening prayers, we purposely remained together longer, in order not to give him time to think about his mother missing him. He seemed to conquer the temptation.

A pleasant silence reigned throughout the house; our friends were practically invisible. Apparently it is considered good prison manners for the jailers to show themselves as little as possible. Or maybe the poor things think that we would not be able to look at them in a fraternal way? Perhaps they believe that religious holidays are a flowering of intense antiatheism? And we prayed for their serenity and for love that is born in a stable, for the people of stables and barns. If only they could understand how very much Christ is intended precisely for them.

By the will of our Heavenly Father I cannot stand today at the cathedral altar to celebrate the family feast of the Holy Trinity: the Father, Begetter, the Son, Begotten, and the Holy Spirit, Beloved. I cannot pay pontifical homage to you, Virgin Mother of God. I ask only one thing: that you, Mary, be present at that service and help those who replace me, to honor the Holy Trinity worthily and gloriously, to serve you better than I, and that the Father be duly venerated by His Holy Church. Gather, O Mary, the glory of God from all the places of worship of both archdioceses, from the lips of all priests praising the Father today and professing to the people faith in Christ, Son of the Living God—cleanse them of human imperfections and offer them as a gift to the Family of the Holy Trinity.

December 27, 1954, Monday*
"What was from the beginning, what we heard, what we have seen with our own eyes, what we have looked upon and what our hands have handled: of the Word of Life (and the Life was made known and we have seen and now testify and announce to you, the Life eternal which was with the Father and has appeared to us). What we have

---

*The feast of Saint John the Evangelist.

seen and have heard we announce to you, in order that you also may have fellowship with us, and that our fellowship may be with the Father, and with His Son Jesus Christ. And these things we write to you that you may rejoice, and our joy may be full" (1 John, 1:1–4). The disciple of Christ, who drew from the bosom of the Master the invigorating stream of the Gospel, first touched everything himself with his own hands before telling about it. Perhaps that is why this persevering disciple stands so close to the Christmas crib in the liturgical cycle, because it was not enough for him merely to share a table with the Master—he sought a close intimacy with Him. Christ did not deny him—he allowed him to rest his head on His bosom.

Was this not why Jesus wanted to be in the Bethlehem manger to encourage us to the intimacy of a religious experience? Is He not an Infant so that we may take Him in our arms? Is He not in a crib so that we may see in Him familiar nourishment? Did He not assume a body so that every disciple John among us could find support whenever his soul was in need of it? John is not so much an abstraction of the Logos as the experience of loving, faithful hands! This great love simply explodes the established pattern of philosophical thought. Bethlehem makes it easier for us to approach the Word—the Infant. And when this rapprochement occurs, the Infant is already the revealed Life!

When the Church reveals to us the Word Incarnate, it wants us—following John's example—to rest trustfully and childlike on the Bosom of God and to draw from it the stream of the Gospel and light. How proper is John's presence at the side of the manger. John, whom we will see in the Upper Room, on Calvary, at the Tomb and at the side of the Mother of the Word Incarnate! John, the way to the Way . . .

———————

December 28, 1954, Tuesday*
Ex ore infantium [Out of the mouths of babes] . . . The great mystery of the world: children and Herod. The Herods are constantly organizing the world against God, and God gives them His answer

———————

*The feast of the Holy Innocents, commemorating the slaying of young children ordered by Herod in an attempt to kill the Infant Jesus.

through children. Man always seems to think that he is more correct than God, that—precisely in this matter—he would have proceeded differently, more sensibly, somewhat more "wisely." And so the Herods build entire structures of arguments to convince God. And God answers like a child. When the world ascended in its pride to the heights of human prudence and might, God sent His Son into the world as an Infant. An Infant is to give a response to the might of Babylon, Cyrus, Alexander, the Pharaohs, Greece, and Rome. When the world falls silent under the heel of Augustus, the Infant will be heard in Bethlehem. . . . When the Sanhedrin is silent, *pueri Hebraeorum* [the children of the Hebrews] will cry out: "Hosanna to the Son of David . . ." And should their lips be sealed, "the stones will cry out." When Nineveh and Babylon, the Acropolis and the Palatine crumble, wild roses will spring forth from the ruins. And in each blossom there is more hope than in that rusting rubble of metal—in those lifeless lips of the sages of this world. How eloquent this shambles when God's fresh shoots surpass technology!

I am busily erecting a whole structure of thought in my soul, I want to convince God. This can make as great an impression on me, as the Palace of Culture* might make on some dimwits. But only because they have never seen five hundred skyscrapers crowded onto the tiny island of Manhattan. How naive these mental acrobatics must seem in the eyes of Wisdom, which is Love. When my skyscrapers tumble, one tear is enough to restore my hope—the tear of a child. Since I am able to cry . . . I am like a child. The way to the Kingdom is open. I will be able to "convince" God only with my tear . . . and myself also, since my tear restores my peace. . . .

December 29, 1954, Wednesday†
King Henry II of England (d. 1189) complained that he could not have peace in this country because of a single solitary priest. This was Saint Thomas Becket, archbishop of Canterbury and Primate of England. But the king was silent about the reason behind his anxiety

---

*A towering and grotesque example of Stalinist architecture in the heart of Warsaw.
†The feast of Saint Thomas Becket.

—about the Constitutions of Clarendon that struck a blow at the rights of the Church. These men often assume there is peace because of the silence of those who, in fact, are prevented from speaking. They forget that even a [jackbooted] leg cannot continue to exert pressure for too long. To rule a state, therefore, force must be abandoned; only then will tranquillity return. It is significant to note how little contemporary men learn from history. Mighty empires fell more quickly as they increased the intensity of their violence.

We can take examples from ancient history: weaker countries often managed to survive longer than states ruling with slavish tyranny. Recent examples could also be cited (Hitler's state). The ruler seeks peace, and so do the citizens. Let the ruler leave the citizens in peace, and he will achieve peace himself and be able to maintain peacefully all he possesses. The ruler fears revenge against his violence. Police states are violent states. In conditions such as these, only a priest can find a way to defend the citizens. This defense is not a reaction against the authorities; it is not rebellion.

December 31, 1954, Friday

This year that will end in a few minutes I offer to you, Holy Virgin of Jasna Góra, so that through your immaculate hands it may be offered for the glory of God—*Soli Deo.* I offer it completely, without sorrow, without sadness, without reservation, although I have spent it in this masked prison. You look at my life and know what this prison is giving me. And I trust in the guiding grace of God, and I know how much I gain by it. I do not ask "for what? or why?" because I trust. God's wisdom, goodness, and love suffice as criteria for all that is happening to me. And besides, why should I know and understand everything? Where, then, would there be room for trust?

This past year has so deeply convinced me of the wisdom of God so filled with love that there is not the slightest space for any resistance to God's will. The mind trusts, the will surrenders. And the heart—if it longs for the altar, the pulpit, for common prayer with the people—very quickly returns to its equilibrium. This is probably the most difficult trial—to be denied the opportunity to profess one's faith in Christ before the people. The greatest loss, since the

Son acknowledges before the Father those who worship Him before the people. But one can profess one's faith in word and suffering. Perhaps Christ will acknowledge me before His Father, since he gives me the privilege of suffering in His Name.

January 1, 1955, Saturday
Soli Deo through Our Lady of Jasna Góra. During our night vigil in prayer, we began the New Year with the name of Mary of Jasna Góra on our lips. In our country, this is a special Jubilee Year, the three hundredth anniversary when Jasna Góra became the force behind the rebirth of the Nation.* It pleased God to save Poland from the "deluge" through Mary of Jasna Góra: the Lord praised the Mother of His Son by mighty miracles and signs. Henceforth, Jasna Góra became a "fortified bastion of the spirit of the Nation." And so it remained throughout the most trying days of history. Today we speak about the Tower of Grace [an epithet of the Virgin Mary], raising our trusting eyes toward Jasna Góra, whenever we are troubled. The visible sign of mercy in the form of an armed victory persuades us that we are right when we appeal to God, to Mary, to the consciences of men. But we aspire to something a hundredfold more: today the "defense of Jasna Góra" is a defense of the Christian soul of the Nation. Such a miracle is a hundredfold more significant, demanding even greater heroism for the struggle

---

*Poland has had a long history of being dominated and tyrannized over by her powerful neighbors. No period in her past was more tragic than the catastrophic twenty-year reign of King John II Casimir (1648–1668), during which Poland suffered a revolt of her Cossack provinces, an intermittent and brutal thirteen-year war with Russia, and in 1655 a devastating invasion by Swedish armies under King Charles X Gustavus. Virtually the entire country was overrun, the King fled to Silesia (then part of the Austrian Empire), and for the moment the Polish state ceased to exist. But an outburst of popular feeling—partly patriotic, partly religious—swept over the Polish people, and they rallied enthusiastically behind their military commanders. In November 1655, Swedes and Poles clashed at the monastery of Jasna Góra in Częstochowa, and after a heroic defense by the hard-pressed Poles, the Swedes were turned back. Within five years they had been driven from Polish soil.
On his return from exile, King John Casimir, calling Jasna Góra's successful defense a miracle, made a public vow to the Virgin, placing the Nation under her protection and proclaiming her Queen of Poland. In 1955, Poland celebrated the tricentennial of this "rebirth" and the vow of her King.

against the enemy that is within us. How easy it is to do battle against an external enemy. And how difficult to do battle against our very selves. That is why we need so much more help from Our Lady of Victory, the Mediatrix of all Graces. Today the "defense of Jasna Góra" calls for victory over self, the real enemy.

Thus the Jubilee Year of the "defense of Jasna Góra" (1655–1955) is to be a year of prayer to the Queen of Poland, whose Image has been given by Providence *ad defensionem populi Polonici* [for the defense of the Polish people], to aid all the faithful of the Nation to gain victory over self and within themselves—the enemy of God, the enemy of their neighbor, and the enemy in their soul. Let this historical proof of God's might be proof for the weak and powerless. Today I offer all my prayers and suffering here in prison to honor Our Lady of Jasna Góra in the name of our Christian Nation, that it may prevail in grace and love.

January 5, 1955, Wednesday
A father's wrath is always a grace, because it is proof of his caring, interest, closeness, and desire to persuade a recalcitrant individual. How much happier is the state of a man who feels the wrath of God upon himself, like Job or David, than one who sees no evidence for the presence of God. When God is angered, it is easy for me to discover just cause for His anger within myself. And then it is better for me to be pressed into the earth, even by the heel of an enemy, since harvest springs forth from a seed that dies. How easy it is, then, to acknowledge God's justice, even if my faults can be discerned only through a magnifying glass. What a pleasure it is, then, to suffer persecution, so appropriate a whipping rod. How useful, then, are my tormentors, who are not even aware that through their services I achieve a reconciliation with God. How much I must love them, since through them God shows how interested He is in me. Love of one's enemies ceases to be a rhetorical ornament and becomes flesh.

January 6, 1955, Thursday
Once again I cannot fulfill my duty: I cannot pay homage to You in the name of my one Bride, the church of Gniezno, and the other, the

church of Warsaw. I can only beg Your forgiveness for having diminished Your glory. You must have said to me: I have no desire for you and will not accept your sacrifice. . . . I implore You, at least let the service of those gathered in the cathedral today be pleasing to You: the cathedral canons, the seminarians, the clergy, and the people. They are worthy to stand in Your Presence. Accept an offering from their hands. Permit, Father, that Your "excommunicated" servant, excluded from the community of saints, may at least nestle his heart to the walls of his bride, the cathedral. And he will beg humbly: *ut Tibi digne et laudabiliter serviatur* [that he may serve You worthily and honorably]. I will ask that all Your servants, who now raise the Body of Your Son in all the temples of worship in both dioceses, inspire love and faith in You. I beg that every priest who now professes his faith in You before the people should profess that faith in word and deed.

You alone are Holy, You alone are Lord, You alone are Most High. . . . I alone am sinner, I alone am slave, I alone am least worthy. Your every deed is sacred, full of justice and mercy. Who better knows the power of Your mercy if not You, whose mercy tempers even justice? Who better knows the power of Your justice if not I who willingly accepts it, so fully convinced You are right that I feel unworthy of mercy? A new miracle of grace is necessary to concede this.

January 7, 1955, Friday
The first Friday of the month.* God's Sacred Heart hides behind the cross: Flowing Blood renders the ground holy; it cleaves the callous rocks, they burst asunder with pain. Muck beneath the cross, satiated with Blood, becomes a treasure. Everything is transformed. Only my heart remains callous; the earth of my flesh remains sinful muck.

---

*A day of special devotion to the Sacred Heart.

I pray for the priests of the archdioceses, especially those of Warsaw. God tried them the most; He allowed their churches to be razed, and today He condemns them to twofold suffering—to build spiritual dwellings and from the rubble* the walls of new temples. Would that they could comprehend this honor. How completely God trusted them, what great sacrifice He demanded of them. If only they recognized this blessed opportunity. The eloquence of our razed Capital must move even the most thoughtless of hearts. These ruins must speak to our priests as the ruins of Jerusalem once spoke to Jeremiah. May they never close their eyes to the truth: God demands of both shepherds and sheep a cleansing of their hearts. I fear lest this time of affliction should pass. Renewal conceals the wounds; might old afflictions hide beneath? How difficult to admit that we are not without sin; to acknowledge that the Holy of Holies has the right to be angered even by the least of infractions. How eagerly we shroud ourselves in the mantles of victimhood originating in human malice, but look with disdain upon punishment coming from God. So much humble prayer is needed to recognize this.

More and more I fear freedom more than prison. Because freedom would mean a summons to work for someone unworthy; it would mean privileges, the use of an instrument, incapable, poor, worthless. How well I know this. Prison, on the other hand, is a natural state; God's junk heap; an expression of God's justice and truth. But there is something pacifying about prison life. Even if my keepers indulge in abuses, God transforms them into His justice.

January 16, 1955, Sunday
I received a letter today from my sister Stanisława and a package of fruit.

---

*The cardinal here probably refers to the razing of Warsaw in 1944. In 1955 reconstruction was still underway.

January 17, 1955, Monday
Ten years have now passed since the last of Hitler's soldiers left behind the rubble of Warsaw. *Dominus dissipat consilium nationum; irritas facit cogitationes populorum* [The Lord brings to nought the plans of the nations; he foils the designs of the people] (Psalms 32:10; Psalms 33:10 KJV).

Neque enim ab Oriente, neque ab Occidente, neque a deserto, neque a montibus: Sed Deus est iudex: bunc deprimit, et illum extollit. Nam in manu domini calix est [For neither from the east nor from the west, neither from the desert nor from the mountains: But God is the judge; one he brings low, another he lifts up. For a cup is in the Lord's hand] (Psalms 74:7–9; 75:6–8 KJV).

January 23, 1955, Sunday
On the third Sunday after Epiphany, the Church reads to its children an excerpt from Paul's Epistle to the Romans:

> Repay no one evil for evil, but take thought for what is noble in the sight of all. If possible, so far as it depends upon you, live peaceably with all. Beloved, never avenge yourselves, but leave it to the wrath of God; for it is written, "Vengeance is mine, I will repay, says the Lord." No, "if your enemy is hungry, feed him; if he is thirsty, give him drink; for by so doing you will heap burning coals upon his head." Be not overcome by evil, but overcome evil with good. (Romans 12:17–21)

Just as the ultimate of Christian truth is the study of the Holy Trinity, so the ultimate of Christian morality is the study of love of one's enemies. "Overcome evil with good"—and so bring forth from within all the resources of a rational being, and when you are wanting, become a debtor to grace. Only this gives birth to moral, spiritual, civic, cultural, and political progress. It is this that bears witness to the greatness of man. And how appropriate this is in a healthy human nature is evidenced by the feeling that comes when we must curb even a just anger. In punishing or reprimanding a subordinate, how often a person in authority searches his conscience: could he not have handled the matter differently, used other words? The voice of conscience is the voice of the greatness of man. To muffle it, one must artificially nurture the feeling of hate. Three years ago we read a resolution in the newspapers: "We must train ourselves to hate: we must hate more." The Polish spirit, carefully nurtured by the Gospel, strives toward love. Only resolutions can change it. The Poles do not know how to hate—thanks be to God and His Gospel!

February 1, 1955, Wednesday *
Frumentum Christi sum: dentibus bestiarum molar, ut panis mundus inveniar [I am the wheat of Christ: let me be ground by the teeth of beasts that I may be found to be clean bread]—the words put into the mouth of Saint Ignatius the Martyr, the bishop of Antioch, are the expression of heroic apostleship. They are certainly also an expression of the hunger of a human spirit that has understood the inexorable consequences of a first priestly step. Actually, the priest can never retreat, even if his mission should lead into the jaws of beasts. God has the right to demand everything. Perhaps we comply with fear, perhaps in panic and trepidation—but it is inexorable. And all our work must be directed not to avoid these final consequences but to approach them with an attitude of trust, serenity, and a full understanding that it must be so because "God's reason of state"† demands it. Wheat and bread—these are the instruments of a priest's sacrificial work. And when there is no more of them on the altar, he who sacrifices now himself becomes the offering, as did Christ when after the multiplication of the loaves, He Himself became Bread and offered Himself "into the jaws of beasts." Beasts feeding on God can become godlike. Oppressors grinding my wheat into bread can become converted. Can they be denied this last chance for salvation?

God demanded of twentieth century priests that they offer their bodies as substitute host; so often in so many concentration camps

---

*Feast of Saint Ignatius, bishop and martyr.
†The cardinal here applies the same concept of Poland's "reason of state" to God's kingdom.

during the last war this sacrifice took place—a veritable hecatomb of the Holy Church.

_____

February 2, 1955, Wednesday
Today I handed the Commandant letters to my father and to my sister, Stanisława Jarosz, as follows:

My dearest and special father!

Please forgive me that only now I thank you for your letter of December 18, 1954, and for the gifts which arrived undamaged on December 23. Your greetings came in time, and thus were a great joy in this solitary life. I thank you from the bottom of my heart for so much thoughtful kindness and anticipation of my needs.

In every letter I try to read between the lines, dear Father, to discover the state of your health and your frame of mind. I would want you not to catch cold anymore and take better care of your eyes, so that they last you as long as possible. It is so important for me that we always reveal to our Heavenly Father our constant serenity and trust, so that the Good Lord does not feel that our trials are in vain. Suffering is a wonderful grace, and since this is not only a "golden thought" but a joyful experience, there is something to be grateful for. The prayer that binds me to you, dear Father, is to entreat God that we should both become worthy of the confidence He has displayed in us. Every day I repeat this during Mass, in the breviary, and during the rosary, when I speak to God of you.

You ask, Father, about my health? Just before the holidays I went through additional blood tests and X rays; the results are good. I have been taking various medications to regain my strength. The disorders that troubled me last winter have not recurred, perhaps because the present house is dry and properly heated. In any case, the climatic conditions in this part of Poland are much better than those where I was before, and this helps to improve my health. My former problems, well known to my loved ones, naturally require extended treatment.

After receiving the clothes, cassock, and shoes, I now have enough of everything, and I ask you not to send me any more clothing for the time being. The overshoes you sent me are quite good. I have no need for money, since I have no expenses; that is probably why they returned the money to you.

There is not much I can write about my life here since it is very simple. I get up at five o'clock in the morning and go to bed at ten at night. Lunch is at one in the afternoon, supper at seven in the evening. Every morning I celebrate Mass at 7:30. After a walk, I work on my book; the same in the afternoon. I keep to a very tight schedule so that not a moment remains for fruitless reflection. That is why it passes so quickly; I do not even notice the passing weeks and months.

The second portion of the books I asked for on October 29, 1954, arrived on December 24. A few titles from this list are still missing, and I repeat them now: (1) Journet, *L'Église du Verbe Incarné*; (2) Bishop Radoński, *Lives of the Saints*; (3) Saint Teresa of the Infant Jesus, *The Story of a Soul—The Little Way*; (4) Dobraczyński, *The Violent Ones*; (5) Merton —a small gray book, I cannot recall the title; (6) the Constitution of the Polish People's Republic; (7) the writings of Norwid; (8) the writings of Claudel; (9) something to read in Italian; (10) Maślińska, *Communist Morality*.

In my letter of October 28, 1954, I also asked for the Ordo for the new ecclesiastical year. I need it very much, since it is difficult to recite the breviary without a calendar, especially during Lent and Easter. I still have not received it— and I now repeat my request.

I am very grateful for the new alb—please thank my sisters—as well as for the beautiful burse with Our Lady on it, and for the pall for the chalice; these pleased me very much. I would be happy to get some altar candles; we have wine and hosts for Mass.

My dearest father, I embrace you with a child's heart and

kiss you in gratitude for all the goodness you have shown me throughout my life. I want you to know that my best wishes flow from the kindness you have shown me; I am always mindful of it. I thank you, Father, for your prayers, your concern, and your heart, as well as for your fatherly blessing. Please accept my filial love and my pastoral blessing.

February 2, 1955
+ Stefan Cardinal Wyszyński

The letter sent to my sister, Stanisława Jarosz, the same day is as follows:

My dear sister!

I owe you thanks for both letters: one dated December 18, 1954, and another (undated) which I received on January 16, 1955. I was very happy to know that my letter reached you before Christmas and served as an expression of my remembrance, wishes, and brotherly love on Christmas Eve. Judging by the last present you sent me, I see that you have been burdened with the task of providing me with "treats." I fear that you might strain your modest purse, especially by sending me fruits. I thank you for everything, but I want you to consider your limited means, particularly since I have all of life's necessities.

I describe my health in my letter to Father. I ask you not to worry. I live prudently and hope that I will preserve my strength. And if God allows, some day I will undergo a full course of treatment.

I became a little worried about the state of Józio's health; but I think that such a self-abnegating person will easily seek a cure. I implore him to do this—please remind him that a person who has received talents from God has the obligation to live a long life.

Thank Tadzio for his kind letter; how good it is to see

handwriting, since in it you can usually read more than what the letters spell out. I don't know why, but I am constantly worried about his health, about which he writes so succinctly. I constantly commend Ania to our Most Holy Mother and trust that with careful treatment the child will outgrow the aftereffects of her illness. Give my warmest regards to all four. I am pleased with the news from Stach and his wife, whom I always hold dear in my heart. I still have not heard anything about Julcia; let her at least sign her name to one of Father's letters.

I send warm greetings to all my sisters and their families; please express a few kind words to Sister Superior. Kindly ask everyone to pray very hard for me and tell them not to worry. I kiss you with all my heart and bless you with my brotherly affection.

February 2, 1955
+ Cardinal Stefan

February 2, 1955, Wednesday
Rubum, quem viderat Moyses . . . [The bush that Moses saw . . .]. "In the Bush that Moses saw, unburnt, we see preserved Your glorious virginity: Mother of God, intercede for us. . . ." It was from that Virginal Bush, burning eternally with immaculate purity, that the Church ignited all the fires that burn today in the Catholic churches of the world. A veritable river of fire, in which our flicker draws strength and brilliance. This river of light flows like water "from the right side of the temple" (*Vidi aquam* [I have seen water]),* and becomes more powerful through the ages as new generations add their own streams. This river of light flows through the darkness of the world which cannot conquer it. It flows, embracing everything

---

*This is a rite that precedes the principal Sunday Mass in which the celebrant sprinkles the altar, the clergy, and the people, reciting at the same time special prayers. In Paschaltide it begins with *"Vidi aquam* . . ."; during the remainder of the year it begins with *"Asperges me* . . . [Sprinkle me . . .]."

that is of light in this world, so that—*Lumen de lumine* [Light of light]—it may return to the bosom of the Father, from whom all light comes. I rejoice that the Father has allowed me to join the river of light. That I can go through life and cry: *Lumen Christi* [Light of Christ]!* That I can praise the true Light, which the Father gave to the world from the unburned bush.

February 3, 1955, Thursday

Today Father Stanisław went to Rawicz to see his father, who is coming from Tarnów. These visits involve a lot of complicated machinations. When we were in Stoczek, Father S. was taken to Barczewo. In his father's presence, he had to pretend to be a prisoner, but in a cassock; it must have been difficult for the father to understand what it all meant. Now they take him from Prudnik all the way to Rawicz so that he may pretend to be a prisoner in Rawicz, although he still appears in a cassock, which prisoners are not allowed to wear. He sees his father not through prison bars but in a special office. Transporting him is rather comical, since on the way to the meeting he must conceal his cassock; but upon arrival he must display his cassock, and this rather ostentatiously, so that his father may know that he wears his cassock, and that he is fine because he is not a prisoner, although the meetings are held in a prison.

What can the poor father think about all this? Why were there meetings at first in Rawicz, in prison garb, and then later in Barczewo in a cassock, and now once more in Rawicz in a cassock? To explain this mystery is to understand the psychology of a man living in a Communist system. It shows how one lie can complicate human relations and how many new lies are needed to support it. *Abyssus abyssum invocat* [Deep calls unto deep: *i.e.* lies call for more lies] ... Father S. always fears these "visits," because other meetings are also arranged with various men from Warsaw who come to talk with him. The conversations are not pleasant.

---

*This is a part of the pre-Vatican II liturgy for Holy Saturday, which the deacon, assisting the celebrant, chants three times.

February 4, 1955, Friday

Father Stanisław has returned from seeing his father and has brought the *Directory** for 1955. My attempts to get the Warsaw Ordo have so far been unsuccessful, even though I asked for it several times. From the *Directory* we at least found out that the Holy Father is alive, that the Catholic University in Lublin is still functioning, since there were church collections for it, and that "the publishing house of Our Lady of Loretto" is still accepting religious studies for printing. From the priest's conversation with his father, carried on in the presence of the deputy, we have learned that again many priests have been removed from the schools because they are "unqualified." So the crushing tidal wave continues its slow and inexorable advance, inconspicuously destroying religious life in Poland. The youth comes to church for religious instructions. Nuns have managed to hold on here and there in the hospitals, but only a few of them. Clergy transfers have been rendered very difficult as a result of the Decree on Filling Ecclesiastical Posts.

In short, hope that my imprisonment would halt the destruction of the Church is fading. Until now this has been a great consolation for me, that my imprisonment might distract attention from the Church. After all, they had made me out to be the chief obstacle to arranging good relations between the Episcopate and the government. It is possible that for a while the conflict did indeed subside. But the ironclad logic of their teaching does not allow this for too long. Strategy gives way to principles. . . . After my imprisonment, it was announced that the propositions of the Episcopate "would be heard." Maybe they were, but the struggle goes on. What is there left for me to do? Lose hope in the meaning of my sacrifice? On the contrary, I should offer my sacrifice to the Church even more resolutely, so that through my sacrifice I may obtain from God His mercy and a little respite for the weary. *Sic volo* [So be it]!

---

*This *Directory* includes the Ordo and other brief information about the Church in Poland and a given diocese.

February 6, 1955, Saturday

The Commandant, who reappeared at Prudnik after a long absence, visited me today and brought me two small books: *The Constitution of the Polish People's Republic* and Maślińska's *Communist Morality*. I had asked for these books a long time ago, as early as October 29, 1954. However, the copies given me were not the ones from my library, since mine were underlined and annotated in the page margins. I noted that other books I requested at that time still had not arrived. Apparently these two books are especially privileged.

Of the books I wanted most and already requested in Stoczek, I still have not received the following: (1) *Annuario Pontificio*; (2) *Caeremoniale episcoporum*; (3) *Dottrina sociale cattolica*—a collection of documents; (4) *Księga Henrykowska*; (5) *Rubricella* (Ordo).

February 17, 1955, Thursday

Today I was given the book of Bishop Radoński, which I had requested October 29, 1954. It appears that my friends have more of my books, but give them to me *data occasione* [whenever they see fit], or else as a result of some mysterious distribution policy.

After some time I was given several letters: from my sister Stanisława, my brother Tadeusz, and my sister Julia, informing me of the illness of my father. At the same time I was given a food parcel and some more books.

My beloved brother!

I have decided to inform you about the illness of our father, who at this moment has almost recuperated, but at his age such an occurrence cannot help but be worrisome. Two weeks ago Father arrived at Miodowa Street in Warsaw; on the following morning he suffered something akin to a paralysis of speech, without losing consciousness or the use of his other organs. The doctor we called diagnosed it as a mild stroke, ordered an extended rest and complete quiet, said that he considered the stroke minor, and did not wish to alarm us. Slowly, his speech returned, but his weakness persisted. He is getting the best of medical attention and therapy; we hope that he will soon be on his feet and back to normal. Sister Maksencja is his chief nurse, and we are very grateful to her for the concern and affection she shows him. It happened that the incident took place on Miodowa Street, but it would be only right that we take care of our sick father. I ask you, my beloved brother, not to worry about him; I am writing you the whole truth, since I feel that this is best, even though I understand how painful it may be for you to think about your father from afar. Because of your father's illness I have sent a petition to the Premier asking for permission for you to see him. I hope the request will be granted.

We wait impatiently for news from you. We have not had a letter from you in nearly two months. We would like to have detailed news about your health and how the time has passed since your last letter.

I send you many affectionate greetings and words of remembrance and love from all of us. We offer prayers constantly in your name, for your health, strength, and endurance. The Good Lord willing, we may see each other soon. We live with this hope and wait.

Commending you to God and His Holy Mother, we ask for your blessing and your prayers; Father sends especially heartfelt kisses and assures you of his fatherly love.

February 10, 1955
Your devoted sister,
Stanisława Jarosz

February 18, 1955, Friday
After I received the news yesterday about my father's serious illness, I decided to write a letter to the Council of Ministers with a request that they make it possible for me to see him. I wrote in my letter that my father had on five occasions asked the Council of Ministers for permission to see me; he had never received an answer. Now, during his illness, he has expressed a wish to see me. I cannot ignore

that wish. The Commandant listened to the contents of my letter and took it.

Primate. I have two other letters: to my father and to my sister who is taking care of my father on behalf of the family. But I ask that this letter not be taken away from my father, as earlier ones have been. This is most inhuman, especially to a man who is close to death. You must admit that such an act, which is incomprehensible even to someone healthy, must be especially painful for someone who is sick. To show him a letter and then to leave, taking it from him, is unconscionable.

The Commandant explained that the last letter was read in the presence of my sister, Mrs. Jarosz, and in the presence of another man. Upon request, certain passages were repeated.

I explained that even a healthy person benefits little from this method. What is to be said of a sick man who has the consolation of seeing a letter written in his child's hand? Furthermore, how can I know what is read and how I appear in these presentations?

Commandant. Everything that concerns you, your family, is read, but not other things—some things are left out.

Primate. Since I do not write statements either to my dioceses or to the clergy, what can these omissions mean? And why are letters, which are my property and the property of my father, held back? This is truly confiscation. A letter written by me is my property, or it is my father's when it reaches him. But so far neither my property, be it only a breviary, nor the property of my father has been confiscated. On what legal basis, then, is the letter retained?

Commandant. I do not know how to explain; I will give you an answer in a few days. There must be an order on the basis of which this is being done.

Primate. You should know them, since in my eyes you are the executor of decisions (unknown to me) that cause me harm. Every decision must be based on the Constitution and on a statute of law. Otherwise, it is lawlessness pure and simple, and gives rise to unlimited abuses. Everything you have done to me constitutes an abuse, since it is a litany of extraordinary decisions. Please indicate to me on the basis of which article of the Constitution, on the basis of which statute, on the basis of what directive, letters are confiscated —letters that are my property and that of my father. What also concerns me is the way the matter is being handled. What have I done to you that you should treat me in this way? What, for instance, have I done to you personally?

Commandant. We treat you with courtesy, and as far as the letters are concerned, is it not better that they are at least read to the recipient than not delivered at all?

Primate. I do not want to get into your concept of "courtesy"; I am not concerned with social conventions. A person can be subjected to the greatest wrong "politely." At your hands, I have suffered every kind of wrong for nearly a year and a half. And I also see this other matter of writing letters in a different light. I seldom write letters—on purpose, because I do not wish to expose my father to the unpleasant ordeal of having my letters read to him by someone who selects the parts he feels should be read and then takes the letter away. For me it is not one and the same thing. I prefer to spare my father such open insults. But what can be the justification for this extraordinary invention, which is not applied to the families of any other prisoners?

Commandant. Something must have happened at the beginning; I think that there was something on the part of your family that caused us to stop delivering letters.

Primate. I doubt it, since my family is too modest to allow themselves anything that could be construed as political. Anyway, they knew my wishes, because in my first letter from Stoczek I wrote my father that no complaints were to come from my family, that they were not to reveal their sorrow to anyone or discuss the subject with anyone. And I know that they followed my wishes— my father referred to this in one of his last letters. But you, on the other hand, organized a boycott against me, as a result of which I did not receive one letter from October 1953 to April 1954. Even for Christmas of 1953 my family's letters were not given to me. Is this not an abuse of power? If you consider yourselves mature enough to rule the Nation, you must be mindful of the fact that nothing can be achieved by force. You must rely on other means; one must be good to the people from whom one expects goodness. But the methods you employ will produce no good.

Commandant. We do not resort to force. And this Christmas you did get letters.

Primate. Please look at the letter I received in April 1954, the first in six months. Cut up, pasted together. Can you be serious? You are afraid that news from me might be spread by my family. But what can you possibly be afraid of when you hand me a letter? To whom can I pass information? What a strange thing to do! Grown men indulging in nonsense of this sort!

Commandant. The illness of a father is undoubtedly a very sad experience. Parents are the most important things we have. I understand that.

I gave the Commandant three letters today: to my father, to my sister, Stanisława Jarosz, and to the Council of Ministers. Copies of the letters:

My dearest and special father!

I don't know how to thank you for adding your signature to the most recent letter from Stasia, which I received today. I am sure that it is difficult for you to write in bed, and that is why your fatherly effort is so dear to me. This week I am offering Mass in our family's intention; today it became clear how very necessary this was. I don't know how to beg your forgiveness that I cannot be at your side at the moment of your suffering and weakness. It is up to me before all others to show you as much affection as possible, so that you do not feel abandoned. But since God has willed it so, I do what I can, I increase my prayers for your recovery. I pray to my mother, who surely is already in heaven, to intercede with the Mother of God to allow me the favor of seeing you. If the Heavenly Father always wishes His Son at His side, He will certainly understand our family feelings, which He Himself blessed. I wish most fervently, dear Father, to fulfill your wishes and that is why I have written to the Council of Ministers asking for permission to visit you. Before this comes to pass, I already accomplish it by desire and in my heart. I also ask you to remain calm and confident which so helps combating this kind of illness. I want you to know, dear Father, that I am with you in every prayer, that I ask the Heavenly Father for every blessing necessary during illness. All your life you have been in the choicest hands of the Father of Light. God has allowed you to spend your life in service to Him; you have never left His temple, but have served it with all your soul—not for personal gain. What can worry us who, to the end, will put our faith in our Most Faithful God? I will not cease to pray to the Healing Madonna of Jasna Góra, asking her to bring you comfort and good health, and comfort to us all. I bow respectfully to your dear hands, kissing them with devotion, asking for your fatherly prayers and blessings. From the fullness of my priesthood I grant you, my most dear father, my bishop's and Primate's blessing.

February 17, 1955
+ Stefan Cardinal Wyszyński

My dearest sister!

What I feared most has happened. I foresaw that our father's sensitive heart would not be able to bear the suffering imposed upon it at so advanced an age. It is a real blessing that it happened in town, where help was more readily available, than at your house. I know that Father has always been ready to meet his Maker, but we must consider it proof of God's love that the attack was not fatal. I am so grateful to you, dear Stachna, that you kept your wits about you and are still watching over Father, even though you yourself—as I see from what you write about Józio's health —are not free of worry. I sincerely thank Sister Superior for devoting her goodness and medical experience to Father. I am writing a few words to Father, not too much, in order not to tire him. But I would like to write more to you. What I am concerned about is that Father should be positively disposed toward all adversities plaguing him, and that he should love everyone until the end. Love is the most important treasure we take with us from this world; all other virtues and accomplishments, however great, we leave at the threshold of our new life. There is as much happiness and glory for one in heaven as there was love in that person's heart on earth. In the face of temporary adversities, it would be a shame to jeopardize this happiness from God. I also want Father to live with the conviction that only God does right, always and in all things, and man does right to the extent that he is close to God. This is an inexhaustible source of our faith and peace. Be good to him. Our father has always been so faithful to the family, and he might now feel his loneliness more than ever.

My letter of February 2 answered the questions you posed about my health. It is stable, with little setbacks. I am grateful for your news of the family. It seems that Józio demands even more of your energy. A few days ago, I offered Mass for his health. I think of you all. Today I pestered Our Lady about Julcia during a Mass I offered for her. I received her note which made me very happy.

I am grateful to you for the books about birds; they will make it easier for me to live with the winged swarm that likes to visit my window. I also received seven Italian books today, which will be very useful for my reading. I thank you very much for the latest gifts of food. For the time being I have no new needs.

All I am left with is a great concern about Father. Please do all humanly possible to keep him alive. I want so much to see him. God desires prayers from all of us and that is why He keeps us in circumstances for which there is but one hope—prayer.

Please kiss Father's hands in my name. Thank Sister for

her goodness, and especially thank Jula and Tadzik for their letters. I commend them all to Our Lady. I never forget any of you during my Mass at 7:30 each morning. I send you my brotherly love and bless you with all my heart.

February 17, 1955
+ Stefan Cardinal Wyszyński

To the Council of Ministers of the Polish People's Republic in Warsaw:

On February 17, 1955, I received news from my family that my father, Stanisław Wyszyński, fell seriously and gravely ill. I know from letters that five times he has asked for permission to see me, and that until now he has received no answer. Now during his illness, my father has expressed a great desire to see me. Since my father is of advanced age, and his illness—partial paralysis as a result of a stroke—is grave and life-threatening, in conscience I must seriously consider my father's wish to see me. I would not wish my absence to contribute to the deterioration of his health and so bring on his death. I ask the Council of Ministers to enable me to see my father, as I want to fulfill his wishes, the needs of my heart, and the duties that are mine as a son.

February 18, 1955
+ Stefan Cardinal Wyszyński

February 18, 1955, Friday
Why do you prefer to wander in thought to those who tyrannize you rather than to me, who am your Immaculate Mother, your Refuge, your Consolation and Protector? Or to my Only Son, who redeemed you with His Blood, drawn from my Heart? Or to the Father of Mercy, who loved you so much that He gave my Son for you? Will your suffering be assuaged by thoughts of the wickedness of your enemies? Is not love—brought to earth by my

Son and mediated by my service to you—the only medicine? Turn away from your thoughts and turn toward mine. Cast your worries into my arms. They bore the Suffering of the Saviour of the world, they will manage to bear your suffering. It is a waste to devote your thoughts to the wicked. Devote them to those who are ready to understand you, hear you out, comfort you. Do not reverse the order of the world: God is your Saviour, not people. You are here to tell people about the Saviour, not to seek their help. It is your duty to lead them to the One Saviour. How can you seek salvation in these illusory shadows and have hope in your helplessness? When it is difficult for you to bear the hatred of men, remember that not all hate you. And even if they all considered themselves your enemies, I remain for you the Mother of Beautiful Love, my Son will go on loving you until the end, and certainly the Father is always love.

February 24, 1955, Thursday
I reminded the Commandant about my request to the Council of Ministers that I be allowed to see my sick father. A week had gone by, when would I get an answer? The Commandant answered that he did not know, that such matters could not be arranged immediately. A few days are needed. . . .

"Death does not wait," I told him. "I will get an answer after everything is over. This is a question of mortals."

"I think you will get an answer on this matter; it is the kind of thing that requires one," added the Commandant.

"But when?" I persisted.

"I don't know, I think soon. I will again relay your concern."

February 25, 1955, Friday
The Commandant brought me the statement: "I am empowered by the authorities to tell you that your father is feeling better and is back on his feet already."

Primate. Is that it—this declaration? Thank you for the news, which lessens my anxiety somewhat, but it does not lessen the anxiety of a sick man who will feel that his request has not been granted. He wrote five times to the Council of Ministers and never got an answer. If he were a healthy man, he might understand it. But the course of the illness will depend on external circumstances. I have yet to fulfill my father's wish, and we are both aware of this.

I consider it my duty to call your attention to my family's experience: my brother was in prison for two and a half years, and as it later turned out, he was there unjustly, for he was released with no explanations. The imprisonment killed his mother, who worried herself to death; and my brother was not allowed to attend her funeral. Our family still feels the wrong. The circumstances now are similar.

Commandant. I am not authorized to say anything more, but for the time being, I am telling you what the authorities have instructed me to tell you, Father, so that you do not worry.

Primate. Thank you, but who will stop my father from worrying? He has written five times. If ours were a dictatorship, a state run by tyrants—there would be no need to talk about it. But in a democracy, whose Constitution speaks about the rights of its citizens in every article, it seems incomprehensible. I myself have written three times and have received no answer. This in itself is contrary to the Constitution, which condemns bureaucracy (Article 73).

Commandant (somewhat excited). I am not authorized to offer clarifications in this matter. You are upset, Father.

Primate. I am not upset, but I tell you unequivocally that this sort of behavior can drive a person to a nervous breakdown. I feel that a great wrong has been done to me—to me and to my family and to my flock, who have a right to their shepherd. You have cut me off from the world, interrupted my work, and are destroying my life. The fact that I remain calm proves nothing. I live with the feeling that a great wrong has been done to me. What is more, you deny me the right to defend myself, remaining silent to all my petitions.

Commandant. Please accept my assurances that you will receive an answer, Father. Please be of good cheer.

Primate. Thank you.

March 8, 1955, Tuesday

John of God realized his mission in life only when he found himself in a prison for the insane. He devoted himself completely to the service of his fellow prisoners. Then the prison guards realized that John was not insane. But he wanted to remain "a madman for madmen" to serve them for the rest of his life. When he was released from prison, he worked for the benefit of the unfortunates whose terrible ordeal he had realized only in prison. Is God not allowed to lead His servants down paths that will open their eyes to the needs of men?

March 11, 1955, Friday

From Your Cross You saw the laborers in the Vineyard about whom You spoke to the Jewish throngs and the chief priests (Matt. 21: 33–46). They did not bring enough fruit for You to leave the Vineyard in their hands. You also saw Your Church, to whom in turn You gave Your Vineyard. Do you get enough fruit? In its great humility the Church prays constantly that "our righteousness may bear more fruit. . . ." We too constantly offer this prayer. And it goes hand in hand with a fear that our present life—at which people who do not know You look—not destroy the rest of godliness in their hearts. We pray for them, so that You may arouse in these thoughts a conscience sensitive to You. Perhaps this is the last opportunity! Or perhaps it is the fatal rock of insult? Because if they recognize my weakness and faults, what will they think of God's Church, which harbors such unworthy people? People who do not know love are easily scandalized by the servants of love. They suffer much hunger not to find their total happiness in bread. Let them not think that a weak man is all of the Bread of Life. Let them realize that only You possess perfect love, that You are love. Let them at least discern as much as a child sees in a blossom: since there is a blossom, there must be a tree somewhere that produces the blossoms. A dreadful fear overcomes the soul—for that final grace of love for people who have observed us for these last eighteen months, bound together with such a poor representative of the law of love. What a great fortune that the whole Church prays for the same thing!

March 15, 1955, Saturday
Oremus pro Pontifice Papa nostro Pio [Let us pray for our pontiff, Pope Pius]. I beg You, Father of Life, for a long life for Your Servant Pius and for great holiness. Show that You are the Lord of Life to all those who lie in wait for the life of Your Servant. Give him strength to work, to write, to speak out and worship You publicly, to bless, teach, carry out His pontifical work. Your obedient prisoner begs You for this favor—a prisoner who cannot speak to his flock, cannot instruct them or bless them. Who understands better the privilege of giving public witness to you than Your prisoner, who does not enjoy this privilege, although it is his duty? Hear Your prisoner, who is obedient to You, when he begs You on behalf of Your Servant Pius. Endow him with all the gifts of the Holy Spirit; grant him great holiness so that he who announced to the world the glory of the Assumption of the Mother of your Son* should himself experience the great glory of holiness.

March 13, 1955, Sunday
Reading the Gospel . . . It is astounding how many satans expressed their belief in the Deity of Christ (Luke 4: 33–41). Christ ordered them to keep silent, but they could not. They had to proclaim the Holy One of God. It is the power of faith that reveals our thoughts and forms them into a mighty voice. This is a reality that not only cannot be denied but cannot be contained within oneself. For how many people does the reality of faith bring profession to the lips. But often things are worse with man than with satan. That is because convention, pride, superstition can seal the lips against a profession. How many satans, stirring up hatred of God in the hearts of men, taught them to believe in God! How many bloody persecutions of the Church opened people's eyes to the power of the Church! This has been admitted especially by writers who have spent their lives writing blasphemies. It was worse with satans in uniform, because that is where one is most

---

*A reference to Pius XII's proclamation (1950) of the dogma of the Assumption of Mary, the Mother of Jesus.

likely to meet ignoramuses, and even satan cannot teach them anything. Stupidity is the most faithful ally of disbelief. But a true
satan is a clever spirit who knows that Jesus is Christ (Luke 4: 41),
the Son of God.

_____

March 16, 1955, Wednesday
The Superintendent handed me a letter from my father, sister, and
little Staś, along with a package of books—six volumes of the writings of Norwid and *The Story of a Soul* by Saint Theresa. I glanced
at the letter and realized that my letter had been read to Father, not
given to him, and the same for my sister. I asked on what legal basis
this had been. In Article 74, the Constitution of the Polish People's
Republic "protects the secrecy of correspondence." The letters I
send are the property of my father and cannot be kept from him.

My beloved son!
Your last letter of February 17 was read to me on February
21 on Miodowa Street, where I still remained in bed.
I thank you, my son, for your words of affectionate, filial
love and solace, thank you gratefully for your prayers on my
behalf. We also pray trustfully to the Comfort of the
Afflicted, Our Lady of Jasna Góra. I have now remained in
my room for six weeks, the doctors have advised little activity and a lot of peace and quiet; for four weeks I felt weak,
since I had to stay in bed, but today I feel much better, and
I hope that I will still be able to return to Zalesie. I am
grateful to Sister Maksencja for her efforts on my behalf. I
cannot write well, as my hands are still weak, but it will
come back, since it was worse before. I thank you warmly
for your pastoral blessing, and I wish you health and
spiritual strength, as well as a speedy return, which we all
await longingly. I enclose greetings and kisses from all your
loved ones as well as my own fatherly blessing.

Warsaw, March 8, 1955
S. Wyszyński

Dear Uncle!

I want very much to write to you, but I don't know what and how. I asked Mommy and Daddy for help, and now I write.

It has been so long, Uncle, since I've seen you, and I would so much like you to return to us. Every day, morning and night, I pray to Our Lady for your return and your health.

I am already in the second grade and am studying a lot. I study catechism, since in May I am to receive my First Holy Communion. Maybe by then you will return and will be the one to administer it. I am an altar boy.

At home I help Mommy, go shopping, and play with Ania. I love Ania a lot, because she is so pleasant. She was a little sick again, but now she is healthy and happy.

Please, dear Uncle, write me a long letter, and I will answer you.

I send many greetings and kisses to you from myself, Ania and our parents; I apologize for my errors in this letter and I ask you to remember me and to pray for me. I will pray hard for your return and I will ask the gentleman who brings your letter to me to let me keep it.

My address is Warsaw, 43 Grójecka St., Apt. 11.

Your Staś

March 19, 1955, Saturday

With Luke in hand . . . "When you give a dinner or a supper, do not invite your friends nor your brothers, nor your relatives, nor your rich neighbors . . . but call together the poor, the infirm, the lame and the blind: and you will be blessed . . ." (Luke 14: 12–24). This is Christ's Manifesto for the social order of the future, perhaps the near future. Beggars until now have been fed only from the pages of the Gospel . . . Until now only Christians held such feasts . . . All others always had hopes of reciprocity: "a welcome, a greeting, a treat . . ."* And yet a genuine social culture is identified only in these words of Christ. What a marvelous description of such a feast. . . . It seems difficult to comprehend. We continue to be Christians to such a small degree. . . . We have so little social awareness. . . . So little faith in real progress . . . So little daring for social initiative . . . So little courage to show that "only one thing"† is necessary . . . Unselfishness in serving the needs of man! I do not ask you who you are: I know you are poor and infirm and lame and blind—this is your social ID. "And you will be blessed because they cannot repay you. . . ." All social programs, even the most radical, are infant babblings in comparison with this courage of the Word Everlasting, Creator of heaven and earth. . . . So now we are only on the threshold of spiritual changes in the world. . . . Thy Kingdom will come. . . . Not by crown and scepter . . . but in service and love . . . A long way to go? Perhaps, but we cannot look back. . . . Only then will the world be ready for God's Judgment, where they will reward a piece of bread, a cup of water, a warm garment—with the Kingdom of Heaven. What little children we still are! How magnificent is the program of the Father of the Future.

March 22, 1955, Tuesday

Today's lesson read to us by the Church for the Tuesday after the Fourth Sunday in Lent tells us how Moses managed to appease Your anger, O Father, which raged against the Chosen People in the wilderness (Exodus 32: 7–14). . . . "Let Your anger subside, and be merciful about the anger of Your people." Moses was a great man, Father, but what was he in comparison with Your Son? Only a prophetic apparition. Before You today stands Reality Incarnate, forever living, to intercede for us. Your Son, encouraged by Mother and Queen, begs You to have mercy. And we trust in this prayer, because Your Son told us sinners that the sun should not set on our

---

*A Polish proverb: *"czapką, papką, i solą."*
†The cardinal is referring to the Mary and Martha gospel story in which Jesus tells Martha that only one thing is necessary: faith.

anger, that we should forgive those who trespass against us not seven times but seventy times seven times. If poor sinners must forgive so readily, should we not expect Your forgiveness even more readily? The lessons Your Son taught are not His, but Yours Who sent Him. And so we wait hopefully. Even though more than once the sun has set on Your anger, even though the blood of the sons of our land has flowed in bountiful currents, even though the fires in the ovens of the concentration camps have gone out, even though the flame of insurgent Warsaw's burning crucible has now turned to ashes, even though the thousands of bloody hands pleadingly raised heavenward have long since fallen! We still cry: *Miserere, Domine, populo tuo: et continuis tribulationibus laborantem, propitius respirare concede* [Have mercy, O Lord, on Thy people, and mercifully grant them relief, who labor amidst continued tribulations]. Our participation in the agony of Your Son is so painful: *et sustinui, qui simul mecum contristaretur* [and I waited for someone who would grieve with me]. . . . We were cosuffering with You, Christ, we atoned for our sins with the thousands of priestly martyrs in the concentration camps, hundreds of thousands of prisoners, the cries of those tortured during interrogations, the glow of burning villages and towns, the misery and abuse suffered. . . . What are Solomon's hecatombs in comparison with this holocaust of a whole people? *Veni, iam noli tardare* [Come, do not delay]. . . .

March 25, 1955, Friday
I sent letters to my father and sister, as follows:

My dearest and special father!
    I am deeply grateful for your last letter of March 8, 1955, delivered on March 16. In it I see proof that your health is improving and that you are capable of such an effort. I scrutinize every letter of every word trying to find you in it, Father, as if it were a mirror. Although illness disrupts our daily life, we must suffer it calmly, as one does the tantrums of a child who will stop crying more quickly that way. I ask you, then, Father, not to rush too quickly into a great deal

of activity, since the doctors recommend that you rest; be careful not to tire yourself out by reading—rather dwell on what you have learned in the past. Fortunately the doctors have not forbidden you to pray, so you are able to enjoy solace for the heart and food for thought. I support you, dear Father, in this effort with my prayers every day, when I offer Mass and say the breviary. Since you pray to Our Lady of Jasna Góra, we meet in prayer before her altar. Prayer will bring us comfort in the face of all adversity, and it is the wisest task to which we can devote ourselves. I pray, dear Father, that especially in the coming celebration of the Resurrection of Christ, you submit yourself completely to the joy that the Living God inspires in those whom He has won with His own Blood. Christ desires this happiness from us because He labored to win it for us. He wants to see our happiness flow from His effort. I wish most fervently, my father, that you achieve this happiness—I pray that you may have it. To you, and to the good Sister Superior, and to the other sisters, and to my loved ones I send words of God's peace for Easter. I include other news in my letter to Stasia. I bless you with all my soul, dear Father, as well as those who provide you with care and kindness. I commend you all to Our Lady of Jasna Góra.

March 25, 1955
St. W.

My dearest sister!

I am very grateful for your letter of March 11, 1955, delivered on March 16. News of the improvement in Father's health made me very happy. I see from the letter that Father's hands were also paralyzed; this is evident in the changes in his handwriting. Father's active disposition is likely to trouble him, and you must watch to see that he does not become overtired. Those trips that Father used to take alone always worried me, but now they must cease, even in the best of health. Even though the air in Zalesie might be good for his frame of mind, it is best not to rush his return home. The experienced help of Sister Superior is indispensable. Stachna, you are trying to influence my thinking about Father's health; I am working on offering my worries to God, and this is good for me.

I thank you for the six volumes of Norwid you sent me; I am a great admirer of his; unfortunately, the things that interest me most are not in these volumes. I also received Saint Teresa's *The Story of a Soul*. But I still have not received Merton's *Seeds of Contemplation*, even though you write that it was sent in July of last year. In the future, please include in your letter a list of the books you are sending.

I was very pleased with the letter from spunky Staś; I will be happy to answer him, but I will do it later. Thank him and tell him that all that he wrote pleased me very much. The name days of Zenia and Józio have passed—I prayed for them at the altar. Now the name day of Naścia is approaching, and I will remember her at Mass. I want the whole family to be very happy on the day of the Resurrection, I want you to find happiness through God's grace and live trusting our Heavenly Father who out of love gave the world His Son to fill us with peace and love. To the whole family, through you, I send my brotherly devotion and my most loving thoughts. I do not cease to pray for you. Do not worry about me—pray patiently and cheerfully, and this will be the best help you can give me.

And now, in conclusion, a word of response about the birds who come to feed at my window. There is a Mr. Woodpecker about whom I was suspicious, because he was too well groomed; as it turned out he is also very well mannered, and although he is the largest, he always patiently waits in the apple tree for the "cafeteria" to be unoccupied. Greedy nuthatches arrive and greedily devour white cheese with the gusto of "leaders of consumption." There are bread-eating coal tits, meat-eating titmice, and my favorite bluebottles, unassuming and trusting. The sparrows do not want to feed at my cafeteria, although they peer into my window to see what I am doing. I observe many things which would be of no use to ornithologists, but which bring me much pleasure. The most interesting of the birds were the starlings, who are now gone; I must give you a full lecture about them some day.

I thank you, Stachna, for the caring heart you reveal to me in every letter. I want you not to worry about me, as I requested in my first letter. God watches over us, and when He tries us, He is within us, because He rewards every suffering with an increase of love. I bless the whole family and commend you to Our Lady of Jasna Góra.

March 25, 1955
St. W.

March 25, 1955, Friday
Today marks one and a half years since my departure from the world into this disguised concentration camp, separated from the world by thickets of wires, cables, barbs, walls, sentries. . . . There is nothing around that does not smack of a mission to censor my mind, my work, my life. . . . This is an especially agonizing realization for a man born to be free. . . . But every suffering has its deeper meaning that is slowly revealed as days pass and as pain subsides. This is God's way, not man's. . . .

The suffering of a priest always makes divine sense, since he is given to serve as a sign. . . . So if this is necessary for You, Christ, and for Your Church, I deny You nothing, even though I know how difficult it is to give even a little of oneself. I write this with fear, wondering whether I would bear up if You choose to take advantage of my offer. But I cannot deny You this, since I cannot deny anything to God the Father, to Love, to the Saviour, the Church, the Holy Father, the saints, my flock. Perhaps my miserable life is needed precisely because it serves as an argument for the Truth. Perhaps this will be the noblest deed of my life. If You are to be glorified by it, I cannot deny You complete right to me and all that is mine. *Benedic anima mea Domino, et omnia, quae intra me sunt Nomini Sancto eius—Soli Deo* [Bless the Lord, O my soul, and all things in me bless His Holy Name—For God Alone]. In the footsteps of Mary, Servant of the Lord.

March 29, 1955, Tuesday
Saint John Chrysostom writes from his exile to the bishops, priests, and faithful: "You are in prison, and you are bound with chains. What better fate can you have? What does a golden crown on the head—what does a chain binding the hand—offer God? What do possessions, what does a prison full of darkness, filth, and suffering? Rejoice, then, and don a wreath, because sufferings prepare you for great happiness. They are the seeds promising a rich harvest, the struggle that will bring victory and palms." (Letter 118)

March 31, 1955, Thursday
Father Stanisław Skorodecki returned from two weeks of medical observation in Wrocław, where he was isolated—imprisoned, together with one of our younger guards, in an isolation ward. He feels well, even though being locked up drained him. He missed "home" and Mass, which he was unable to celebrate. His isolation was so complete that he could not see or hear anything other than what the guard, who had been quite civil, told him. And he had a tendency to talk a lot; but, having learned from experience, Father S. had no inclination to reciprocate. In any case, slight innuendoes led us to suspect that some kind of change was in the air; this explained the increasing politeness of those around us. In prison everything is important. And the "diplomatic protocol" of our guards slathered meaning onto slightest actions, with a pedantry worthy of the courtiers of Louis XIV.

I have still not received an answer to my request to see my father. This in spite of assurances from the Commandant and the Superintendent that I would get an answer. To the series of lies to which I was treated from the beginning now comes another lie—and this in so delicate a situation.

I have decided, in view of this turn of events, not to take up any further matters and not to make any more statements or present any requests.

April 3, 1955, Sunday
Palm Sunday—*Gloria, laus et honor Tibi sit, Rex Christe* [Glory, praise, and honor to you, Christ the King]. . . . My heart and thoughts leap to the Cathedral of St. John, to stand at the threshold and experience the joy of congregational* prayer. But I must hold back my heart and mind. Let them remain here, where God permits the body to be imprisoned. Even though I learn, I do not wish, my Father, to be opposed to Your will. You allowed me to be confined behind these wires, You allowed my cathedral as well to be without my service today. *Fiat voluntas Tua* [Thy Will be done]. Return, O heart, and do not trespass the boundaries of these walls, remain faithful to God, as the body is dependent and gazes only to heaven, because it is not enclosed by wires.

April 4, 1955, Monday
"And the house was filled with the aroma of oil!" Mary's deed in Bethany, recalled by the Church on Monday of Holy Week, is profound in its historic perspective. Grateful for her brother's life, Mary anointed Christ's feet and wiped them dry with her own hair. The fragrance flowed not so much from the alabaster urn as from the soul. The Bethany house is an image of the Church. And the fragrance—the glory of the Lord which fills the entire House of God, the whole Church. The fragrance of grateful hearts, devoted to God, is God's greatest joy. Christ defends Mary before Judas, as the Church will defend its servants against those who are scandalized by a life devoted to God. Surrender everything to Him, not only the fragrance of your life, but the whole beauty of life, to bow down to the feet of the Master, not deny Him anything—this is the fragrance that fills the whole house. This is the fruit of the centuries-long work of the Church. To this day this fragrance amazes all those

---

*That is, prayer in which everyone present in the church joins in.

who look calmly at the Church. His greatest glory is that He inspires souls and sows about Himself the fragrance of sanctity and God's glory. The world pays its due to God. Open the martyrology, the missal, the breviary, the history of the Church, the annals of hagiography, ascetic and mystical writings—we experience this fragrance. In the face of this, is it possible to ask: Why this waste?

April 7, 1955, Thursday
Maundy Thursday—the day of the Last Supper, the day of the institution of the Eucharist, of the first Mass, the first Holy Communion and the first ordinations—a most special day for priests, that embraces the total priestly soul in its arms and expects the priestly deeds to which I am called. Christ wished to be with his disciples today: with a great desire He desired this Passover. From this desire of Christ there remains so much in each soul that inherits its priesthood from Christ. What intense pain for a bishop to be far from his priests, from his cathedral, and his diocese. No day of this imprisonment torments more than this day. What a great effort of humility and docility is needed to spend this day in the spirit that the Father has a right to expect of me. How very unworthy I feel of this grace of the altar to which I once stepped so boldly—I feel this today.

My Maundy Thursday: "How do you feel today, Father, well or poor? So you have taken to working in the garden, Father," says the Commandant of the camp.

"You do not allow me to hear confessions or teach, so I do what I can!"

"That's good, you will feel better, Father."

"Everyone feels best doing what he was called to do," I answered.

"That's true," agrees my smiling visitor.

Mandatum novum do [I give you a new Commandment]. . . . My Dearest Teacher and Leader, when I cannot fulfill my duties, when I cannot imitate You, by washing on my knees the feet of the children whom You have given me, accept my greatest wish to kiss the feet of all those you entrusted to my episcopal care. . . . *I kiss* with reverence the feet of brothers for whom the Father prepared a body for You. *I kiss* with reverence these feet for which You told the Father: "Behold, I go to do Your Will, O God." *I kiss* with reverence those feet for which You did not disdain the Virgin's womb. *I kiss* with reverence those feet for which You Yourself took on human feet. *I kiss* with reverence these feet for which You traversed the Holy Land. *I kiss* with reverence these feet for which You did not cringe before the torture of Your flogging. *I kiss* with reverence these feet before which You knelt at the Last Supper. *I kiss* with reverence these feet for which You allowed Your Holy Feet to be nailed to the cross. *I kiss* with reverence these feet for which You sent throughout the world *speciosi pedes evangelizantium pacem* [the beautiful feet of those who preach the gospel of peace]. . . . *I kiss* with reverence these feet for whose salvation You established the Visible Head and allow us bishops to kiss Your Holy Feet in his person. *I kiss* with reverence these feet for which You appointed me pastor of my sheep and told me to serve them in love. *I kiss* with reverence the feet of all my sheep; all those who love You and who hate You, all who are in a state of grace and who are in a state of sin, all who walk in Your ways and those who deviate to evil ways; all who out of hatred toward You have become my enemies; all to whom You command me to show love in order to save their souls. . . . All—without exception. Allow me to cross Krakowskie Przedmieście* on my knees, and I will do it without delay.

April 8, 1955, Friday
Good Friday. "In pain shall you bring forth children. . . ." There were no pains, O Mother, when You gave birth to your most pure firstborn Son in Bethlehem. But how they multiplied when on Calvary You became the Mother of the whole sinful, though redeemed, human race. You gave birth to us in pain—look upon us with the love that every mother feels toward the fruit of her suffering. Mother of Sorrows—what a Mother of Joy You are for us.

You would have every right, Teacher and Leader, to turn everyone against me, even the worst, in order to fulfill the glory of the Father. It was the Father—Love—who used against You Judas,

---

*A main Warsaw thoroughfare.

Annas and Caiphas, Pilate, Herod, cohorts of soldiers, men and women servants, street rabble, false witnesses—in order for the Scriptures to be fulfilled. And You accepted this with submission, with trust. You repaid everything with a silent love. You—Holy, Innocent, Immaculate, different from sinners. And what could I say about my own case? If You delivered me to those who slap my face, spit on me, beat, kick, and besmirch me, I would have to admit that You have a right to do it. Could I defend myself against You? I would have to acknowledge signs of Your will in everything. And in them, see the lasting instrument that I must revere, in the way one kisses Your cross and nails.

Proprio Filio suo non pepercit [He did not spare His own Son]. When He forgave Abraham, taking into consideration the feelings of the faithful heart of the Father of Faith, he did not forgive His own Son, since He did not reckon with the feelings of His own Heart. God has the right to ask from his Highest Priest the ultimate sacrifice for the people, even the sacrifice of his life. This happened on Calvary, during the first Sacrifice of the New Order. Today Christ called upon the servants of the altar, whom He endowed with the power of sacrifice, to help Him. Showing us to the Father, He says: *sacerdos alter Christus* [the priest—another Christ]. What God demanded from the Highest Priest he also has the right to expect from His ministers. He did not forgive His own Son, and he has the right not to forgive us, to demand the sacrifice of our life, when this is required for the good of the people. It befalls us to bear the sins of the people placed in our care, befalls us to protect them, befalls us to sacrifice everything for them—even our own life. This is the law of inheriting our priesthood from Christ, whom God did not forgive. We cannot demand for ourselves more consideration from the Father than He gave to his own Son.

April 9, 1955, Saturday
During Holy Week we concluded a three-day retreat, which permitted us to spend all our time in the chapel of our prison. I had to speak simultaneously to myself, to Sister, and to Father S.—an audience well-chosen but diverse. Subjects had to be presented in

such a way as to avoid giving the impression of speaking *ad personam* [to an individual person], even though a retreat devoid of personal contact lacks real meaning. My listeners were most patient and indulgent. We spent Holy Week in the chapel, trying to identify with the experiences of the Church as closely as possible. On Maundy Thursday there was a festive Mass with Holy Communion for "the people"; every day we sang the Tenebrae.* On Good Friday, apart from the Tenebrae, we made our Way of the Cross, which was devoid of sorrows and complaints but was permeated by a spirit of unity with Christ in His way. This was the way of Christ, not ours. On Holy Saturday I allowed myself the privilege of offering Mass in the hope that the Church would have permitted it in these unusual circumstances.

We had serious problems in decorating our chapel for the holidays. In the garden we found some variety of mountain flowers that had just barely managed to peep out of the earth. Transplanted into small pots, they did all they could to decorate our bare altar.

At twelve o'clock the Superintendent brought me my letter and holiday packages. And so we held a grand conference of our Commission of Three, which accepted the gifts. The number of letters was also an indication of some loosening of the net of isolation. My hands now held letters from my father and my sister Stanisława, my brother, and my sister Janka. It was an unusually exceptional feast of reading.

April 10, 1955, Sunday

Valde mane [Early in the morning] we celebrated the Easter morning Mass in our little chapel, without a procession, but with chanted Matins and the *Te Deum*. Again, we spent this holiday together—in the chapel, at table, and during the afternoon meetings. There was much singing and joy on the second floor, deep silence and solemnity downstairs and on the third floor. People bereft of religious joys sit like birds with their wings tied back. We pity such

---

*Literally "darkness"—the solemn services performed on the evenings of Wednesday, Thursday, and Friday of Holy Week.

people. Today I risked saying to the deputy who visited me, "I wish you much joy and happiness." He responded in a whisper, "Thank you." Downstairs, on my way to the garden, I said to the Old Gentleman, "God grant you good health." I heard the same answer: "Thank you." We stopped for a moment at the desk of the guard on duty. We implored him to fight off sorrow, since it was not proper for victors to wear such glum faces. And, we added, everything on earth is resurrecting. One must retain his will to live. He smiled with antiseptic caution.

The companions of my fate are serene and happy. I hear their melodic voices. The sister is puttering around in the corridor and humming, *O Filii et filiae, Rex caelestis, Rex gloriae, ex morte resurrexit hodie, Alleluia* [O sons and daughters, today the King of Heaven, the King of glory, has risen, Alleluia]. And Father S., pleased that he was "home" and not at the clinic, takes up one Resurrection hymn after another. When Christ rose from the dead, he revealed so many possibilities to men that we no longer even care about our present situation. We know that all possibilities stand before us. And he who "can do all things in Him Who gives strength" does not remember what is happening today.

April 11, 1955, Monday
Surrexit Dominus vere et apparuit Simoni, Alleluia [Truly the Lord has risen and has appeared to Simon, Alleluia]. This was Peter's genuine happiness, because it was proof of forgiveness. It was enough that Christ looked at Peter; this was absolution granted to the visible Head of the Church by Christ. It is also our happiness, because it is related to hope. Christ forgave Peter; hope mounts that He will also forgive us. He who commanded us to pray for our enemies and does this Himself knows that we are not His enemies. All the more can we count on Christ's gaze of mercy.

Alleluia, gavisi sunt discipuli, viso Domino [Alleluia, the disciples rejoiced when they saw the Lord]. Joy is characteristic of the Easter season. Because "it is finished." Because the sentence hanging over the people has been suspended. Because Christ, condemned to death, dies no more. Because what had been imminent for the Son of God from the beginning now is imminent no more. Because the Father's wrath against His Son has ceased. Because the horrible visions of the passion that the Son beheld since the promise made in the Garden of Eden have dissipated. Because the blows and buffets will no longer pummel God-made-Man. Because the horror has passed. . . . Alleluia, Alleluia!

April 12, 1955, Tuesday
Refuge of sinners—please tell the Lamb and His Father today that God's judgments are just. So recently I was able to wonder why they were testing me so painfully. Today I wonder no more. God's grace has revealed to me how much I have harmed the Church and its members. But only one of these faults would be enough to give the just Judge reason for removing me forever from grace. And if God does not do it, I see in this a measure of His mercy. As distant as are all the sufferings of this earth from eternal punishment, so great is God's mercy toward me. And that is why, Mother, tell Him that I praise the justice God metes out to me. I recognize God's undeniable right to punish me. I also ask for one thing: Together let us defend Your Son and the Father Most Good before the people, so that they may not allow themselves to question God's justice, whenever they think of me or pray for me. You can do it, so that —by internal inspiration—You can persuade those closest to me that God punishes justly. Give them, Mother, a clear vision of all my faults. Let them recognize my worthlessness so that, together with me, they could praise God's justice. Do not defend me before human judgments, but defend God at my expense. I would rather be harshly judged by men than have the slightest thought arise against the justice of the Father and the Son. You can do this. . . . I will not pray: *Ne respicias peccata mea* [Look not on my sins], but I will pray: Look at my sins, Father, so that You may confirm Your conviction that the punishment You mete out to me is just.

April 18, 1955, Monday
I do not know why, but I must record this, in spite of my fear. You command it; I am not capable of doing it myself. You direct me to

want it and You direct me to write it, even though I struggle against both of Your wishes. And thus, verily: If You, Father, need more than has already happened to me thus far, do it. If You require my imprisonment, a dungeon, the tortures of interrogations, trials, a spectacle made of Your servant, slander and derision, the contempt of the rabble and whatever all you wish. . . . Here I am! I have written it, and . . . the burden is lifted from my heart.

April 19, 1955, Thursday
Nihil proficimus [We make no progress]. All day we have had a blizzard, one wave after another, with sun in between. And once again darkness swallows the earth. And when new snowflakes fall on the green grass, tossed by the force of the wind, they seem to say, "We have accomplished nothing." The April earth warmed the icy flakes and conquered them. Oh, because the snow falls to no avail in April, since the time of cold is past, and everything longs for warmth, light, greenery, and flowers, the most violent hurricanes accomplish nothing. There is a time for winter and a time for spring. . . . You can manage nothing, you flowers of the cold, when the earth longs for warm ones. Of no use is your furious toil, your obstinacy and persistence. Oh, if you only knew how the earth longs for the sun, warmth, love, and peace. . . . Nothing will be able to turn back the time, turn back the centuries, release from the embrace of goodness, from the habits of the heart. . . . For two thousand years, the Sun of Justice kissed the earth with the caress of loving lips. We have fallen in love with this caress. Our lips, our eyes, our thoughts, our words, our actions give birth out of love. The whole world searches for a good heart, a kind look, a friendly word. . . . This already is in the blood of the world. . . . Today is not the time for snowstorms. . . . Warm the world with the glow of your heart, even an April one. It might be weak, but after April comes May, not March. The sun will gain in strength, love will sink deeper roots. . . . Forward, to the sun, to warmth, to goodness! Enough of the cold, enough of harsh words, enough of blustering winds! We open the door of our country to warmth and to flowers. . . . "For see, the winter is past, the rains are over and gone. The flowers appear on the earth. . . ." (Song of Songs

2: 11–12). Do not retreat! On to light! You cannot turn back the course of human longings . . . *Nihil proficimus*—and the white frost died in the embrace of emerald winter corn. . . .

April 25, 1955, Monday
Today I answered the holiday letters of April 9, 1955, at least those from my father and my sister Stanisława. I must leave unanswered the letters from little Staś, my sisters Anastazja and Janina. Trying to imagine the procedure followed in the reading of my letters, I do not wish to expose other members of my family to the brutalities of having a letter waved in front of them and then stuffed into the pocket of some policeman. I am especially anxious to keep little Staś from such a shock. He is too young to be exposed to such a drastic restriction of his civil rights.

My dearest father!
In a few days you will be celebrating the feast day of your patron, Saint Stanisław; I wish to assure you in advance that on this day I will be united with you in prayer and in my filial devotion. I will offer Mass, Father, in your name on May 9, since on Sunday it is my duty to offer the Mass for the people of my diocese. I will also think of all the Stanis-laws in the family.
On the day of your Patron, dear Father, I will thank God for returning you to health and for graciously letting me continue to count on your prayers, the only help I expect of you. I will ask our Father to continue to infuse a living faith into your soul—a faith that questions nothing, and only trusts, like Abraham; a faith that desires nothing, and gives all, which does not permit any fear to enter the heart, since it knows that the experiences of this life are nothing in comparison with the joy that God grants His servants. Let us both be bolstered by this hope, certain that although we are separated by distance, we are joined by Our Heavenly Father who is the master of space and can conquer it by a single beat of His loving heart.

All the members of my family and all my loved ones have shown me so much kindness and thoughtfulness at Easter time that it embarrasses me. I show my gratitude to them through prayer, especially during Mass. As for my loved ones, I hold them gratefully in my heart and support them with prayers to God. I remember each one of them specifically, and commend them all without ceasing to Our Lady of Jasna Góra, Support of the Faithful, since this Special Woman—*Virgo Auxiliatrix* [Virgin Helpmate]—does not forget those of her children who give themselves to her trustingly.

I see that I am incurring a huge debt of gratitude toward our sister, who is supporting you, dear Father, in your recovery and who accompanies you to the hospital. With such care I am not at all worried about you, Father, since I know that you are in good and experienced hands. My heart is full of gratitude to her, as well as to all those who are helping you. I only ask one thing, that you do not attempt anything too ambitious or begin to work too early; you have always been very industrious, and so your rest is fully justified.

Do not worry in the least about me, dear Father; I lead a busy life, in the fullest meaning of the word. I do not leave myself one free moment—I do everything with an eye on the clock, from awakening in the morning to retiring at night. The life of a Carthusian monk is probably most like mine; there is nothing new about my health that is worth mentioning.

Please accept, my dear father, my warmest greetings, words of affection, filial respect and devotion. I kiss your hands with love and gratitude, and I send blessings to you and to my loved ones. I commend you all to the Holy Mother of Jasna Góra and Support of the Faithful.

April 25, 1955
S.W.

My dearest sister!

I will again burden you with many intermediary duties, but I console myself that the fault lies with your goodness. I want to show my gratitude with the wishes I send you on the day of Saint Stanisław, your patron. Through you I send greetings to Stach and little Staś. In a few days I will offer Mass for you: For Father, May 9; for you, May 11; for Stach and his family, May 13; for Staś and Ania and their parents, May 18. All that I wish for you I will tell our Heavenly Father at the altar, trusting that this carries more weight than human emotions. Since I am writing about Masses, I ask you to tell Sister Superior that I will offer Mass for her on May 20. For Julcia, June 2, and for Tosia and the whole family, June 13. I do not know if I will have a chance to write before then, so I ask you to convey my greetings to Julcia, Janka, and Cześ; I will support them with prayers on their name days, during Mass.

I was so pleased with all the letters I received from the family for the holidays. I would be happy to answer them, but I do not wish to add to their troubles. Please tell Naścia that I am very pleased with the determined decision of her youngest child. I pray that he may persevere; she should take care of her own health, so that she may look after the family that God has entrusted to her for a long time. I was happy with the signatures of Janka's family. I see that Stefanek writes more legibly than I did at his age. I am very grateful to Zosia for the picture which I always keep on my stand. Thank Tadzio for the nice photographs of Staś and Ania; indeed, the children look somewhat serious, but they appear healthy. I cannot bring myself to answer Staś's letter, which has been such a joy for me. But I do not have the heart to expose the child to having the letter read to him, when he already has the ambition to read himself. Perhaps God will permit me to answer him one day. I would like to know what day he will make his First Communion, and then I will offer Mass for him. I thank you very much for the fifth

volume of Chrobry;* this book is truly a milestone in Polish literature. What artistry! Since Tadzio sees the
Romeks, please have him tell them that I have not forgotten my little goddaughter and that I am praying for them.

The two holiday packages delivered to me on Holy Saturday, in which I found everything you listed, aroused
mixed feelings in me. Naturally, first gratitude and delight,
but also a fear that I will start to live too ostentatiously.
Every new item that appears in my simple field of vision
expands the world of my observations. Only now did I
notice how pleasant tomatoes are in their freshness, even
though they are such a common fruit. I was delighted with
the three lovely painted Easter eggs, so carefully made that
they are worthy of being put on exhibition.

Do not misconstrue my silence about my health; there is
nothing worth reporting. I feel much better than last year.
Only certain symptoms remain that demand systematic
treatment—these you know about. I have no problems with
my teeth. Please keep Father from rushing into work; he has
worked enough in his life. How did Julcia's stay in the
hospital turn out? Thank the youngest children for the
lovely picture and for their good hearts. I send words of
brotherly devotion to all members of the family and to my
loved ones. I commend you to Our Lady of Jasna Góra,
Support of the Faithful, and bless you with all my heart.
S.W.

May 1, 1955, Sunday
Confiteor . . . Beatae Mariae semper Virgini [I confess . . . to Blessed
Mary ever Virgin]. The Church tells me to confess before Mary. It
gives her the right to look into my soul, to self-accusation, to open
revelation of all that is in me. Refuge of Sinners, what a painful task it
is to be a confessor; I sympathize with you when you have to hear me
out. But what a great solace for the sinner when he finds a good

---

Bolesław Chrobry (second king of Poland) by Antoni Gołubiew.

confessor. And what am I to say when you are supposed to hear my confession? Your mercy will gain forgiveness for me and bring relief to my heart.

May 3, 1955, Tuesday
The closest Companion of the Holy Trinity, Virgin Mother of God and Queen of Poland, today we desire, through your motherly hands, to pay grateful homage to the Holy Trinity for the fact that you are our Mother, that you are the Queen of Poland, and that you reveal God's Merciful Heart in so many favors bestowed at Jasna Góra. Thanking You for everything, we ask you for the grace of fidelity to the Holy Trinity, for the grace of fidelity to the Heart of your Son and to your Immaculate Heart, for the grace of fidelity to the Church. Remember, Mother, that we offered our Polish Nation and Church to your Immaculate Heart, as soon as the invaders were ousted. Soon after we offered the Nation to the Heart of your Son through your immaculate hands. We wish to be granted a bit of a respite, so that we may fulfill our vows. Accept this plea, O Mother, and let your queenly Heart manifest a motherly understanding for your distressed children.

I bring you, Mother, my whole burden and cast it from my shoulders at your feet. Look upon it as you would upon a laborer who must carry great loads. And so I have brought it, cast it off, and look at your hands. . . . I can do nothing better, so I carry heavy burdens. Not only my own—but these are your burdens and those of your Son. When I cast them before you, I will be somewhat relieved. Will I receive a laborer's wages . . . ?

May 12, 1955, Thursday
On the ninth anniversary of my consecration as bishop, celebrated at Jasna Góra before the throne of Our Mother Most Holy, I gave thanks to the Holy Trinity through my Queen and Patroness for the grace of consecration and the fullness of the priesthood. Pontifical*

---

*The book used in the consecration of a bishop. It contains the text of the ceremony, which includes a scrutiny (interrogation) about the faith of the candidate and his readiness to be consecrated.

in hand, I renew my bishop's scrutiny, repeating from the bottom of my heart: *Volo—Credo* [I will—I believe]. I examine my conscience and admit with humility that not all has been accomplished in me during these nine years. The question *Vis mores tuos ad omni malo temperare, et quantum poteris, Domino adiuvante, ad omne bonum commutare?* [Do you desire to abstain from every evil in your way of life and turn to every good, insofar as you are able, with the help of God?] serves as a reminder of how far I still am from this exchange of good for evil, despite the fact that being a bishop is such a great help with one's own sanctification. What a weak vessel God has chosen for Himself, since the most powerful means of help fail. And in its every word the consecration preface is an excuse for the faithless servant, who for nine years has not managed to put this program into action. I am still lacking in this *puritas dilectionis* [purity of love]. Life went by *in persuasibilibus humanae sapientiae verbis* [in the persuasive words of human wisdom]. Have I not deserved the admonition: *ut utatur, non glorietur potestate?* [to use but not glory in your power?]. Was I a *fidelis servus et prudens* [faithful and prudent servant]? . . . Oh, but that the desire of the Church should be fulfilled in me: *Multiplica super eum benedictionem et gratiam tuam: ut ad exorandam semper misericordiam tuam tuo munere idoneus et tua gratia possit esse devotus* [Multiply your blessing and your grace upon him: that by beseeching you he may always be fit to gain your mercy, and by your grace be able to be faithful] (P.R.).* I come back to the preface, in order that it may serve me as a plan for my interior life. . . .

A great consolation in my misery is that I was born as a bishop at Jasna Góra, that *origine* [by origin] I am *claromontanus* [of Jasna Góra],† or that I can look at my Homeland, reigned over by the Blessed Mother. She will not deny help to her child who struggles in his battle for fidelity.

Pontificale Romanum.
†*Claromontanus* is a Latinization of "Bright Mountain," which is what Jasna Góra means in Polish.

May 19, 1955, Thursday

The Ascension of Our Lord—the open gates of Heaven allow all wanderers to gaze at the heavens with the insight of faith, with the eyes of hope. When Heaven is open, one's entire life seems to be but a tear rolling down the face of a newborn. The Sun of Life will soon dry it and embrace it with the rays of its fervent love. And love is without end.

Cleanse me, then, as You cleansed the Samaritan woman, Mary Magdalene, the public sinner. Give me Your hand, as You gave it to Peter on the waves of the sea. Open my eyes, as You opened them for the blind man of Jericho and the man blind from birth. Lead me from the grave, as You led Lazarus. Let me touch Your side, as You let Thomas touch it. Increase my faith and teach me to pray, as You taught the Apostles. And give me love, as You did to Mary, so that I may love much. Love is, after all, the greatest virtue of Heaven's inhabitants.

Let it be as You demand: "Think of Me, and I will think of you." "You will free yourself of unnecessary worry, fruitless considerations, useless thoughts. And you will gain much time which you may devote exclusively to Me and to my Church. You wish more time? Think only of Me, and you will see how much more time you will have." Let it be as You wish, my special Teacher!

May 29, 1955, Sunday

Our days pass in good order and routine. We both work diligently. Father S. has become enamored with his work on books and writing; Sister distracts him a bit, slipping away from the books to household chores of which she manages to find a great number. I have managed to finish "Reflections on the Liturgical Year" and have already begun work on "A Letter to Those I Have Ordained." It is an extensive work divided into four parts, each of which emphasizes the supernatural bond existing between the priest and the Holy Trinity, the Church, the bishop, and the parish. I address this work to the priests whom I ordained. I write very slowly and with no little trouble; I lack the conditions necessary for this type of work. Father

S. continues to work on the reflections for school youth. He is planning a short guide for altar boys. We have both seriously taken up Italian conversation; all meals and walks have become opportunities for practice. Father S. is making rapid progress.

Our official relations have so diminished that there is less and less to say during the official visits. But our meetings with the Old Gentleman when we go down for a walk are becoming more and more natural. We talk about health, about the weather, and about birds, but at least we say something. Aesculapius has become totally mechanical; it seems he does not even see us when he asks: "Your health? Any requests?" And he leaves without waiting for a reply. The Commandant is becoming more and more human. He once

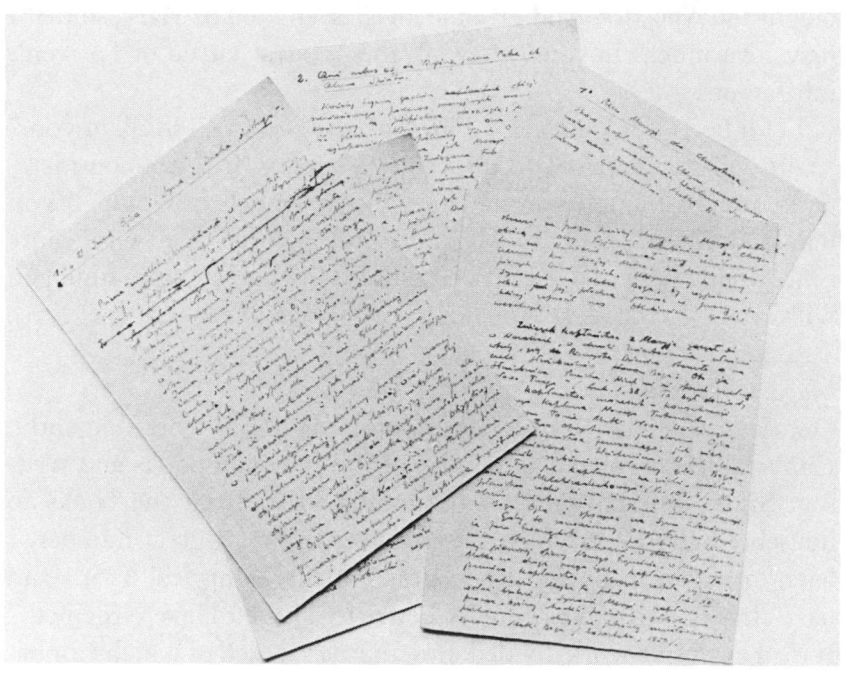

The manuscript of "A Letter to Those I Have Ordained," written in Prudnik.

even used the expression "like a human being." There are no conversations with the Superintendent either—except perhaps about
the flycatchers that have made a nest in my window frame and are
awaiting a new generation. Today I was handed a letter from my
father and from my sister Stanisława:

My beloved son!
   Your letter of April 25 was read to me on May 3. Thank
you very much for the letter, for celebrating Mass in my
intention and for your name day wishes. I returned to Zalesie on May 4 in the company of Fr. Franciszek* and Fr.
Hieronim.† Here, at home, I am recovering very well. It
seems that the spring air is doing me good, all I need now
is some warm weather.
   Sister Maksencja fell ill and went to Poznań, where doctors found an internal illness that required surgery. After
two weeks of preparation, the operation took place, and it
was successful. Tadeusz and his wife thank you for the Mass
you offered for them; they are well and little Ania is recovering well. Yesterday, Staś received his First Holy Communion.
   Fr. Padacz has asked me to inquire whether on August 3
of last year you were given a letter from him sent together
with the letters from us. Stasia will elaborate. I thank you
again for your prayers and pastoral blessing, and I want you
to know that we are praying for you and trust that the Good
Lord will grant our petitions. I kiss you, my dear son, wish
you health and perseverance, commending you to the care
of Our Lady of Jasna Góra.

Zalesie, May 23, 1955
S. Wyszyński

---

*Father Franciszek Borowiec, who was the administrator of the Primate's house.
†Fr. Hieronim Goździewicz.

My dearest brother!

Your letters of April 25 were read to us on May 3. I thank you personally and in behalf of all those for whose name days you offered Mass, and for the kindness you have shown us all. On the days you mentioned, we all joined you in our thoughts before God; your intercession on our behalf is the most precious name day present we could ask for. On May 8 of this year I went to Jasna Góra, on the second Sunday —the Sunday of your consecration—nine years ago. On this day two Masses were celebrated before the picture of Our Lady in both our names, at ten in the morning and with the May devotions in the evening. I also requested a Mass for May 12—the anniversary of your consecration. In a package I am sending you hosts with the image of a lamb and the expression you will remember from the day of your consecration: *Volo in coelo et in terra* [I wish this in heaven and on earth]. I add the request, if possible, that you should celebrate Mass with this host on May 31, the day of the feast of *Regalitatis Mariae* [the Queenship of Mary]. I would be very pleased if you would fulfill my request, and if you do, please mention it in your next letter. [Excerpt]

May 29, 1955

May 29, 1955, Sunday

Sometimes trifles mean more to the little ones than great revelations to giants of the spirit. A trifle might be the fact that so far I have not received a letter from my loved ones, although for the holidays I usually received them a day in advance. But God granted me the grace to offer this deprivation with serenity. I accept with confidence everything that comes from Your hand. Since morning I keep repeating to myself: Everything is a grace, You are Goodness and Wisdom, which is present in everything. I surrender this consolation, You have the right to demand everything. Am I to deny You that which is a need of the human heart? Even if I were without fault, You would still have the right to send me trials. Besides, You know how to offer consolation in Your own way. . . .

Completely calmed, I concentrated on my companions, who were sad. Soon we were all comforted. A letter filled with the best of news arrived. They had prayed for us on May 8 on Jasna Góra, in the chapel of Our Lady; two Masses were celebrated before the Miraculous Painting, one at 10:00, the other during the evening May devotions. The Blessed Mother saw fit to hear the prayers offered for her slave before her Royal Throne. My sister Stanisława attended this Mass, as she had once (1924) attended the first Mass I celebrated hopelessly ill, like Lazarus, before the Miraculous Painting. They sent us many small items, which are a delight to children. Sister received a letter from Mother Getter. So there was great joy. Consolation for the children who were granted the grace of trust. The imprisoned Primate did not know that night and day on Jasna Góra prayer vigils were being held for him, that hundreds of Masses were being offered for him.

I sometimes think that You could stop by our prison and say: "Lazarus, leave your grave." Our hands and feet are bound, I see barbed wire from my window. My sisters pray to You and plead with You. You delay until the fourth day. But if this delay would bring You glory, I will wait in my grave.

May 30, 1955, Monday

"God so loved the world . . ." When the Church on the second day after Pentecost recalls that little word "so," it seems to expect our response. Christ did not find a better word for describing that which cannot be compared with anything, which is so profound, which has no *terminus a quo* and *terminus ad quem*. This is a sign of a depth that cannot be comprehended without God. And the Son of God, who knows His worth in the face of His Father's love, must see in God's Gift to us the immensity of God's love for this world. "So" will always remain an abyss, even though it seems to be filled with the Son, like the stone jars at Cana. This "so" (*tak* = so) may only be

224

answered with another (*tak* = yes) "yes"—that is, the "yes" of man.*
It too is without measure or bounds, unfathomable. It can always
permeate inward and upward, in breadth and in height. It is a lifelong
work; it is cooperating with the Holy Trinity. It is something that is
always increasing, which never says "enough." It might be compared
with that *unum* [the one thing] which is necessary and with this
primum [the first thing] which must be sought. These three words are
enough to consume the energy of the most willing heart.

May 31, 1955, Tuesday
Today the Church allows its children to gather all the names, titles,
and appellations that it showers on Mary and, during a Mass in
honor of the Mediatrix of All Graces, allows us to say everything
that a believing and loving heart is capable of saying. Today there
is full freedom of words and feelings; all will be understood. Today
one name, even if it be the most beautiful, will not be enough. Today
we receive all and must return all.

What can be most beautiful in this valley of tears? It is the Virgin
cradling God-made-Man in her arms! It is the priest transforming
bread and wine into the Body of Christ and the Blood of the Virgin's
God! It is the Virgin offering her body and her heart to the King
of Virgins! It is a Mother nursing the Fruit of her womb.

If I were to be born again today and were asked what path I
would choose in life, without a moment's hesitation I would choose
the path of priesthood, even if from the beginning I knew clearly
that I would end in the chains of Christ, in the scorn of the gallows.
Better a scorned priest than a praised Caesar.

---

*The Polish word *tak* can have two meanings: "so" (intensive) and "yes." The
cardinal plays on the ambiguity of the meanings.

*June 6, 1955, Sunday**

The Holy Trinity—the First of Love, blazing eternally like Moses' burning bush in the wilderness. The Light of this Fire—*Lumen de lumine* [Light from light]—is the Son, and the Spirit in the form of fiery tongues is the sparks from that fire which, falling on human hearts, spread the fire of God all over the world. All that is mere straw is consumed in this fire; all that is gold is cleansed. Souls radiate God's light, from God's fire. Fire unites—our little flames unite with the fire of Love. Thus arises one Fire of God, which is the Light of all people. This Fire is eternal.

Heart of the Holy Trinity. He came as the fruit of the love the Father bears for this world. Born of great Love, to give birth to love. He came as the radiance of His Father's perfection. He allowed His Heart to be opened on the cross. That Heart is from the Father. In that Heart we recognize the Heart of the Father. The Father has a Heart, and that is why He gave His Son a Heart. We can and must speak of the Father's Heart. Can there be love without a heart? The Spirit is the love of the Father and the Son. The Heart of the Spirit, from the Heart of the Father, and from the Heart of the Son. These three Hearts are one Heart, which beats with mutual love. We live on this love, we act and are in it.

June 9, 1955, Thursday

Corpus Christi. *Notre Dame* [Our Lady]—a cathedral, the synonym for "cathedral." *Templum Domini* [Temple of the Lord] in which dwells the Everlasting Word. *Sacrarium Spiritus Sancti* [Sanctuary of the Holy Spirit]. And in Poland nearly all the old cathedrals are named for the Mother of God-made-Man. How fitting this is! Priests are consecrated in cathedrals. The first consecration of a priest took place in *Notre Dame* Cathedral on the day of the Annunciation, when the gift of the Father flowed onto Christ's humanity—priesthood, according to the order of Melchizedek.† All the servants of the altar have taken their priesthood from this priesthood of Christ. They

*The feast of the Holy Trinity.
†Psalms 109:4; 110:4 KJV.

participate in this gift from the Father, which made Jesus a Priest forever. How fitting it is that they should persevere in this *Sacrarium Spiritus Sancti,* that they should do everything with the Mother of the Eternal Priest. Mary was present at Her Son's First Mass on Calvary. How close she should stand to the altars on which we offer the Most Holy Sacrifice. How proper it is to invite her to take part in every Sacrifice of the Mass. The Church reminds us of this when it tells us to confess to *Beatae Mariae Virgini,* when it mentions Mary so often in the prayers of the Mass. Christ's priesthood was realized in Mary. An *Alter Christus* cannot forget this.

June 10, 1955, Friday
To experience the grace of comprehending the greatness of priesthood it is necessary at times to experience, too, the grace of one's own wretchedness and unworthiness. Christ, to whom we say during Mass, *quoniam Tu solus Sanctus* [for You alone are Holy], will show me who I am: *quoniam tu solus peccator* [for you alone are sinner]. How useful *felix culpa* [happy fault]* is, then; it allows me to free myself of this improper presumption that I have a right to the altar. Only Jesus Christ has the sovereign right to the altar, the God-made-Man, *Sacerdos et Hostia* [Priest and Victim], adorned in His humanity with a priesthood forever. I am only a "vessel for abuse" from which *solus Sanctus* feeds His children so admirably as to protect them from all my uncleanness and degradation. *Misericors et miserator Dominus* [Merciful and compassionate Lord].

June 12, 1955, Sunday
In the Octave of Corpus Christi. *Etiam passer invenit domum, et hirundo nidum sibi, ubi ponet pullos suos* [The sparrow has found a home, and the swallow a nest for itself, where it will place its young].

Altaria Tua, Domine exercituum [Your altars, Lord of hosts] . . . (Psalm 83).

When I look at the flycatchers' nest, which the winged parents

---

*This term is used during the Holy Saturday services to describe the sin of Adam.

wove into the frame of my window and where they placed five of their nestlings, I begin to understand better the significance of the altar for the priestly soul. These helpless fragments in whom the spark of life is barely smoldering only know how to open their beaks —so wide and passionately, so greedily and spontaneously—whenever they hear the flutter of their parents' wings. How secure they feel in their nest, although they are separated from the inside of my room only by a pane of glass. How ready they are, how watchful. . . . How they never have enough! Where can a baby bird feel better than in its own nest? Small wonder that he is so hesitant to attempt that first flight.

I am even more than a helpless nestling at the altar. I know but one thing—how to open my mouth. But I cannot give anything from it. It is Christ who gives the words: *Hoc est enim Corpus Meum* [For this is My Body]. . . . All my strength comes from this Winged Seraph who nails my hands and feet to the altar: *altaria Tua, Domine virtutem* [Your altars, Lord of power] . . . Where am I happier than at the altar? Where do I live more magnificently than in this nest of grace? What remains for me? To open my mouth with the greed of nestlings! To hold on to the altar as nestlings hold on to the edge of the nest! Open my heart, trust, wait, desire, anticipate. . . . The altar—it is my home. . . .

July 9, 1955, Saturday
I still have not answered the letters received on May 29, and now I have received new letters dated July 7. Together with the letters from my father and my sister, I received a food parcel. Father's letter brought me the sad news of the death of Archbishop Jałbrzykowski.* I sat down immediately to draft my answer. It is most difficult to write a letter that will tell the whole truth as well as express my sincerest feelings, knowing that this truth and these feelings must pass through the insensitive throat of a police reader. What a torment!

One motive moves me to struggle against this resistance; one

---

*Archbishop Romuald Jałbrzykowski of Białystok in the area of Wilno.

must consider the feelings of those who love, who are concerned. On the other hand, this resistance is a protest against the violence done to a citizen's right to freedom and to privacy of correspondence. This right continues to be violated in spite of my protests. I don't know what is read from my letters and what is omitted; and maybe the text is supplemented by their own comments and observations, which may put me in a false light? Under these circumstances would there be any sense in writing letters? Instead of relief, they may bring new anguish.

You can expect anything from people for whom the difference between truth and falsehood does not exist. I cannot understand how a system that forces its officials to lie to the people does not fear that this talent for lying, this "virtue" in lying, some day may be used against the leaders themselves.

My beloved son!

We sent a parcel and letters in May. You probably received them, but we still don't have a letter from you. We are concerned; more than five weeks have passed.

I am slowly regaining my health. A few small discomforts cannot be avoided at my age. There is nothing new in the family; Stasia will elaborate.

Please write about your health—that is most important to us. *Słowo Powszechne* of June 21 printed the news of the death of Archbishop R. Jałbrzykowski. He died on June 19, 1955.

We entrust you to the care of Our Lady of Częstochowa. We pray, trusting in God's mercy that He will hear our prayers. Please offer a Mass for the late Jadwiga, who prayed for you with the others.

I conclude these few words asking that you pray for us. I wish you good health and speedy return and ask for your holy blessing.

Zalesie, June 30, 1955
S. Wyszyński

My dearest and special father!

This letter answers your letters of May 23 and June 30. I was so pleased that after so many trials and so much suffering you were able to return to Zalesie. I thanked God for your recovery; I hope that summer weather and fresh air will contribute to your complete recovery. I pray for it to God and Our Lady. I am grateful to everyone who helped you, Father, during your illness, with their help, care, and good hearts, especially Sister Superior and Fathers Franciszek and Hieronim, who took you home. I will show my thanks to them by offering Mass for them. I was sorry to hear the news of Sister Maksencja's latest illness; the news of her recovery and return home was a source of joy.

The first Holy Communion of little Staś is a great joy. I could not serve him, but as it happened, on May 18, I offered a Mass for him, and I asked God to keep him faithful to Him all his life. Please, my dear father, tell little Staś that although I did not answer his letter, I think of him constantly. The children's photograph that was sent to me is on my table, and often during work I commend them to the Blessed Mother. Let him be a good Christian, truthful, of pure heart, righteous toward all and brave in battle with himself. I bless him with all my heart.

To the question of Father Władziu Padacz—whether I received his letter for my name day—the answer is no, but I thank him for his good heart and ask him not to stop praying for me. I often offer Mass for him. On July 4 I offered Mass for you and the family. You, Father, share in every Mass. I ask you, dear Father, to conserve your strength, to refrain from hard work, not to succumb to sadness, to be peaceful, trusting, and patient with our faith, and Heavenly Father, and to know that I am always with you in prayer and love. Other details are in my letter to Stasia.

The news of the death of Archbishop Jałbrzykowski

moved me very much; he was a man of great heart and engaging simplicity. I will offer Mass for the soul of Jadwiga on July 29.

I kiss your hands with reverence and devotion, blessing you.

July 8, 1955
St. W.

My dearest sister!

I answer your two letters of May 23 and June 30. Please excuse the delay, but I want to spare you the indignity of having my letters read to you, and therefore I write less frequently. With a shadow of envy I was happy to hear that you were able to go to Jasna Góra and pray before the picture of Our Mother; but my envy was an honest one, because I knew that I would benefit from your prayers. Thank you very much for the three Masses offered for me, especially for the one on the ninth anniversary of my consecration as a bishop. Your pilgrimage reminded me of my First Mass in Częstochowa thirty-one years ago, when we were there together. I was happy to receive the Mass hosts and was able to fulfil your wishes exactly on May 31. I believe that the Support of the Faithful unites us and helps us to remain faithful to God the Father in Heaven and to good hearts on earth. Truly—*Volo in coelo et in terra*—without a shadow of hesitation, even stronger than on the day of my consecration. It is a happy coincidence that in my breviary I have a small picture of the hands of Jesus, which always reminds me of that. When a person sees how similar the hands of God became to human ones, he experiences great comfort that such a thing is possible.

You must all be very happy at home that our dear father is again with you and, I hope, in satisfactory health. During the school year he must be rather lonely, but now you can keep him company. You must always watch that his passion for work, which has consumed him until now, does not exert him beyond his strength. Maybe both our convalescents will encourage each other to be prudent; I am so happy that Józio is also recuperating. The news about Julcia made me happy; I think of her and remember her in my Masses. I feel so sorry that Sister Maksencja has had to endure so many severe illnesses within such a short time; with all my heart I wish her a speedy return to permanent well-being. I often offer Mass for her and the other sisters and try to repay in prayer all the care I received from them. To Tadzio and his wife give best wishes for their growing son, and tell them that on the feast of Saint Anne I will remember their little Ania at Mass. It's good that they finally have an apartment.

Thank Włodzio very much for such a beautiful picture and for such happy news. Tell him that on June 8 I offered a Mass for him to Our Lady of Częstochowa into whose care I commended him for the rest of his life. He has to prepare himself for a difficult life as the nephew of a cardinal, because he'll have to be the most humble among priests, never thinking that he is better than others or looking to get special favors. In Christ's Church everything is measured by God's graces, not human ones; he has to learn this rule from the start. I trust that we think alike, and I bless him especially with all my heart.

I am happy for all of you and for Janka and Romek and his wife—that you are going on vacation, which will help recoup your strength after a whole year's work and a chance to look out for yourselves. Thank you for extending my wishes to Zosia; I did not forget her day here. I think of Cześ and will offer a Mass for him on July 20. For the children I will offer Mass on August 16. I send warmest greetings to Naścia's family, to all yours, to the family of Janka, Julcia, and all my dearest ones. Console Janka—tell her that in our family we already have one Stefan, who gave us a lot of trouble.

I am very grateful for the food in both packages; you take such trouble and I could get along very easily without it. But

I accept it as an expression of our unity. There is nothing new about my health; the old troubles bother me. I don't have any new ones.

Because this is vacation time, I too must boast of one summer achievement. I managed to rear five little flycatchers, whose parents trusted me and built their nest on my windowsill. For a month I had practical lessons in God's wisdom in such minute detail as the life of these little ones. Christ used sparrows to teach us that we are more important in the eyes of the Lord. My little ones have already gone from their nest, but I meet them from time to time in the garden.

Be patient, because you need to be for yourself as well as for our Father. You have more than you think. I will pray that the Lord will give you even more.

I think that's it, as the journalists say—all of my life that can be of interest to you. I offer myself to you with all my heart and prayer, remembering and blessing you.
S.W.

July 16, 1955, Saturday
Saturday, the Commemoration of Our Lady of Mount Carmel. I will conclude my Thanksgiving after Mass on this Saturday, the day of the week that honors Jesus as well as Mary, with the words of the woman from the crowd: "Blessed is the Womb that bore you and the breasts that gave you suck." Here the lives of Jesus and Mary are one; as in the story of Redemption so in every soul. And that second sentence: *"Ave verum Corpus, natum de Maria Virgine"* [Hail to thee, true Body sprung from the Virgin Mary's womb]. And that third one, a prayer of the Church: *"Beata viscera Mariae Virginis"* [The Blessed womb of the Virgin Mary]. And this fourth one from a simple folk song: "Hail, Jesus, Son of Mary, truly God in Sacred Host." Can there be a better way of honoring a Guest who comes into your soul on a Saturday morning?

Today we decorated our poor little altar with lilies from the garden. *"Florete, flores, quasi lilium"* ["Blossom, flowers, like the lily"]. Jesus had beautiful praise for the lilies, on which sparrows sit so willingly in the garden, perhaps sensing their evangelical kinship on the lips of the Word? The lily is the real glory of the Creator, whose fate was superior to even that of Solomon himself. Murillo, quite appropriately, borrowed colors for his "Purissima" from the lily. Three blushes of virginal modesty cover three purest inner petals that are so immaculate that even with closest scrutiny one cannot find the slightest taint. The marvelous design of the flower: three snow-white petals arranged in the form of a triangle, embraced by three narrower petals softly pink on the outside. These intersecting triangles: The outer one—*"Tres sunt, qui testimonium dant in terra: spiritus et sanguis et aqua"* ["There are three things that give testimony on earth: spirit, blood, and water"]—is the fruit of the Spirit of the Creator, which renews the face of the earth through blood and water. The inner one—*"Tres sunt, qui testimonium dant in coelo: Pater, Verbum, et Spiritus Sanctus"* ["There are three who give testimony in heaven: the Father, the Word, and the Holy Spirit"] (1 John 5:7–8)—shelters their common creation, the Word Incarnate. And the whole symbolizes the Palace of Virginal Modesty—the true Temple of the Lord— because the calyx of the lily as seen from below gives the impression of a gothic cathedral, whose snow-white ceilings are upheld by the pink arms of the ribbing. Christ says: "Behold the lilies of the field. ..." It is a good idea to heed His words. ...

August 1, 1955, Monday

The bound Hands of Christ. I received such a picture on the way to my installation as archbishop in Gniezno, when I stopped at a church in Podgórze, a suburb of Toruń. In the picture, Christ, His Hands bound, stood supported by a soldier at His right Arm. In my breviary I have another little picture of Christ with Hands bound; I received it on the day of my consecration. Today they are both very relevant to me. They raise my spirits when I think how similar to human hands are those Hands of Christ. Those who originally bound Christ's Hands would still like to see Christ with His Hands bound. How many labor at trying to bind Christ's Hands! But they have no power over God. So they reach for the hands of those whose vocation it is to untie God's Hands. The greater the effort to find Christ's blessed Hands, the greater must be the priestly struggle to unbind Them. O Christ, help me to unbind Your hands in human souls, so that You may act freely, so that You may bless and heal. ... But have mercy on those, too, who shackle Your Hands. Unbind their hearts so that they may know Your love.

August 3, 1955, Wednesday
A practice has established itself here in Prudnik: letters and parcels are delivered *ipsa die* [the same day]. That is why the Superintendent came today with my name day letters, and his face was a little friendlier than usual. It seems to me that to a certain extent he is sharing in the little bit of joy that the sight of a letter brings.

We are spending the feast of Saint Stephen in a family atmosphere. My comrades in grace did all they could to show me their love. Father Stanisław chanted the Mass, and Sister rendered a series of hymns known by members of the Family of Mary. We spent the day together: at table, in the chapel, and during tea. Supplied generously by the parcels I received today, we could set a "luxurious table."

The weather did not cooperate, so we could not go to the garden. It is becoming more and more difficult to walk there; there are no adequate paths, and the air is very stuffy—a real quagmire, even though it is situated up on a hill. Sister does not like it when we go to the garden; she prefers that we stay inside. Besides, there is nothing drawing us there. We are really watched less than we were in the beginning, but some eye is always hidden somewhere, suspiciously tracking our steps. We are fighting a plague of grass snakes that make this place their home; we meet them everywhere.

By your loving will, Father of life, last night I completed fifty-four years of life on this earth and thirty-one years of priesthood.

I want to thank You for life: for my whole life, the part submissive to Your grace, and the part that is rebellious. In life I learn to know the Love that makes my existence possible, and Your Mercy. Did You also say this about me: *Paenitet me fecisse hominem* [I regret that I made man]? Why did I give him life? Father, if my life were an even greater failure than it is, it would be my happiness. Without the grace of life, I would have no hope of Heaven. And all that is born of my weakness, sin, and stubbornness will fall from my soul like a leaf from a tree. Life is a greater gift than anything else, because we can struggle through it, as through a jungle, to You. My clothes are torn, I am covered with wounds, as if I were returning from a battlefield, but you will cure and heal all. Please, Father, do not regret that You gave me life. Add Your grace; it will be sufficient for me. I am grateful for my life, for all my life, even my present life here in prison. Even this is better than nonexistence.

I thank you for the mother, whom You gave me, and who fifty-four years ago endured suffering and pain to endow me with Your Fatherly Love. Through her arms You embraced and nursed me. She was obedient to You in this Father's right. As once she suffered for Your right to life, today show her Your Heart and bring her to the throne of Your grace and happiness. You summoned her from this earth at an early age; You gave her all the pains of childbearing without the joy of seeing the fruits of those pains. Give her the joy of gazing into Your Fatherly Eyes.

Thank You, Father, for my patron Saint Stephen, whom I received at baptism. Perhaps I besmirched that name made famous by his martyr's blood? I want to garnish it with my good life and suffering. Give me, Father, the grace to turn heavenward, so that I may know how to pray for my enemies. Saint Stephen, the first martyr, in my life I have brought you little glory; ask the Father of my life to insure that only glory will flow from my life onto your name, to insure that Stefan will be a liability to no one.

Thank you, Father, for the grace of baptism, priesthood, and the office of bishop, for life in the Church, for my Blessed Mother, whom you gave me to replace the mother of my body. All of this is such a great grace that for each blessing I want to offer you the highest price, even if it be paid in blood.

August 6, 1955, Saturday
Yesterday the Superintendent offered to allow newspapers to be delivered to me. I asked which ones I would be allowed to receive. I requested *Trybuna Ludu*. Today they gave me an illustrated weekly, *Stolica [Capital]*.* It is the first newspaper I have had since the moment of my isolation.

August 7, 1955, Sunday
During the usual visiting hour the Superintendent turned up in the company of a man whom he introduced as a representative of the UB, who had come to talk to me. After the Superintendent left, my unexpected visitor said that he would like to talk about the two appeals I had sent to the Council of the Ministers. He brought a response with some related proposals. He would start with the first one, the more important one, concerning changes in the conditions of my isolation.

The decree read as follows: "Return home is impossible, the decision of the Council of Ministers is irrevocable. However, the Council of Ministers is willing to relax the conditions of your confinement so that it need not be implemented as it is now in the company of these people. It, therefore, proposes that (1) you take up residence in a monastery, one mutually agreed upon, (2) you be confined there without any leave of absence, (3) you will not be allowed to attend any public functions or make any public appearances, (4) you promise not to allow any petitions or any kind of demonstrations where you will be staying or by any visitors you might receive. Such is the proposal of the Council; I now await a response."

My response required some explanations. Not two but three of my letters to the President of the Council of Ministers had gone unanswered. I wanted to know on the basis of what law I was

---

*An illustrated weekly devoted to the history and culture of Warsaw.

detained in prison. I had requested it several times and to date had not received a copy of the government decree.

The representative of the UB explained: "On the basis of the resolution of the Presidium, in agreement with a decree concerning the appointment to Church posts and removal from Church posts by the government, Article Six." He read it.

I insisted that "Article Six does not apply here; more so because it does not provide any punitive sanctions, and I am affected by punitive sanctions without having had my guilt established. The principle *audiatur et altera pars* has not been observed, and [in effect I have been condemned] in my absence. Restrictions are placed on me which are not even placed on ordinary prisoners. Every prisoner (1) knows his rights, which I still do not; (2) he knows the basis of his punishment and the term of his sentence, he knows how long he will remain in prison—which has a profound effect on one's mental health—but I have yet to know this; (3) he is able to correspond [freely]—my letters are confiscated; (4) he can visit with his family, and of this I am deprived. I want to understand my situation —that is why I tried to get a government representative to hear me out. The usual answer was 'Your request will be forwarded to the authorities.' And this is where it has ended—with no answer at all. My three letters—of July 12, 1954, of October 1954, and of February 1955—are still unanswered. You are the first representative of the authorities with whom I have been permitted to talk, and that is why I explain my position to you now, before answering to your proposal.

"I consider the behavior of the national authorities incompatible with the principles of basic justice. In the past I had the opportunity, on my own initiative, to conduct many conversations with President Bolesław Bierut and Marshal Franciszek Mazur. Also in this case, instead of a two-year wait, a half-hour conversation would have been enough. Why did the government depart from our established procedures? Even in cases where the authorities demanded the dismissal of a certain priest from his office, we always had an opportunity to learn the charges and present a defense. This was the accepted procedure. Either the diocesan chancery or the individuals involved settled the matter. Many times I instructed the accused priests to inquire about the charges against them. Explanations always led to a settlement of the matter.

In my case, no one has told me precisely what the charges were, no one asked for any explanations, no one ever sought a meeting. I was fallen upon at night and taken away, although the decree does not state that it was the government authorities who were to take me away. Why were the most elementary rights not preserved? Even criminals have a right to be presented with charges, given a defense, judges, the possibility of explanation—finally a just verdict."

My interlocutor recorded my remarks. He then said that for the present he was interested in my answers to the specific proposal at hand.

I requested some clarifications:

(1) As far as the location of my stay was concerned, could it be within one of my dioceses? Answer: "Of course not! It also cannot be in any city, only in the country, far from any heavily populated areas." I was to live with others and enjoy a homelike atmosphere, which it was said I had requested in my letter. I explained that that was not what I had asked for.

(2) If I was to be denied the right to leave the premises, it would be impossible to undertake health treatment at Krynica or Zakopane.*

(3) I did not understand how I could "prevent petitions and manifestations," since I was denied any contact with people. I could not assume an obligation "for others." He explained that I could influence those who visited me not to undertake such actions.

After these explanations the interlocutor pressed me for an answer, but I requested a few hours to think it over. We settled on three o'clock as the time I would give him my answer.

After praying, I came to the conclusion that agreeing to the new arrangement, which was supposed to mitigate my isolation, added

*Both cities lie south of Kraków in the Tatry Mountains.

up to: approval of the situation created by the decree, that is, approval of a deprivation of freedom, of home, of work; an exchange of "involuntary captivity" for "voluntary captivity"; the creation of conditions which might invite recriminations and conflicts with authorities; complications and potential unpleasantness for the monastery where I would be located; and a provocation of rumors and public scandal.

In view of these and other reasons, at three o'clock I gave the interlocutor the following answer: I could not give a response to the proposal. I considered the arrangement offered a new punishment after two years of imprisonment—during which time I was unable to commit any other "crimes"—because I would continue to be deprived of home, work, and freedom. I asked the government for justice.

The representative insisted that it was not a new punishment but a mitigation of the former one.

I replied, "By accepting it, I would be approving a punishment that I have been subjected to without having my guilt proven."

The representative stood up, "Well, then, I'll see you in a year."

"This is a threat?"

"It is not a threat."

With that he left the room. I must add that throughout the conversation he addressed me as Cardinal,* whether it was necessary or not.

I placed the whole affair in the hands of our Blessed Mother, in the spirit of the message of today's Mass (Tenth Sunday after Pentecost): *Iacta cogitatum tuum in Domino et Ipse te enutriet. De vultu tuo iudicium meum prodeat: oculi Tui videant aequitatem* [Cast thy care upon the Lord and He shall sustain thee. Let my judgment come forth from thy countenance: let thine eyes behold the things that are equitable]. It seems to me I could not act otherwise. I could not become a collaborator with the government in arranging this new

---

*The Polish usage, *Ksiądz Kardynał*, literally means "Father Cardinal"—a title recognizing full respect.

form of my imprisonment. My place, assigned by the Holy See, is the bishop's cathedral; I cannot "choose" another place of residence when it is my duty to reside by that cathedral.

I informed Father S. about my decision, and explained the reasons for it. I think in the beginning he was bewildered and did not appreciate the motives behind my refusal. He thought that even a little freedom would enable me to do some work for the Church. But after thinking it over, he agreed that I could not have given any other answer. Slowly he regained his composure, and we resumed our normal life. I spoke to Sister briefly, telling her that it was better not to talk about the matters discussed with the representative of the UB, since they were not pleasant. I asked her to trust me and pray for me.

Tenth Sunday after Pentecost. They proposed that I select a monastery in which to stay, a new mutually acceptable place, to promise not to leave the premises, to abstain from any declarations and statements, to counteract any petitions and manifestations. I declined to answer.

My place is in the cathedrals of Gniezno and Warsaw. I can discuss only that. I cannot cooperate in deliberations newly depriving me of my freedom; that would only make me a voluntary prisoner. The voluntary surrender of freedom is an expression of a citizen's moral ruin. If today I refused to defend my right to freedom, I would not be able to defend the freedom of my country if the need should arise. Only a free citizen is able to defend his freedom. A citizen oppressed in his own country cannot hope to defend it.

August 9, 1955, Tuesday
My rejection of the UB's proposal made a profound impression on the people around me. Obviously, everyone was convinced that I would eagerly accept it. The Superintendent stopped Father S. and asked him, "Well, did the Primate agree?"

Father S. expressed surprise: "Agree to what?"

"To go to a monastery."

I concluded that my "acceptance" would have been considered a political gain for the regime and perhaps even for the press. Perhaps the foreign representatives, many of whom were now in Warsaw for the festival,* would have regarded it as such, too.

In the garden they began a big project on the path. Evidently the UB representative became acquainted with the conditions in which we take our walks and recommended the construction of the path. The turf was removed from the sloping ground and replaced by gravel. This created a path which would soon be washed away by the water running from the fence and gate down the side of the hill to the ponds. All the inhabitants of the house joined in this work, in accordance with their talents and physical attributes. Even the Commandant turned over a few symbolic shovelfuls. The Old Gentleman helped the workers and kept a watchful eye on them.

A major attraction for us were the newspapers, which we continued to receive. Although after the visit of August 7, the regularity of their arrival was affected, some papers still reached us. Thus, I received *Świat, Przekrój, Stolica, Problemy,* and *Przegląd Sportowy* [*World, Cross-Section, Capital, Problems,* and *Sports Review*]. Everything was a revelation to us. It was a whole new way of writing, extraordinarily critical toward things that had been untouchable before; it was startling and provocative. How was it that today the press was allowed to discuss openly the sore spots in the Citizens' Police [MO], the National Agricultural Administration [PGR], and the bankrupt Union of Polish Youth [ZMP]? Two years ago even to think these things was dangerous. Some radical change in strategy must have occurred to allow public opinion a voice. Between the lines there were even such messages as "Do not stifle criticism." It seemed that today one could do what I had been hoping to accomplish sitting in prison for these past two years.

Was it possible that I knew the spirit of Communism better than my keepers? If the enemies of the revolution today were those who were condemning criticism, then it must mean that I had been its

*The International Youth Festival held in Warsaw in 1955.

"friend" from the beginning, and I knew better what served it best. To understand what was happening, I read those few banal publications from beginning to end, missing nothing, not even the advertisements. Because everything teaches us something and leads us to understand these new currents in Poland.

August 15, 1955, Monday

The Feast of the Assumption. "A Woman dressed in the Sun"—it is a kiss of the Book of Apocalypse for the Book of Genesis, a great-granddaughter's kiss for a great-grandmother, Omega's for Alpha. How consistent God is: He revealed hope to our forefathers in Paradise. "A Woman will crush the head of the serpent." It is she today, "dressed in the Sun!" What long-range thinking God employs, how marvelous His programming! The Lord of ages! Only humans are always in a hurry; their time is running out. God programmed it all millions of years ago. But not one of His words will be changed until it has come to pass. The Holy Spirit safeguards it, the Father of Genesis and the Apocalypse. The Word safeguarded it, so that Scripture might be fulfilled. How much joy is poured into our hearts by this power of God over the ages, His fidelity to His promises. This admirable unity of thought in God's plan is the power of God's cause on earth. So constantly we expect tests for the faith and trust we place in God. So constantly we want God to justify Himself to us: *ut iustificaris in sermonibus Tuis* [that you may be justified in Your words]. . . .

September 1, 1955, Thursday

Today's conversation between the Superintendent (Katz) and Father S. was no small event. Contrary to all prevailing customs, the Superintendent called Father S. out of his apartment and spoke to him in a most surprising way: "Father, I am leaving, and someone else will come to take my place. I was supposed to stay with you until the end, but by the first of the month I must report to my new assignment. Soon you will be released. The Primate will go home, and you will too. Because this is vacation time and the government is off we must wait. But at the end of the month the government will return from vacation and issue a resolution concerning the Primate. This has to be passed and then the Primate will return home."

Father S. maintained restraint and caution. The Superintendent noticed it. "You don't believe me, Father?"

Indeed, the priest did not believe him. "There have been so many rumors, none of them true," he answered.

"You will see for yourself soon. You will be free, we will meet again someday, and then you will see, Father, that I told the truth."

In this way the Superintendent tried to persuade Father S. of his goodwill, but the priest had been treated to lies for too long to be able to believe this "truth." This time the Superintendent did not ask that the news be kept from the Primate. He must have wanted me to hear about it right away.

Father S. was composed when he came to me and repeated the conversation with the Superintendent. We decided that for the time being this news should remain between the two of us. Our behavior should continue as if the conversation had never occurred. We would work normally, quietly, systematically, without excitement. I would write a letter home asking for books. If this conversation was to be another trick, this would let them know that we could discern such tricks. After all, having been subjected to so many daily lies, we had a right not to believe.

I must admit one thing, that since my memorable talk with the representative of the UB, everyone around us was most courteous. The Commandant did everything he could for us. He even tried his hand at small talk, expressed interest in my successes with feeding the birds. He came in full of smiles and went out to greet Father S., very satisfied. Both of us agreed on that. All the workers downstairs, starting with the Old Gentleman, were also extremely polite. We hardly saw them, they were very quiet. The checkpoint by the door was not operative. It had always been assiduously occupied before; today there was no one there—books, papers, pens had all vanished. And even the symbolic temptation of the 100 zlotys which had been ever present* was evident no more. The watchman disappeared down the corridor when he heard our footsteps. Our requests for wine, hosts, light bulbs were filled right away, whereas before we had had to wait weeks for everything.

Indeed the Superintendent did leave. The sister saw him depart with his suitcases. His place was taken by a "miserable little man" of unheroic pose and modest manners. We didn't see Aesculapius (the physician) anymore either. Our only visitor was the Commandant who visited us every day.

September 9, 1955, Friday
I handed the Commandant a letter to my father:

My dearest and special father!

I received all your letters, wishes, and parcels on the morning of August 3, 1955. I do not know how to express my gratitude for all the goodness I receive from the family. I am in a position where only paper and pen are at my disposal, and that is not enough. Nothing can express my feelings or show what is in my heart. So obviously I must convey my feelings through the best possible way, the most lasting bond —the Heart of God. Letters decompose, ink will fade, but what lives forever will always retain its freshness. We can discover one another only in prayer, and therefore I consider prayer the most valuable name day gift; I am so grateful for every Hail Mary, every part of the rosary, every Mass. Your prayers, dear Father, are my most vital support. You gave me this life and now you fear it may not prove worthy. Do I need to assure you that this is my greatest concern too? I have but one life, and must not sully it in any way. Pray for this, dear Father, because your prayer is my most precious support and the only help I ask of you. So that you would be free of fear and doubt—I pray for you, especially

---

*This was a symbol of the benefits that would accrue to anyone cooperating with the government.

at every Mass and at each third part of the rosary which I recite for your intention.

I derived great joy at the thought that you are feeling better every day: your body, accustomed to a lot of work, did its job. Now you have to try to be cheerful and full of hope. Do not be sad; it only tires you mentally and exhausts you physically. Live in the spirit of Christian hope, which always remembers that God's fatherly hands guide all human affairs. Be grateful and praise God, as the Church teaches us in the Gloria—we give you thanks, Lord, for your great Glory. Let the Psalms help you. They are full of praise for God. When a man frees himself from his small worries, how much serenity he gains for the struggle against great suffering! Take God's advice: Think of Me, and I will think of you.

Do not worry, dear Father, about what I sometimes tell Stasia of my health. I do it only to be truthful and to spare you uncertainty. I need to be home rather than in a hospital. Under these circumstances, I am doing unexpectedly well, and I am able to cope with my minor discomforts. Maintaining internal peace and not thinking about the past or the future help me very much. I read a lot and do some writing; but it is difficult because I do not have my library. I am sure that is good! As of August of this year, I received a few publications (*Stolica, Świat, Przekrój, Problemy*), so I know some of the things that are happening in the press.

I am happy, dear Father, that you are home, that Julcia and Stasia are with you, that you are not lonely, that you are so close to the chapel with the Blessed Sacrament, which you can visit from time to time. I am happy that your children are with you to give you the love you so deserve. So much to be thankful for to the Heavenly Father. Remembering this I often recite the *Te Deum*.

Let us continue in our unity of prayer, especially during Mass which I offer each morning at 7:30. I offered Mass for the happy repose of Jadwiga, whom I remember often.

There will be a Mass on the anniversary of Mama's death, but I remember her always; she helps me a great deal.

I kiss your dearest hands, beloved Father, with filial devotion and give myself in prayer. Thank you for letters—you and Juleczka. To the whole family I send words of love and blessing.

September 9, 1955
St. W.

September 14, 1955, Wednesday
"Father, forgive them. . . ." The cry from the cross is urgent. Having experienced the most painful indignity, the Holy of Holies expressed His whole relationship to His enemies and persecutors in a prayer to the Father. He remembered that He was dying for them as well. Could He deny them the fruits of Redemption? This is the example left for us by *Sacerdos in aeternum* [the Priest forever]. Can the relationship of a priest to his persecutors be any different? After all, they too must redeem themselves, they too must experience the love and grace of God. Who will make it easier for them? Since God has joined us together, enemies and priests, it might be because He wants us to pray for our persecutors. Indeed, we must follow the example of the Shepherd of Shepherds! After all, these people usually "know not what they do." They lack faith in God, they lack the ability to tell right from wrong, they do not know the Gospel, they do not know what exactly is the Church, they have completely mistaken notions about the duties and lives of priests, they are full of prejudices; perhaps they are scandalized by us, perhaps full of anger and the spirit of revenge, full of weakness and ill will. It is difficult to act human when you wear such handcuffs. They are their own slaves. They deserve sympathy!

Would my own actions be any better if I lived without faith, without the help of grace, without Christian moral principles? And even now, so richly blessed, do I not also deserve the accusation "he knows not what he does"? I have faith, I have knowledge of theology and philosophy, I was brought up as a Christian, I spent my life in the

Church, I was strengthened by the Sacraments, I was ordained a priest—and yet? Do I please God in everything? Do I not sometimes seek forgiveness, hiding behind Jesus's words: "Father, forgive me for I know not what I do. . . ." How very much more must I repeat this prayer for my enemies who truly do not know what they do!

My dearest son!

Your letter of September 9 was read to us on September 17. Many thanks. We had no letter for two months; that is a very long time. We are happy that the parcels and letters reached you in time. August 3 was a great family holiday, because on that day we commended you to God and Our Lady, praying for your health and a quick return to your duties which await you. Father Władysław celebrated a special Mass for you, which was attended by many people praying fervently for you.

For your advice, warm, meaningful, honest, and thought-provoking, I thank you very much. The encouragement you gave me to recite the hymn *Te Deum*, for example, was a reminder to me to recite it often; from now on I am going to do it every day. Until now I did not pay much attention to it. Thank you for saying part of your rosary for me. In the spirit of the dedication in my prayer book, I offer all my deeds and daily prayers for my son. As far as my health is concerned, I still feel well, but I am afraid of the approaching winter, because for the last few years my health seems to fail then. His Excellency Bishop Michał always reminds me that when the cold weather comes, I should move to Warsaw. Your beautiful sentence about enduring suffering I would like to incorporate somehow into my life. I have suffered often in the past but lately my suffering has been unusually onerous; I trust in God that with His help I will be able to survive this cross too. I was encouraged by your comments about your health, because that is our greatest concern, that in your critical condition, the Good Lord would give you this precious gift; for this we constantly pester Him.

For the Feast of Our Lady of Sorrows, I made a pilgrimage to Częstochowa; kneeling before her miraculous picture, I asked Our Lady to protect our Country, the Church, all the Clergy with you, my son, at their head, as well as the needs of our family, and my own needs. The head auxiliary bishop asked me to send you his greetings, assuring me that he remembers Your Eminence in his prayers. There were many bishops there making their retreat. A few words now about your house on Miodowa Street. The historic gazebo is covered with new shingles, the garden is well cared for, the lawns are reseeded, many new bushes were planted, beautiful roses bloom along the paths, cannas dominate the flowerbeds. The entire view is impressive. On the square in front of the palace they have added two lawns with four flowerbeds of cannas and other flowers. Both buildings, on the right and on the left, are beautifully replastered. Now the masons are plastering the part facing the street. It is obvious that the administration wants everything to be beautiful when they welcome Your Eminence. Thank you very much for the Masses offered for the soul of the late Jadwiga. Jula thanks you for the Mass for the soul of Mama. Stasia will write about other matters concerning the family.

In closing, I'd like to thank you once again for your prayers, I commend you to the protection of the Heart of Jesus and Our Lady of Częstochowa. I add heartfelt greetings and warm kisses with gratitude for your priestly blessing.

S. Wyszyński

September 25, 1955, Sunday

It is two years today since my imprisonment. During this time I came to the firm conclusion that whatever God did, He did with divinely just judgment. And therefore I end my years with the words of the *Te Deum*. . . . I praise with all my heart the Lord's justice, which was present in all that happened to me. Looking at my entire priestly life, with all its insufficiency, I grant You, Father, that You were right to take me away from your altars and pulpit. Thank you for standing in defense of Your Church, for defending it for me; for defending the sanctity of Your altars from my unworthy service, for defending Your flock from such a poor shepherd. I am Your ally in Your battle against me, Father—a very sincere ally. So wage Your battles against me, Father, I will aid You against myself. *Rectum iudicium tuum* [Your judgment is just]. . . . You are absolutely right. . . . And for that, be praised.

The days ahead I will spend in a spirit of gratitude. I will offer You all my prayers, so that I can praise the Holy Trinity with a hymn of glory. And as I praise Your justice, I cannot hide the signs of Your mercy with which You have filled these two years of my imprisonment. If I must regret something, it is only that I was not able to take full advantage of Your enormous mercy. Let me continue my life full of devotion to You—*tacere, adorare, gaudere* [to be silent, to adore, to rejoice]. Our Lady of the Rosary, I began my prison life with you. During my farewell in front of St. Anne's Church, I asked the little group of faithful for a rosary. Keep me faithful to your rosary. *Refugium peccatorum, ora* [Refuge of sinners, pray]. . . .

October 15, 1955, Saturday

The last few days were rather spirited in our Carthusian silence. First, on October 9 I received a letter from my father, my sister, Stanisława Jarosz, and four parcels with books and food. I received the books I so wanted, yet I did not know how to ask for them in my letter. Several times I had noticed that there existed a special bond of communication between my family and me, which fortunately could not be censored. In some matters, it was enough just to think of a particular thing, and it would come to pass. But there were others for which I might offer many prayers, and still they would go unanswered.

As a result of a cold, a large sore developed on my face, which I could not get rid of with the usual home remedies. I was forced to request medical treatment. This time the response was immediate. It was decided that we should go to a clinic in Opole on the evening

of October 13. We left at 11:30 at night. The treatment took place in
the clinic of the provincial office of the UB. The doctor who took
care of me came from Warsaw. There was a young woman there
who looked like a nun. The doctor was talkative, the woman full of
smiles. Our Commandant, who had accompanied me to the clinic,
was on very friendly terms with the doctor, a man full of bustling
vigor and self-importance. All the security conditions about which
I had previously written were still carefully observed. The cover of
night, the empty streets, courtyard, corridors, and staircases, all—
as before—insured security.

We made another visit the next evening between six and eight.
This time the doctor was alone, without the help of the sister,
although always in the company of the Commandant and the Old
Gentleman. Both were solicitous and polite. I even had a chance to
glance through the weekly *Świat* [*World*], lying in the waiting
room. Apparently they already knew that now I was "allowed" to
know what was being written in some magazines. This time the
doctor was more open, more able than his predecessors to add the
human touch in the administration of nationalized health and medicine. But to be cured, I had to seek help from "the system." How
strange, yet how simple it all is!

We returned at night in deep silence. My comrades at home were
waiting for my return and were genuinely happy to see that I was
back. The previous night they had stayed up until I returned. When
I scolded them for not going to bed earlier, they were surprised that
I had expected them to do so in my absence. Every time I returned
from Opole to my "monastery," every time the wire fence emerged
from the darkness of night, I would feel as if "my drawer" had once
again been shoved deep into some cavernous desk. And here again,
in silence and isolation, I had to survive, not knowing how soon the
doors would again open for me. This time once more the chauffeur
was from Warsaw, probably the same one who drove me from
Miodowa Street.

Today I drafted a reply to my father's letter of October 1,
1955.

My dearest and special father!

I want to thank you for your letter of October 1, which I received on October 9, and for everything it contained. I chose this day to answer, to let you know right now that I did remember the anniversary of Mama's death and I will offer Mass for her on October 25, another one on October 31, and a third on November 2. I am convinced that Mama is happy in heaven: God takes into account everything very carefully, takes suffering and prayers into consideration, and likes to hasten His graces. I also wanted to assure you that I remember Grandmother Katarzyna; I often remember the moment when I saw her for the last time and received from her a stern encouragement to be an exemplary priest. I remember it as the greatest of God's favors. It is significant how such moments are long remembered. I once read that we should never deny anything to anyone, when they ask us, because there will come a moment when we won't be able to forgive ourselves this refusal. This is a great truth, especially with the dead, because you can never repair the harm done, and then only prayers remain. Fortunately, prayer is a gift which you need not learn; it is enough to want to pray, and it comes. With its help it is easier to take care of all matters and duties. Through prayer it is very easy to get in touch with dear ones and be reassured of their well-being. It is also the easiest way to repay favors received. When pain and anguish overcome us, prayer helps us conquer their burden by enabling us to place everything that hurts into God's Fatherly Hands.

I am very glad, Father, that your health has improved. Do take advantage of the friendly advice of Bishop Michał and move to the city for the winter. I am very grateful to him for his solicitude for you, which I myself cannot show, even though it is my duty. But God will not leave you without friendly people; He was the first to worry about you, even before your children. I often pray for those people who show you their goodness. Autumn is here with its foul weather, which you tolerate very poorly. Take care of yourself and do not risk catching a cold. Limit unnecessary travels and trips to town.

In the September 23, 1955, issue of *Stolica*, I saw photographs of the façade of St. John's Cathedral. I was very glad to see the work started and also that they finally accepted the solution developed by Prof. Zachwatowicz.* Sometime when the weather is good, please visit the cathedral, say a prayer at the grave of the late cardinal and in the chapel of the Blessed Sacrament and, if possible, describe in your letter how the interior looks. I trust that during the last two years progress has been made. Thank you very much for the news of the work done on my home; I am a little afraid that it may look too showy compared with the surroundings. Maintaining a proper balance is a social virtue, especially now when we are rebuilding our city. There are many churches; St Florian, for instance, could use some help for its walls.

I ask Juleczka to add to your every letter a short note about her health, which I always miss. And if she added a word about Tadzik, I would be really grateful, because the thought of his health haunts me.

I was so happy that you, Dad, could be in Częstochowa and could pray in the chapel of the Virgin Mary. [letter not sent]

October 25, 1955, Tuesday
Even if I found myself in the pit of Hell before the face of Satan reigning in all his glory and inhuman power, You, Christ, would still be King of my heart—You, scourged, humiliated, and crucified. As I reflect upon this today, I look upon Your neglected Kingdom as higher than the greatest glory of the kingdom of darkness.

---

*Professor Jan Zachwatowicz was the chief architect for the reconstruction of all of Warsaw after World War II. He was responsible for directing the restoration of Saint John's Cathedral and recently of the Royal Castle in Warsaw.

If today I were to choose anew the paths of my life, I would choose from among the most magnificent gates opening before me the one that opens to the priesthood, even if at the end of that road I could see a guillotine prepared for me.

If I had the choice between owning the entire library of the British Museum and owning one missal, I would choose the missal.

If I had the hope of regaining my freedom at the cost of the slightest humiliation of the Church, I would choose a life of endless slavery.

I believe in life everlasting, in life that changes but never ends; I have a lot of time and a lot of patience.

October 26, 1955, Wednesday

To strive for inner peace. To maintain complete silence during work hours which I spend alone in my room. To increase my output of written work.

I must repeat more often to Our Father—so that He will know how submissive I am to His will—that I feel God's justice is being done to me and that I accept it with mind and will. I want to submit my heart to it, so that my feelings would be in harmony with my mind and will. I am on the side of God's justice with mind and will; I want my heart to be on the side of the just God, against myself.

To You, Christ, I give full right to my joy and pain. My priesthood, by which I participate in Your Priesthood, demands that I offer suffering in union with Yours, that I be one with You. As long as Your Church requires my suffering, I want to submit to Your will. I want to sacrifice my personal good for the good of the Church. The worse my situation, the better that of the Church. The Church protects my suffering from the virulence of God's enemies. I am the prey that distracts the wolves and gorges their throats so that they cannot devour others. I appreciate how my imprisonment impedes the hands of the Church's enemies who until now blamed everything bad on me. Perhaps *prudentia carnis* [prudence of the flesh] would ease my situation, but I will not resort to it lest I make the situation worse for the Church. Give me strength, my Teacher and Leader, to be faithful to these resolves.

October 28, 1955, Friday
At 5:30 I had a visit from the Commandant, who apologized for coming at "an unusual hour." He announced that a representative of the government had arrived from Warsaw and wanted to see me. I told him I had no objections. Soon a tall, awkward man entered my room and asked to talk with me. A paper folder was in his hands. He seated himself at the table, removed a sheet of paper from his folder, and declared that the government had decided to alter my living conditions in accordance with a decree. He proceeded to read out loud.

Office of Religious Affairs
Warsaw, 27 October 1955

Decree

I declare that the Government of the Polish People's Republic has allowed Archbishop Stefan Wyszyński to change his place of residence and to relocate to the convent of the Sisters of Nazareth in Komańcza, Province of Sanok. He will not be permitted to leave this new place of residence.

If any attempts are made to exploit contacts for actions against the government, the guilty parties will suffer the consequences.

The ban, contained in government decree No. 700 of September 24, 1955, on performing any functions related to formerly held Church positions and the ban on public appearances, is still in effect.

Director of the Office of
Religious Affairs
Marian Zygmanowski

After he finished, he asked me to consider the text carefully and respond to it. I asked him to define "place of residence." The official said that it meant the whole village of Komańcza, where I would be able to take walks. But I would not be allowed to get into a car and drive anywhere else. He added: "Please get your things together, because tomorrow morning at six a car will take you to your new place of residence." I inquired about their plans for Father Stanisław Skorodecki and Sister Leonia Graczyk, my prison companions. Both of them were ill and needed home care. The official was surprised to hear that the sister was ill too, and added, "Both of them will be released, especially since Father S.'s father has been trying to get him released for some time. The government, applying the principle of amnesty, will free most priests, many of whom received rather severe sentences. Such is our present policy."

I asked whether I might copy the decree. The official agreed. He must have sensed my doubts, because he drew another paper from his folder—a letter from Bishop Michał Klepacz, as the chairman of the Episcopal Conference, to the President. He allowed me to read it. This letter—the original—assured me that the measure was being undertaken in cooperation with the Episcopate; its goal was to remove me from the prison in which I had spent the last two years and secure better living conditions for me. The official also presented me with a list of conditions that the Episcopate had accepted for itself in exchange for my release from isolation. Both texts provided for the possibility of visits with my father, sisters, and brother, and with Bishops Klepacz and Choromański. I asked him to elaborate on the reference to "contacts" with outsiders, since I took offense at the implication that I might take advantage of these meetings to incite "actions against the government," and felt uneasy about the threat of consequences for "guilty parties." The official explained that all bishops who wished to visit me could do so. I had the feeling that others would also have free access to me.

After weighing these explanations, I did not express any valid reservations about the other limitations of my freedom. I only added that many charges had been made against me and that I was still unaware whether these are understood as "actions against the government." The official replied, "The government invited all the bishops and presented all its charges against you. Bishop Klepacz, who will visit you in the next few days, will explain everything. He will also provide additional details about your living conditions." Hearing this I decided not to voice the other doubts the new decree had awakened in me. I preferred to talk with a bishop rather than with an official with possibly slanted information. I said, "Gentlemen, you will do with me what you have decided to do, just as you have until now." I was asked to write, "I accept this information" on the decree. I wrote, "I have read the above—Stefan Cardinal Wyszyński, October 28, 1955." The official assured me that the local help would pack my things for me, and then he left the room.

I shared the news first with Father Stanisław, who was making the Way of the Cross. He was obviously very moved but in control. We decided to dispose of our household goods after dinner. We wondered what to do with our chapel. I was ready to leave everything so that Father S. could offer Mass until he was free. But the second deputy soon informed him that he would be able to go home as soon as the Commandant returned, so there was no need to leave anything behind. "What's more," he added, "this house will be evacuated, and everything must be removed." Sister Leonia received the news without surprise; we all said nothing for a long time. I remembered the words of the representative of the UB on July 7, 1955: "We'll see one another in a year."

And so this was the way that the government, without my cooperation, decreed a partial change in the extraordinary decisions that had been applied to me for two years. It was all happening without my consent. I was still merely an object of the arbitrary actions of the government. I was aware that I could not enter into any negotiations concerning the place of my residence, because my duty was to be at my cathedral and with my flock. I would feel free only when I could return to Miodowa Street. I could not consider the new arrangement as presenting me with the opportunity to return to work nor as any redress of the injustice that had been done. The violation of canonical jurisdiction still obtained.

After supper we conducted our last common service. We concluded our novena to Christ the King. We acknowledged the graciousness of our Heavenly Father, who gave us a sign of His goodness precisely in showing us His power over us in the course of this novena. Moreover, we were able to say that truly "never was it known" that anyone who turns to Our Lady is not heard. For a long time we were sustained by our prayers to Our Lady of Częstochowa, Our Lady of Perpetual Help. Nothing calms a person's heart like prayer through Mary. How many Masses we offered to return to the duties of our vocation! Sometimes it seemed that our prayers were not heard, but they always left their mark on our souls, and we were never bereft of hope and peace. Our prayers during the past year here in Prudnik were more thanksgiving than petition. We now know that prayers of praise bring greater joy and strength than prayers of petition.

We made a pact with Our Lady, requesting that the grace we awaited would fall on a Saturday or in the month of May. We were prepared to stay in prison even longer, just so that God's mercy on us would devolve to the glory of Mary. God showed His special goodness, because our first day of freedom would fall not only in the month of the Holy Rosary, but on the day of *Sanctae Mariae in Sabbato*, which is actually tomorrow.

October 28, 1955, Friday
With your rosary in my hand, I await, O Mary, the feast of your Royal Son. Help me to prepare my heart, will, and thoughts. All that I have comes from you; I desire that the homage proper to a King should pass through you to the throne of my King.

(1) When I see the suffering at Gethsemane, I am amazed at the obedience of the Royal Power to the Father. But there is no kingdom without obedience. I want to be obedient so that I may praise the King.
(2) Monarchs don magnificent coronation robes. Your Son, Mary, cloaked Himself in His own blood. His scourged shoulders were His most precious ornament. With reverence I kneel on the floor of the praetorium, to pay homage to the tatters of his royal robe of Blood, drawn from You— as if I impressed my lips onto the chalice of the Mass.

(3) What a singular crown of thorns draws blood from the forehead of this King. All other crowns draw blood from subjects. Only Your Son spares them. But He does not spare Himself. And yet a fragment of one thorn from this crown is more precious to me than all the crowns of the world.

(4) What king was followed by such crowds carrying their crosses? People follow kings, but triumphant ones. Only You, Christ, are followed by crowds prepared for pain. How numerous are the ranks of Your cross-bearing faithful!

(5) You transformed the gallows into a throne. We see thrones decorated with gold and precious stones. Kings know their worth, and so they add something to increase their value. Only You, Christ, discarded everything. You alone are the highest value of the naked Wood of the Cross. This was the Throne that became the glory of the world.

V  KOMAŃCZA

October 29, 1955, Saturday

Prudnik Śląski–Komańcza. A Mass of Thanksgiving to Our Lady
of Częstochowa at 4:30 and a second to Our Lady of Perpetual Help
were our last opportunities for prayer in common. Two years in the
lives of three people had been spent in prayer. Although we were
victims of coercion, we were able to create a true Christian community, free from internal coercion, full of peace and serene harmony.
This period of time passed with unusual speed. The daily schedule
never changed and was maintained with greater than monastic pre-
cision.

A.M.

5:00	Rising
5:30	*Prime* and morning prayers
5:45	Meditation (I would usually suggest themes based on the liturgical year)
6:15	*Angelus Domini.* Preparation for Mass
6:30	The first Holy Mass, on occasion a High Mass with Gregorian chants, especially during Advent and on more important feasts

7:15	The second Mass. Thanksgiving
8:15	Breakfast
8:45	Breviary, one part of the rosary (often in the garden)
9:15	Work on a book
11:15	Visits of the administration

P.M.

1:00	Dinner. *Adoratio Sanctissimi* [Adoration of the Blessed Sacrament]
1:30	Walk and free time
3:00	Vespers and a part of the rosary, usually during walks
3:30	Work on a book
5:15	*Matutinum cum Laudibus* (Matins and Lauds)
7:00	Supper. Readings in German
8:00	Rosary in the chapel and evening prayers. Singing of religious hymns
8:45	Work, reading, retiring

This daily program would change on Sundays and holidays; in the afternoons at 3:00, we would gather for coffee and reading. These meetings touched on many subjects: Mariological lectures, history of religious art, reading (*The Story of a Soul*, Ricciotti, Sienkiewicz, Parnicki, Church history, K. Michalski). During Christmas we would sing carols for hours; we also studied Gregorian chant.

For Christmas we would prepare Christmas Eve *Wigilia*,* with the Christmas wafer, mushrooms, and even a Christmas tree. At midnight we would celebrate Midnight Mass. During Holy Week we held services, which had to be modified because of the lack of

---

*Polish tradition calls for a special Christmas Eve meatless supper, consisting of an odd number of courses and begun after the youngest child sights the first star in the sky. Before supper begins, the Christmas wafer is shared.

ministers. Sometimes Father S. and I sang *Matutinum cum Laudibus*. We accepted as a rule to do everything within our power not to depart from the life of the Holy Church, to keep in closest contact with the public prayer of the Church beginning with morning meditation and continuing through evening prayers. This heightened awareness brought great variety into our lives and enriched our prayers.

We left at six o'clock; our route led us through Katowice, Kraków, Tarnów, Jasło, Sanok.* One of the two Warszawas† was occupied by a gentleman unknown to me. He was an imperious man who exercised his authority over the driver of his car. My companion was the Commandant, who had been with me for two years. He behaved very politely, even tried to maintain a conversation, and seemed enthusiastic about the Stalinogrodzka cathedral,‡ which was to be consecrated that Sunday. We stopped only once, for a quick "visit to the woods," where all the requirements of security and caution were observed.

We arrived at Komańcza at 3:30. A woman ran out of the house to greet us, who—we later learned—had appeared only that morning to tell the sisters about my arrival and to prepare the apartment. Everything was being done at the last moment. The sisters were surprised by the announcement of my arrival and were visibly confused. We waited for quite a while in the corridor before someone appeared. I sensed that they must have been told quite a bit to cause them to lose their usual convent composure over a visiting bishop. The two-person Warsaw delegation—a man and a woman—had arrived that morning and was busy with the details of my future residence in Komańcza. Finally, a sister did emerge; she greeted me and left without saying a word. A few more minutes passed; my companion was impatient and upset. At last, two sisters appeared,

---

*A route leading from west to east and then south.
†A Polish make of automobile.
‡During the time of Stalin the Polish city of Katowice was renamed Stalinogrod. The reference is to the cathedral in Katowice.

The house of the Sisters of Nazareth in Komańcza. This was the fourth and last place of Wyszyński's internment. It was his Golden Cage, where those with special passes were permitted to visit.

one of them the superior of the convent, whom I had not met before. Together they took me upstairs to a large room, where I was finally left alone. And so here I was, finally, in a convent, as the government bulletins had proclaimed I had been for the past two years. This time, their convent was a reality: a large building with a normal convent life, with real nuns—not prisoners—who lived their own monastic lives.

I learned from the sisters that only this morning two people in a Warszawa had appeared in front of their house, telling them about my arrival. They both examined the house carefully, chose a room on the second floor, and issued orders that it be prepared for me. They also insisted on making arrangements for a chapel, stubbornly maintaining that "the cardinal must have his own chapel." They must have read the Code of Canon Law rather carelessly. The sisters were still so unnerved by what had befallen them that a normal dialogue was very difficult. My escorts proceeded to prepare for supper and rest. My suitcases and boxes of books were brought in. All of the men were polite. From the Prudnik contingent there were the Commandant (Colonel), his deputy, so-called Mo-Mo, and a helper whom I did not know. In the truck there were several more men from Prudnik, but I did not recognize them.

At five o'clock a stranger entered my room and declared in an officious voice: "From this moment on, our protection over Your Eminence ends and is transferred to the Episcopate of Poland." He also asked whether I had any other requests. I requested an explanation of what "Komańcza" meant, so that I could know the limits of my freedom of movement. From his hesitant answer I deduced that I could walk in any direction, through woods and over mountains, but I could not get into a car and drive away. I attempted a joke: "You could not take me out any farther?"*

---

*Except for his brief stay at Rywałd, all the cardinal's places of confinement were at the nation's extremities—Stoczek in the far north, Prudnik and Komańcza in the far south. Komańcza, in fact, is located at the very farthest southeast corner of Poland, and in his joke the cardinal is apparently teasing his jailers to the effect that they have stashed him away as far from Warsaw as they could get without actually crossing a border.

"Oh, yes," answered the escort. "We could go to the province of Przemyśl."

"As far as I know, Przemyśl lies to the north of here." I also inquired what I should do in the event I became ill or needed medical or dental attention.

"In that case," came the answer, "you should contact Bishop Klepacz." I understood that from now on my life depended on the bishops, so I asked no further questions.

A curt and authoritative good-bye indicated that the man had fulfilled his mission. My answer was equally brief: "Good-bye, Sir!" From that moment I felt free from police-controlled isolation. What form it would take now only the future would reveal. I was inclined to think that this was not the end, that my status as a prisoner still existed. But it would take patience to discern it. All of this was so new and different from my previous living conditions that it was a great relief, which must be regarded as a favor undoubtedly from God.

I would put it this way: For two years the three of us had prayed for divine intervention, granting us the right to return to the work to which we had been called. For the past year we had especially prayed that the grace of freedom would come to us on a Saturday or in a month dedicated to the Blessed Mother. The Good Father in His sensitivity had given us a sign that our prayers were dear to Him, since He released us not only during the month of the Holy Rosary, but also on the day of the *Officium Sanctae Mariae in Sabbato.* * Furthermore, the Good Father chose to have it fall on the eve of the feast of Christ the King. It is impossible not to think that God, our King, tipped the scepter of His power to claim a favor for His children. These signs of grace tell us to have faith that what was begun will come to its conclusion by the power of God. Once more I want to express my readiness for anything. With total peace I trust the wisdom and goodness of God. Will He lead me from here to my orphaned cathedrals, or will He demand new renunciations and

---

*On a Saturday for which no specific saint's feast is designated, the priest recites the *Officium* (the Office—the prayers) in honor of Mary.

sacrifices? I know that He will do all for His greater glory and that of the Church of His beloved Son.

October 30, 1955, Sunday
The Feast of Christ the King. I celebrated Mass at a normal altar, with a real altar stone, among normal people freely singing hymns. I give thanks to God for everything that has happened and express my readiness to accept everything that will come to pass. Because I am not allowed any public appearances, I heard High Mass* from a small choir loft. I was happy at the sight of God's people praying, who came for the service in rather large numbers. The local parish priest celebrated the Mass. I considered it a great favor to participate, even in this form, in our collective homage to the King of Ages, the Immortal and Invisible God. . . .

I want to review my year in Prudnik. Although the conditions had not really changed, the atmosphere of Prudnik had been different from that of Stoczek. It was possible that this impression flowed from a growing familiarity with the UB people and their methods. After all, the Security Police are a new type of person not encountered in normal life; you have to get to know them and get accustomed to many things. This adjustment made it easier to accept the style of those UB men. And yet, even admitting that we had become accustomed to having these people around, everything was still not clear to us.

As to their relationship with me, I must admit that the only things that encouraged any communication at all were my tendency to tell the truth and my attempts to change the minds of those inclined otherwise. Our exchanges were actually monologues on my part, listened to with composure (except the incident with Katz), and with much effort to avoid any polemics. If it had not been for my personal initiative, I could have remained silent all year, been asked about nothing aside from the ritual associated with the daily visits. My "friends" sentenced me to complete isolation from everything,

---

*The Polish *suma* is the principal Sunday High Mass with full choir, many parts of the Mass sung or chanted, and some additional rituals.

even from the simplest, most casual forms of courtesy. I was convinced of all this when, beginning in March of this year, I had decided to be silent after they had ignored my request to see my sick father. From March on, there had been absolute silence between us, so that one of the men was moved to tell Father S.: "Too bad that both sides are so stubborn." In spite of this official silence, the occasional exchange of pleasantries at other levels grew more natural.

The guards downstairs did not avoid us; the Old Gentleman, in particular, volunteered remarks on such topics as the weather, health, aging, and his artistic successes. We knew that he sometimes arranged little exhibitions for us, displayed his jigsaw works on a table, put out his paintings, hoping to catch our attention and start a conversation. It seemed to me that he was becoming more human and natural. It certainly became him more. Aesculapius did not change at all; for him a person was still a form to be completed, something hardly to be noticed, something to be left behind as quickly as possible. On the other hand, the Commandant became more pleasant every day, especially during the spring months of this year. We also noticed some changes at the checkpoint, the guards' table. Then, in May, the guards at the table disappeared entirely. We saw no one there at all; if there was anyone downstairs, he would withdraw to the end of the corridor when he heard us descending the stairs to the garden. The table was abandoned and empty. No longer did we see flowers, ashtrays, or white tablecloths reminiscent of a girls' boarding school. Even the chair disappeared. It gave the impression that supervision had been relaxed. We also did not see anyone at the window watching our every step in the garden. There was no manipulation of the drapes. Official interest in us had diminished. Our guards more and more often were bored and did not hide it. Almost everyone allowed himself to smile and to move with a certain kind of freedom and natural courtesy.

Father S. had a more varied life this year. He was often ill; he had problems with his teeth, kidneys, pancreas, liver, joints; he spent several weeks in bed with lumbago, had a very bad cold, and constantly complained of rheumatism. Finally, just before Easter, he spent two weeks at a clinic in Wrocław. He obtained medical care with great effort, only after delays and reminders. It seems that many of these frequent and legitimate illnesses of Father S. were met with skepticism. They thought that he himself had carelessly brought some of his illnesses on himself. The sister could have unwittingly added fuel to these opinions. Father S. was treated politely but rather casually, although he himself tried to be very courteous. He was often off the premises, mainly to see doctors or to see his father. For some time his visits to his father, usually in Rawicz, in prison, were curtailed; we had the feeling that this was a punishment. They tried to force Father S. to make all kinds of statements about me. He always used the defense that he was my confessor. It always worked, although they tried to point out to him that they were not interested in my conscience. Here, for understandable reasons, I won't go into details.

The sister was rather cheerful in Prudnik, and I came to the conclusion that the troubles she went through in Stoczek were not a problem here. She was more reticent with me this year than she had been the year before. She spent more time in the kitchen, where there were very loud conversations and laughter with the housekeeper and the management, who visited there most willingly. Because my room was right over the kitchen, I could not help hearing all these noises. I often reminded Sister not to waste her time in conversation and encouraged her to study and read. But this was difficult for her; she always found odd jobs to keep her occupied, and as a result, the books lay idle. The more diligently Father S. worked on his book, the less Sister worked. She became enthusiastic about the Old Testament and later was interested in the history of the Church, but she wasted much time on novels. She gave herself wholeheartedly to housework; she washed clothes again and again because our wardrobe was limited, did general cleaning, waxed floors and long corridors, and often had to cook when the housekeeper went to Warsaw. In the last months of our time together, Sister became more serious; we would find her in the chapel absorbed in private adoration. Her lively disposition often caused her to speak out boldly, in spite of herself, on our conditions and their shortcomings. She would often ask about my health, and I would avoid answering, fearing that through her impulsiveness it would go further. When, through her hard work, she wore out her habit, they brought her material so that she could sew herself a new one. At first she became indignant, but later she sewed the habit and wore it. At that time I received a new cassock from home, which I had not requested. Maybe this happened at the initiative of the sister, who thought that my old worn-out cassock with its ragged sleeves contrasted too much with her new habit.

On several occasions she tried to find out where I would most like to be; afraid to say anything, I remained silent. One day she said to me, "Your Eminence would probably feel best on the French Riviera in the sun." When she repeated this some weeks later, I was disturbed. "Sister," I said decisively, "please remember that if there is no other place for me in my country, I prefer a Polish prison to any place abroad." She was surprised. I added, "The place for a Polish bishop is either at his cathedral or in prison, not abroad." She tried several times to persuade me to write to the government and ask them to free me. Eventually she gave up. Knowing the tactics of the UB, I am sure that they tried to manipulate her for their own backstage intelligence. I am also certain that she did not let herself be used. She was capable, however, through sheer vivacity and impulsiveness, of unknowingly giving away valuable information to anyone interested. But one could not accuse her of ill will. Maybe she even believed that she was helping me; and, after all, what news could she give to people who already were thoroughly informed about my life? More than once during conferences at the Belweder and Wilanów* palaces, I had given them my opinions. They knew how I felt and what they could not count on.

Were Father S. and Sister recruited by the UB with the hope that they would be "useful"? I doubt it very much. Maybe some of the functionaries, like Mr. Nazi, may have counted on using them; but the Superintendent certainly did not—unless their roles were meant to be completely different. Mr. Nazi was far too simple in his behav-

---

*Residence for foreign dignitaries six miles from downtown Warsaw.

ior to be considered by his superiors as an instrument for intelligence. This simpleton immediately poured out whatever bothered him. His deputy, Katz, had no such official duties; his only responsibility was to drive Father S. around to various offices. I am certain that the UB, if they ever counted on my companions, had to have been very disappointed in them. I emphasize this because I want to protect my companions from any suspicions of those who might try to guess why they were chosen to be with me. I had the opportunity to get to know both of them well enough to be convinced of their moral integrity. Here I also want to emphasize that Father S.'s spiritual life far surpassed even a very good one. He was a man of fervent faith, somewhat emotional in prayer, who loved the Church and was dedicated to it completely. He devoured books on theology, especially in the field of Church history. He had his own apostolic and missionary ideals. Perhaps his only distraction was a love of sports. He had a very strong vocation to the priesthood, which he loved with all his soul. He was not interested in politics and knew little about it. His natural inclination in a conversation was to speak on Church subjects; our conversations were always limited to these.

Our work in Prudnik, which started in Stoczek, took on great intensity. Neither of us had time for idle talk and social loafing. Despite a very modest collection of books, we were able to begin a program of systematic studies. Father S. studied Church history, reviewed his theology, began to write various liturgical articles, a small manual for altar boys, sermons. He took up the study of Italian most enthusiastically. We carried on conversations in Latin and Italian during our meals and walks. In the evening we read in German from an old geography textbook that was a thousand pages long.

I continued to write my Liturgical Sketches and the Letter to Those I Have Ordained. This Letter grew and eventually became a full-length book. I managed to finish the first draft of the Liturgical Sketches for the whole Church year, both for *Proprium de Tempore* as well as for *Proprium Sanctorum*. In this way I filled about three thousand 4×6 slips of paper and wrote first drafts for about eight hundred sketches. The first part of the Letter was completely finished; the second part was almost completed, as was the third part. Still unedited was the fourth part. I returned to a subject I had started before World War II in Włocławek: "The Sanctification of Our Present Life." This work never went beyond my gathering notes and excerpting from books. On Saturdays I worked on meditations on the Litany of Loretto.* I also produced many short outlines for sermons and conferences. I worked through the whole Bible once more, and I read many French books, among them the two volumes of *Maria*, which I read twice. As in Stoczek, I carefully followed the order of the day, moving from one activity to the next, from one book to another, with no interruptions. I asked my companions not to visit me between 9:00 and 1:00 and between 3:00 and 6:00. The order changed only on Sundays and holy days. As a result time passed very quickly so that I did not dwell on the past; I was free of doldrums and did not long for another kind of life. I managed to get accustomed to prison. This is no exaggeration. Given such a life, the appearance in Prudnik of a new representative of the government came as a surprise, since we had already psychologically prepared ourselves to spend a third winter in prison.

There was less possibility for physical work in the garden than in Stoczek. Here the garden was small and overgrown with weeds; there were no tools and little space. We took care of the grapevines on the wall, which were protected for the winter. But the results of this work were meager, because during the summer all the grapes dried out, destroyed by a white fungus. We were unable to grow flowers, because there were so many weeds, and we had no seeds. Our only joy was the bed of lilies, which grew out of the ground and bloomed luxuriously. We hoed the paths by the vineyard, but even here we were overcome by weeds. We built a gazebo under the shed but did not use it often because it had been a dismal summer, cold and rainy. We had very little sunshine in the garden or in our rooms. Our social life was a bit sour too; it picked up in

---

*A litany of titles of Mary.

the fall when there was fruit in the garden. Then even our "gentle-men" came out to the garden and noticed the trees, which were collapsing one after another for lack of care. Our example even encouraged these materialists to prop up the plum trees, heavily laden with fruit. Although the sister and the housekeeper mentioned it, no one tended the strawberries or grew any flowers. Whatever came up by itself grew and disappeared.

Only in Komańcza did I learn that Bishop Antoni Baraniak is in prison. There are even some who had seen him there in very ill health. Supposedly he is in the prison hospital for a year. They say that he is holding up bravely despite illness and exhaustion. The bishop had never been in very good health, although he never said anything about it. He was always noticeably pale. In general, Bishop Antoni did not like to talk about himself, and when asked directly about his health, he would exhaust the subject in one sentence and turn to pressing matters. It cannot be said that he did not take care of himself, but he managed to do so without involving others.

One can imagine what he must have gone through in the prison hospital. The people who first told me about Bishop Antoni saw him from a distance in the Mokotów prison* while he was taking a walk. He wore his cassock, walked alone, was pale but composed. In Mokotów the opinions about him were the best; they all knew that Bishop Baraniak was taking it very bravely and was comporting himself with dignity in the face of his interrogators. It was common knowledge that the bishop had been under indictment, that this period of indictment had been long and difficult, and that the bishop had not implicated anyone. They said that he was a good influence on his fellow prisoners, cheered them up, and impressed them with his priestly bearing and optimism: "He is in total command of himself" . . . "he amazes us with his spiritual strength," even though he was so weak that all his fellow prisoners feared for him.

---

*In Warsaw.

In Mokotów they frequently compared the bearing of the two bishops, Baraniak and Kaczmarek. The prisoners were very friendly to both of them. When they did Bishop Kaczmarek's laundry, the women prisoners would try to do as good a job as possible, "because it is for the prisoner-bishop." This continued until the trial. These same women prisoners were deeply hurt by what was "revealed" at the trial.* They openly expressed their antagonism toward the "traitor bishop." But others did not believe the accusations. They continued to be on his side. In this atmosphere of prison rumors and gossip, the personage of Bishop Baraniak rose to the level of a symbol. So much for introductory information about Bishop Antoni.

Now I can relate this information to the behavior of the security people who tried to lead me astray about Bishop Baraniak's fate. On Miodowa Street, when they had asked me, "Who is the head here?" I answered, "I do not know whom you are taking. The head during my absence is Bishop Baraniak." They did nothing then to reveal what their plans were for Bishop Baraniak. When I gave the bishop my statement, the men present did nothing to try to correct my assumption that the bishop would remain on Miodowa Street. When a few days later, while I was already in Rywałd (October 10, 1953), the question of the checks and paying the construction workers arose, I again asked directly about Bishop Baraniak, who was authorized to sign checks. Then the man from the UB, when asked directly whether Bishop Baraniak was at home, answered me, "We left Bishop Baraniak on Miodowa Street." He either lied outright or used a mental ploy: "*We* left him—what others did with him was their business."

Still, I continued to wonder what had happened to the bishop. My doubts were reinforced by the fact that it was not the bishop but Father Goździewicz who drafted the first list of things sent to me from Miodowa to Rywałd. The bishop, so careful and sensitive,

---

*He was accused of betraying Poland to a foreign power. In December 1956, he was fully exonerated, and this was announced in all the media.

would certainly have done this himself if he had remained at home.

During the two years of my isolation, the fate of Bishop Baraniak remained a mystery. There was not the slightest attempt—in letters or things sent to me—to let me know that the bishop was not at home. When in subsequent packages I received Tolstoy's *War and Peace* from the private library of Bishop Baraniak, it surprised me to see that the books were identified by Father Hieronim with the initials "A.B.," the bishop's usual way, but in the handwriting of Father Goździewicz. This sign virtually changed my doubts into certainty that the bishop was not at home. With his attention to detail, the bishop could not have given the books to Father Hieronim to initial. He would have done it himself.

Only today I also learned that after I was taken from Miodowa Street, they searched the house and confiscated a lot of things. For the time being, they were not able to give me closer details except that the search continued through the night and all day Saturday, and that it was only toward evening that the cars, filled with files, departed from the courtyard of the archbishop's residence. This fact adds to the gravity of their lawless behavior on Miodowa. Government officials are obliged to follow the rules of the Constitution (Article 17) and the Penal Code when conducting a search. The officials knew that they were to carry out a search, so they were obliged to act in accordance with Article 136, Paragraph 2, which clearly states: "The person in whose house the search is to be conducted must be informed of the purpose of the search and is summoned to be present during the search." In defiance of this regulation, first they took away the owner of the house and then proceeded to search it. To the long list of violations which I had been protesting now was added a whole new string of them of which I had not been aware. This typified the behavior of the authorities most eloquently.

I must work out for myself a detailed picture of the legal powers within which the representatives of the UB acted. I must also be fully aware of the provisions of the Constitution and the Code [of Canon Law] that were involved here, in order to judge the behavior of people fairly, since the government believed that it acted within the limits of the law. What law was it thinking about —the Constitution, or some authorizations that are unknown to me, or which it ascribed to itself by virtue of its own decrees? One should not accept a priori that the government wanted to ignore the provisions of the Constitution, which is the fruit of the human mind. Could it have had so little respect for it? I would try hard to understand this.

October 31, 1955, Monday

I received a telegram from Bishop Klepacz: "I will come with Zygmunt* and your father for a private visit, Wednesday, November 2 about 3:00 P.M.—Bishop Klepacz." Yesterday I sent a letter to Bishop Barda, informing him that I was currently within the limits of his diocese. The text of this letter:

> His Excellency Bishop Fr. Barda
> Przemyśl
> The Chancery Office
>
> Your Excellency, Venerable Host Bishop!
>
> I consider it my duty to inform you that last Saturday at 3:30 P.M. I was moved by the Security Authorities of the Polish People's Republic from my former place of enforced isolation in Prudnik Śląski koło Nysy and placed in the house of the Sisters of Nazareth in Komańcza. Since I am not allowed to leave the new place of my enforced stay, I cannot personally ask Your Excellency, as the local ordinary, for your kind indulgence toward me so long as I have to stay here. The sisters received me kindly even though I am a very unexpected guest. I am comfortable here. I commend myself to Your Excellency's kindness and your pray-

---

*Bishop Zygmunt Choromański.

ers—with respect and brotherly devotion *in Christo Rege* [in Christ the King].

Komańcza koło Sanoka, October 30, 1955
+ Stefan Cardinal Wyszyński

I also considered it my duty to send a letter to Bishop Klepacz, to Bishop Choromański, and to my loved ones—my father and my sister, Stanisława Jarosz, who have suffered the most anguish and humiliation during my imprisonment. May these letters be witness to my feelings and be included in these memoirs.

His Excellency Bishop Michał Klepacz
Warsaw
17 Miodowa Street

Your Excellency, Beloved Bishop!
  I hasten to inform you that on the basis of an order of the government of the Polish People's Republic dated October 27, 1955, of which I was informed in Prudnik Śląski koło Nysy on October 28, at 5:30 P.M., I was moved by the Security Authorities the following day to Komańcza koło Sanoka and located in the house of the Sisters of Nazareth. The head of the transport group informed me that "the care of the Security Authorities ends here and what follows is up to the Polish Episcopate." I am not allowed to leave my new residence. Also remaining in effect is the "ban on performing any functions related to formerly held church positions and the ban on public appearances." As I discovered from the letter shown to me from Your Excellency to the Premier, I owe the improvement in my living conditions to the intercession of Your Excellency and the Polish Episcopate. I wish to thank you most sincerely for this fraternal interest in my fate shown by you and all the members of the Polish Episcopate. I commend myself most fervently to Your Ex-

cellency's prayers, with deep respect, gratitude and devotion *in Christo Rege.*

Komańcza koło Sanoka, October 30, 1955
+ S.W.

His Excellency Bishop Z. Choromański
Warsaw

Your Excellency, Most Beloved Bishop!

The news of my release from prison will come somewhat belatedly to you, but I cannot deny myself the joy of hastening to thank you for the defense undertaken on my behalf before the State authorities and the efforts made to change my living conditions. I have learned from a letter shown to me by a representative of the Security Committee from Bishop Klepacz to the government that the bishops have reserved the right to visit me. I hope that I will soon see Your Excellency in Komańcza, but I realize how fatiguing and troublesome such a long journey would be. For the time being, please accept these few words of my gratitude, brotherly devotion, and deep respect *in Christo Rege.*

Komańcza, October 30, 1955
+ S.W.

Mr. Stanisław Wyszyński
Zalesie koło Piaseczna

My dearest father!

You probably already know that the government authorities have released me from police-supervised isolation in prison and placed me in the house of the Sisters of Nazareth in Komańcza. I am not allowed to leave this place or to fulfill any functions related to my pastoral duties. Thus my living conditions have improved somewhat, but what is most important to me continues to be a source of great trial. Before, I could not write you what was in my heart; I do not know whether what I did write was understood in the sense in which I meant it. But I do want you to know that everything I did had for its purpose to represent the Church with dignity, even in prison, and to fulfill God's will as it is expressed wherever one finds himself. And there is but one fundamental obligation of a Catholic bishop, whether he is at a pontifical celebration, in the pulpit, or in prison—*nos Tibi semper et ubique gratias agere, Domine Sancte, Pater* [that we should at all times and in all places give thanks unto thee, O Holy Lord, Father]. Father, always and everywhere to give Thee thanks, Holy Lord. I was of the opinion that my stay in prison had to serve as an expression of truth and gratitude. The first could have aggravated my situation, but was absolutely necessary for the good of the Church and for its glory; although I had to keep silent, it was within God's power to speak for me. And it is in the nature of suffering that through it God speaks more eloquently to every conscience than through the best sermon. I was and remain assured that my situation will not bring harm to the Church, but rather a benefit that can only be wrought by the Holy Spirit who rules the Church in everything. The suffering of people, as an eminent way to help the Church, is so integrated with the Church's History that it can almost be called the Eighth Sacrament, drawing its power from the Sacrament of Christ's Agony on Calvary. Could I refuse Christ the right to call upon my suffering for help, since He considered it necessary for the good of the Church? Finally, the essence of Christ's priesthood is expressed in sacrifice, and all His servants are called not only to sacrifice Christ's Body but to give themselves for the Church, as Christ gave Himself for mankind.

We must be happy, then, dear Father, that it was given to us to suffer abuse for Christ's Name. I expect that I will see you soon, although I fear such a long trip for you. But I have no right to prevent you from it. I trust that we won't cry because we should not appear sad before our Heavenly Father, where there is only happiness and glory. You shared in my suffering, felt it deeply, but I know that you do not regret anything, since everything that God's wisdom and goodness does is love and wisdom itself. I thank you, dear Father, with all my heart, that you put your faith to good use, that you continued to love and trust in God, that you did not cease in prayer that helped me so much.

We both owe a special debt of gratitude to Our Lady. In our prison chapel, we always prayed that the grace of freedom should come on a Saturday or during the month of Mary. We were even ready to remain longer behind bars to have this clear proof of the power of the Universal Mother —this sign of her grace. And God took this childlike plea into account, allowing me to leave the prison walls on a Saturday, during the month of the Holy Rosary. I asked the faithful in the church of St. Anne to pray the rosary for me. I reminded a group of young people who stopped me in the church corridor of a detail in the fresco of the "Last Judgment," when an Angel of God draws a soul out of the depths by a rosary. Apparently my beloved youth of Warsaw took this request to heart, since it was just at the end of October, on the eve of the feast of the Victorious King of the Ages, I experienced new personal freedom.

Certainly, this is not all. There remain my orphaned cathedrals, the clergy, and the people of God. I do not cease to trust that God Himself will bring this work to a conclusion. Let us never cease to trust and be thankful. Since during our imprisonment our most beautiful prayer was the *Te Deum*, let us continue in it.

Please accept, my dearest Father, these few words of filial encouragement, which I intend only for you, since they most appropriately belong to you. I kiss your hands with respect and love, commend you to the Sacred Heart of Jesus, to Our Lady of Jasna Góra, and I bless you through the powers granted me as a bishop.

Komańcza, the feast of Christ the King, 1955
+ Stefan Cardinal Wyszyński
Primate of Poland

On the forty-fifth anniversary of the death of my mother, looking at her hands, I thank You, Father—Giver of Life—for the dear arms in which I came to know Your special providence and goodness. With their help you carried me in my infant helplessness. These Hands kept me from falling, these Fingers wiped my tears, gave me to eat, served me in every need. May Your Fatherly Arms be honored in the hands of my mother. May she stand before Your Throne today and be my advocate. So many times in life she commended me to You, Father. You know the agony of mothers in this world because You announced it to Eve. Today reward this agony undertaken to fulfill Your Fatherly plan—to share life. Once again, let my mother speak to You, Father, about the fruit of her womb.

November 1, 1955
I rejoiced at the sight of the people praying today in the chapel of the Sisters of Nazareth. The Church praying in common has its value for the individual; it comes to the Father of mankind more readily when brought by people praying as one. Seeing others praying helps us to pray, makes it easier for us to find our way to God. People praying as one are drawn together more closely and intimately, and a community of love is born.

Recalling the last two years, I could see clearly how important for my spiritual equilibrium and internal peace were the letters of my younger sister, Stanisława. God endowed her with unusual equanimity and womanly wisdom, with a generous dose of courage and strong faith. All of these qualities radiated from her letters. She must have gone through a lot of trouble to send me letters and packages. I do not know how it was exactly, but I can well imagine that she did it at considerable personal risk and maybe even with considerable humiliation. As I pondered this, I thanked God for the benevolence He revealed through the people whom He has bound to me with ties of blood and faith. Let these few words that I have written to my sister bear witness to my gratitude.

Mrs. Stanisława Jarosz
Zalesie koło Piaseczna

My dearest sister!

You will receive this letter after having heard the good news; but to this favor that God has granted you as a reward for your kindness and courage, I would like to add a few words of fraternal gratitude that I feel I owe you. Now that our hopes have been realized, at least in part, it is the proper time to acknowledge that I saw in you the courageous woman of our family. You filled this role admirably; the letters you wrote me during the two years of my isolation were an expression of your valor, composure, trust, and living faith, which always bear fruit. I am so grateful to you for this attitude, worthy of the sister of a persecuted man and a Primate. God demanded a great deal of me, but He had every right to do it. From whom could He make demands if not His chosen servants? What tremendous demands He made of His Only Begotten Son. Could He not expect cooperation from His adopted sons? All the more so since He did it with justice and Fatherly love. I have received so many favors in my life from God and His Church. I owe my advancement in the Church, so undeserved, solely to the mercy and grace of God. Such great favors must be paid for with something. Today I feel much more honest before God, who has demanded the compensation of suffering, fidelity, and trust for His bountiful graces. I emerged from behind the barbed wire tremendously enriched. Such are the mysteries of God. Let us praise together the inexpressible goodness of God. Please accept, my dearest Stachna, words of my fraternal gratitude for all the kindness you have shown me and, in my absence, our dear father, for whom you acted as guardian and support. With all my heart I bless you, your husband, your household, and all your works.

Komańcza, November 11, 1955
+ Stefan Cardinal Wyszyński

I am beginning to enter the wide world of my new life. I enjoy my first leisurely steps during a walk. My Prudnik cage has been enlarged to a beautiful forest, in which I may stroll freely. The habit I acquired in prison forces me to study the trees closely to make sure that they are in fact—surprisingly—on this side of the invisible fence; I see no barbed wire, nor do I feel the great ear, which used to listen with all its being: behind the fence, the hedge, the gate, and perhaps even by mechanical devices. There is none of that here. But I prefer to speak more softly, even though my talk is childishly innocent and nonthreatening even to the weakest.

I read the papers—the new ones which I can choose freely. I don't understand everything in them, because I have no sense of continuity in the events. But I must analyze the back issues of at least the most important government dailies and weeklies. I would especially like to see *Trybuna Ludu* and *Słowo Powszechne*—these two workhorses of opinion, both touching upon "the truth."

November 2, 1955
I happened upon a back issue of *Słowo Powszechne* (October 29, 1953, Tuesday) today, in which four documents relating to my arrest were reported in the first column. They are "The Communiqué of the Presidium of the Polish People's Republic," "The Declaration of the Polish Episcopate," "The Election of the Head of the Episcopate," and "The Statement of the Vice-President of the Council of Ministers, Józef Cyrankiewicz." Until now I had been familiar only with a fragment of the communiqué, which fell

Komańcza. The statue of the Virgin Mary in the forest. Wyszyński used to visit it on his walks.

into my hands "in a certain room." *Słowo* reported the news of
the plenary session of the Episcopate and listed all the ordinaries
present at the session, including Bishop Choromański. Then it
gave a synopsis of the declaration of the Episcopate. I deduced that
the bishops must have been very upset to have agreed to make a
declaration so quickly.

Today I read these documents with the composure of a man
who already knows the outcome. This detachment allows me to
appraise more objectively that which took place two years ago.
But I strongly believe that the bishops did not have the benefit of
this composure, because it was not given to them; they could not
predict the further fate of the Church. The customary methods of
intimidation and threats were probably used against them—methods in which Messrs. Franciszek Mazur and Edward Ochab ex-
celled. I can imagine how this must have looked, recalling the
many meetings of the Joint Commission. It is possible that the
bishops had to listen to a whole litany of accusations and charges
against me, that they were overwhelmed; the government probably demanded that the bishops make immediate decisions, as had
repeatedly happened before, so that they did not have a chance to
analyze the situation thoroughly and determine their options. This
situation was potentially dangerous for the government; because it
had resorted to such drastic moves, the Catholic population was
bound to have been offended, and the government wanted, therefore, to extricate itself as quickly as possible from an uncomfortable position. This was the bishops' chief source of strength. Were
they aware of that strength?

Probably the pressure for haste did not allow them to discern
their strength and the trump cards they were holding. This led to
the painful "Declaration of the Polish Episcopate" which sharply
delineated—against the will of the authors—all that I had been
doing until then. Today, as I looked at these documents, so perfi-
diously set side by side, I must confess it pained me. How painfully the very juxtaposition of these texts must have touched our
Catholic population. And perhaps it was not so much their content that was so unpleasant but the very juxtaposition. And then

the Episcopate's request "that Archbishop Wyszyński be allowed to reside in one of the monasteries" today proves the government's brutal behavior in so delicate a situation, casting the responsibility for my stay in a so-called monastery onto the bishops. I did not understand this fully when the Commandant declared one June day in Stoczek that "the Government does not conceal the fact that you are in a monastery." The government had not concealed the fact since September 29, 1953, when it "expressed its consent to this proposal" (*Słowo Powszechne,* as above). In this way the bishops fell victim to their "trust" in the truthfulness of this government, which had transformed my "monastery" into a "concentration camp."

November 20, 1955

Help me, Father, to eliminate from my life anything that is only for me, only to my liking, for my satisfaction, for my indulgence, or for the fulfillment of my own desires. Teach me to act in such a way as to recognize at once that such feelings are too selfish, that from these no one profits—not You, nor Your children, nor even I. Let me always reserve time for myself, so that I may always have time for You and Your affairs. Inspire in me a desire to forget about myself—about whatever suits my comfort, sensuality, selfishness. I do not know if I will be able to do this, but I know that I want to very much, I know that it is the only way, that time and energy spent on oneself are a waste. Life can only come from two: I with You, Father. Two young parents with You, as one body. And when I am alone, what can I give birth to? And I wish, I desire only to be with You, because only then can I give birth for You, for Your glory—*Soli Deo.* . . . And so, I repeat, nothing for me! I do not wish my soil to be unproductive! And so only with You, because all fatherhood evolves from You. Free me, Father, from the Sisyphean labor of toiling on my own barren ground. Grant that we may always stay together, You and I—You in me, and I in You. This is what Your only Son wanted for me, who am always with You.

November 30, 1955

Having printed every kind of invective against the Primate in his paper, Mr. Piasecki* thought it appropriate to visit me on the eve of my arrest and offer the opinion that "it will go easily for the Primate at the trial." From this he drew optimistic conclusions about the future. He even asked me at that time not to make any public appearances in the near future and to see him again on Saturday.

At the same time that the painful trial of Bishop Kaczmarek was taking place, *Słowo* took it upon itself to publish (September 21, 1953) an article entitled "After Six Days of the Trial" by Father Wacław Radosz, a priest of the Kielce diocese. This is a typical illustration of what a "policy of fear tactics" can do to people. Father Radosz admitted that he had vowed obedience and respect "not only to my consecrator, but also to his successor, Bishop Czesław Kaczmarek, who now stands accused and on trial." This vow did not prevent Father Radosz from attacking the bishop, at a time when he could not defend himself. This did not hinder a publication that considers itself Catholic from publishing attacks on the accused bishop even before a verdict was rendered, thus having a negative effect on the nature of that verdict. It is hard to imagine anything more hideous or painful. That same *Słowo*, during the course of Bishop Kaczmarek's trial, loaded its pages with articles written, or at least signed, by priests. Even such level-headed people as Father Eugeniusz Dąbrowski and Father Rector Józef Iwanicki of the Catholic University of Lublin saw nothing improper in publishing their interviews with reporters of this paper, *pari passu* [keeping pace] with the publication of whole columns of reports on the trial.

In this journalistic atmosphere there appeared in *Słowo Powszechne* (October 29, 1953, Tuesday), on the front page, one after another: "Communiqué of the Presidium of the Polish People's Republic," "The Declaration of the Polish Episcopate," "The Election of the Head of the Episcopate," and "The Declaration of the Vice-President of the Council of Ministers, Józef Cyrankiewicz."

---

*Bolesław Piasecki, head of Pax and publisher of *Słowo Powszechne*.

Further declarations by the editors of *Słowo* were veiled under the guise of lectures on the rights and duties of progressive Catholics in the country; mainly, priests were solicited to make declarations on the defense of the Western Territories, as if they were in danger at that time. So, in response to all those concerned about the situation of the Church after September 25, 1953, *Słowo* put forth these arguments on the defense of the Western Territories (*Słowo*, October 2, 1953; in an article entitled "The Declaration of the Episcopate and the Enemies of Poland"). In a word, what was [at that moment] of the essence in the concern of the Catholic world in Poland* was passed over in silence, and, instead, a convenient argument that no one was challenging at the time was taken up. There was a similar implication in an article by Father Stanisław Huet—after the Conference of the Episcopate (*Słowo*, 3–4 October 1953)—which, for the first time, listed a whole litany of Polish bishops taking part in the Episcopal Conference of September 28, 1953, just to convince the Polish people that great numbers of bishops were still free.

Similarly, Father Czuj, a professor, directed the whole internal problem to the level of the international situation in his article entitled "There Does not Exist and There Cannot Exist a Conflict Between the Dictates of Faith and Social Duties Toward the Nation" (*Słowo Powszechne*, October 9, 1953). It might be added parenthetically that such a title might be forgiven a patristic scholar, but a sociologist or moralist has no excuse. It seems the author took foreign propaganda to heart, since he wrote about "spreading fantastic gossip, or the bleakest forecasts for the future." This propaganda was certainly supplied, with a lot of ammunition for its arguments, by the moves of the government.

In the middle of October, *Słowo* shifted the weight of its arguments to the subject of the National Front.† There began a whole series of meetings and conferences, beginning with Bolesław Pia-

---

*That is, the recent arrest and sequestration of the country's leading churchman.
†A national organization created and supported by the government—*Front Jedności Narodowej*, the National Front of Unity—which drew its members from all walks of life and from a great variety of philosophies and points of view.

secki's lecture on "incorporating Polish Catholics into the building of a Polish People's Republic" (*Słowo Powszechne*, October 15, 1953). At these meetings the matter of "Church-State incidents of the past few months" was passed off as a mere fragment of the larger problems discussed. But it is easy to sense that this "fragment" was the real reason for organizing the meetings. On these occasions the inside story of this whole matter was surely discussed, but the issue was never fully treated in *Słowo*. These meetings were described as "reviews by the people," who required explanations and reassurances. Naturally, Father Czuj, supported by his minions from the Department of Catholic Theology at Warsaw University, was the front man for these people. A few members of the Department of Catholic Theology at the Jagiellonian University* were added, as well as some from the Catholic University of Lublin. A regular phenomenon at these meetings was a team of professors from the seminary in Nysa. Priests predominated at these meetings, interspersed with a few so-called Catholic activists, primarily people in the employ of Pax.

In my entire review of the press, I did not find one trace of any kind of regret for an event as shaking for the Church as the disappearance from the public eye of the Primate. One got the impression that for the editors of *Słowo* nothing noteworthy had taken place, nothing that would demand taking a "Catholic" stand. There is also no trace of concern in the speeches of the priests; their speeches are formulated in a way that indicates not the slightest concern for the fate of Poland's Primate. They write about everything else. They revile the whole world, execrate Adenauer and the German cardinals, discuss factories, tractors, corn. But the careful reader of *Słowo* will find nothing about their position on the forcible removal of a representative of the hierarchy of the Church.

Did these priests really not try to question, to demand an explanation, to protest? The answer cannot be determined from *Słowo*. In this manner, the editors brought forth from these "patriotic priests" a black document, demonstrating the extent to which they were the

---

*Another name for the University of Kraków.

slaves of fear, having lost all sense of duty to the Catholic "reason of state."

In *Słowo* of October 16, 1953, Father Eugeniusz Dąbrowski, a professor, published an article entitled "Polish Catholicism and the Problem of the Western Territories" (No. 245). It is a transcript of a lecture. The author falsifies history when he claims that in a seven-year period (1946–1953) the Polish Church hierarchy exerted no efforts to stabilize the Western Territories. And yet, during this period, the Mutual Understanding was reached, a spiritual renewal of the clergy was carried out, and the Cathedral canons in Wrocław and Olsztyn were restored. Apparently Father Dąbrowski chooses not to know anything about all this.

It is significant that in October 1953, commissions of clerical and lay Catholic activists began to emerge in the Committees of the National Front, absorbing the Union of Fighters for Freedom and Democracy and the Catholic intellectuals. These two centers, having given birth to a new creation, ceased to exist. A long list of officers and members was announced. Voivodship Committees began to emerge. Bolesław Piasecki delivered a prototype lecture entitled "Present Tasks of the Episcopal Declaration of 28 September, 1953" (*Słowo Powszechne*, October 24–25, 1953); it became the subject of the so-called discussions held at voivodship meetings. In his lecture Mr. Piasecki felt it proper to reprimand "responsible Catholic centers" for "demonstrating more than once their lack of social maturity, and their inability to appraise situations realistically, which is a basic condition for proper leadership." He gave himself credit for the fact that "the social-progressive movement in Poland daringly and directly drew attention to the political shortsightedness of these leaders." Mr. Piasecki's lecture, which was to be an expression of the thinking of progressive Catholics, includes an attack on Bishop Kaczmarek and the Primate of Poland. He is of the opinion that the September Declaration of the Episcopate "creates conditions for the nonappearance of the phenomenon of divergence in appraising sociopolitical events between our movement and the views of our hierarchy." In short, he sees the hierarchy as serving the purposes of Pax.

December 2, 1955

I continued to read the government press hoping to learn more about the accusations formulated against me. The most authoritative was the statement of *Trybuna Ludu* signed by Edward Ochab, National Secretary of the National Committee of the National Front (Saturday, September 26, 1953,* No. 268), entitled "Who Stands in the Way of Normalized Church-State Relations?" The article was written with the trial of Bishop Kaczmarek in mind, but it was aimed directly at me. If one considers that I was abducted late on a Friday night and that *Trybuna* had to appear early Saturday morning, one can easily deduce how quickly the whole police-propaganda apparatus must have been assembled.

The prejudice of the article is obvious: "The reactionary and adventurous elements in the hierarchy that condoned the activities of Bishop Kaczmarek and his accomplices against the people and the state" are responsible for Bishop Kaczmarek's actions.

The following accusations against me can be drawn from this article:

(1) Exerting an overwhelming influence over the activities of the Episcopate, which were directed at destroying national unity, bringing discord between believers and nonbelievers, and negating—in practice—the principles of the Mutual Understanding.

(2) "For the head of the Episcopate, Primate Wyszyński, the signing of the Mutual Understanding was only a maneuver, designed to mislead the government and public opinion."

(3) The Mutual Understanding served only as a screen to conceal political activities that were inimical to the people and the nation, activities directed against the People's Republic.

(4) Despite agreeing to counteract the revisionist activities of some of the German clergy, "the leadership of the Episcopate actually did nothing to fulfill their solemn promise...."

(5) In keeping with the wishes of the Roman Curia, Primate

---

*That is, the day after the Primate's arrest.

Wyszyński did all he could to prevent the stabilization of church administration in the regained Western Territories."

(6) "No canonical sanctions were invoked against priests faithful to such activity"—that is, against the government.

(7) During the trial of Bishop Kaczmarek "the Primate did not condemn the criminals with even one word, nor did he attempt to disassociate himself by even one word from the hostile American-Vatican action undertaken against Poland."

(8) "Primate Wyszyński bears prime responsibility for sabotaging and disrupting the Mutual Understanding, for actually helping the West German Teutonic Knights* and Anglo-American enemies of our nation in maligning and undermining the Polish People's Republic."

The article is to be one more warning, since previously "the numerous warnings from the government and the public did not curtail the rowdy pupil of the Vatican." Mr. Ochab warns that "the brawling of crimson-dressed noblemen" could not go unpunished in Communist Poland.

Thus the article was intended to prepare public opinion for what was to take place during the night and what was to come to the people's attention in the morning.

In the same issue of *Trybuna Ludu* (September 27, 1953, Sunday, No. 269), two articles were published in the same column: "Celebration in Honor of an Outstanding Progressive Leader of the Renaissance, Primate Jan Laski"† and "Vatican, the Primate, and the Regained Territories." The deceased Primate was praised as a progressive person "who was not frightened by the papal bull condemning him"; the living Primate was criticized for "representing not the Polish position in the Vatican, but the Vatican position in Poland."

The anonymous author [of "Vatican, Primate, etc."] claimed that

---

*Ochab here makes ironic reference to the Teutonic Knights of Prussia and Pomerania, who were known, particularly in the fourteenth and fifteenth centuries, to press the conquest and conversion of pagans with extreme cruelty.

†Archbishop Jan Laski (1456–1531), Primate of Poland, famous for his revision of Church law at the beginning of the sixteenth century.

the Vatican's policies had always been anti-Polish. Examples? Ratti, Cortesi,* Kaczmarek, *Papa tedesco* [Papal stooge] . . . Today the Vatican does not wish to allow Church affairs to be set in order in the regained Western Territories, and "in Poland it attempts to conspire against the power of the people." "And this was the very policy the reactionary part of the Church hierarchy in Poland pursued, with Primate Wyszyński at its head."

The following accusations were made in this article:

(1) Primate Wyszyński, who so often maligned the authorities of the People's Republic,

(2) did not protest against Adenauer's declaration on the subject of the Western Territories, which was supposedly made "in full accord with the Vatican."

(3) Primate Wyszyński not only did not keep silent, but "raised his voice contrary to the interests of the nation."

(4) "He torpedoed in every way possible the liquidation of temporary Church positions in the regained Western Territories."

(5) "In the Vatican, where he supposedly went to plead the cause of doing away with the temporary status, he took in fact a strong anti-Polish stand." Proof of this allegedly came from "well-informed sources among the West German clergy" (*Echo der Zeit*).

(6) The Primate persecuted and opposed clergy "who took a position on the revisionist affair."

(7) The Primate fiercely worked against the authority of the People's Republic by protecting and shielding priests— criminals condemned for crimes by the courts.

(8) The Primate attempted to "deceive Polish public opinion and hide from it the real policies of the Vatican" on the Western Territories.

(9) The Primate took a "consistently anti-working-class, pro-Vatican, pro-imperialist, and thus anti-Polish position."

---

*Papal nuncios in Poland during the inter–World Wars period.

December 4, 1955

I found in the press the declaration of the "expanded conference of the Presidium of the Chief Officers of the Clerical Commission of the Union of Fighters for Freedom and Democracy," published in *Trybuna Ludu* of October 1, 1953. The servile Clerical Commission had already held its meeting on September 29, 1953; "more than forty priests, representing all the district commissions" had taken part in it. The Reverend Dr. Edward Korwot delivered a lecture at this meeting on the "tasks of the Catholic Church in the Polish People's Republic." Those present passed a resolution in which they expressed happy accord with the September 28, 1953, declaration of the Episcopate. They attacked the Apostolic See, which "denied Poland the right to lands on which seven million Poles lived."

Finally the declaration described the attitude of those priests belonging to the Union of Fighters for Freedom and Democracy toward the Primate's case: "Responsibility for the atmosphere revealed during the trial falls on the current leadership of the Episcopate, on Archbishop Wyszyński, who by his attitude helped create this atmosphere."

December 8, 1955

A small note from *Trybuna Ludu* entitled "Why Do They Froth at the Mouth?" (October 2, 1953) was to be an introduction to the argument that "they froth for no reason." *Trybuna Ludu* began to publish lengthy, interminable articles depicting me as a diehard enemy of Communism. To this end, they reached onto my bookshelves and removed books that they had already taken out of circulation, not excluding the National Library; and there began a "campaign" against "the Reverend Dr. Stefan Wyszyński" on the basis of his prewar activities. The anonymous author (C.S.) cited the following works of mine: *The Book in the Struggle with Communism; Can a Catholic Be a Communist?; How to Combat Communism Effectively; The Intelligentsia in the Vanguard of Communism; The Catholic Plan of Action Against Communism; Pius XI in the Struggle with Communism; The Culture of Bolshevism and the Polish Intelligentsia; Catholicism-Capitalism-Socialism.*

This material was used arbitrarily, as were the conclusions drawn from it. In these conclusions the author accused me of ill will toward the workers' movements and of sympathizing with Nazism. One can sense that this accusation was meant to serve later as material for a possible trial. A whole string of accusations that had already been published earlier were repeated on this occasion, and I was made out to be a confederate of the *Hakata*.* The conclusion: "Most obviously Cardinal Wyszyński served an evil and harmful cause." (The article: "Let the Facts Speak.")

By the will of God I am once again with a group of women. I must remember: Whenever a woman enters the room, always rise no matter how busy you are. Rise, whether it is the Mother Superior, or Sister Kleofasa, who tends the heater. Remember that she always reminds you of the Handmaid of the Lord, at the sound of whose name the Church rises. Remember that in this way you pay a debt of respect to your Immaculate Mother, with whom this woman is more closely associated than you. In this way you pay a debt toward your own mother, who served you with her own flesh and blood. . . . Rise and do not delay, overcome your manly haughtiness and sense of power. . . . Rise even when the poorest of the Magdalenes enters. . . . Only then will you do as did your Master, who rose from the Throne on the right hand of the Father to descend to the Handmaid of the Lord. . . . Only then will you do as did the Father Creator, who sent Mary to help Eve. . . . Rise without delay, and you will be the better for it.

December 10, 1955

Your Will be done in Komańcza as it is in heaven—I desire to state this clearly, Father, since you know where Komańcza is and that I am in Komańcza. Your Will is so powerful that it leads me

---

*A German chauvinistic organization formed in 1894 for the purpose of eradicating Polish elements in the Poznań province.

to admit this fact fully and wins my full compliance. I feel Your power over me. . . . I humble myself before it. I do not wish to oppose Your Will in any way. You know, You know everything. . . . I am happy that Your Will is so powerful. I am proof of the power of Your Will. It is good to gain yet another proof in Your favor, even if it be gained by so painful an experience.

When I find myself capable of even one act of love, I am no longer worthless. Even if my whole life were one sin, this one act of love offers me to God. No, I am not worthless. . . . I am greatness, because I love. And love does not die. On the junk heap of my life, I have found something godly. . . . It is God himself who has lost this pearl of great price. And even though it lies in the soil, in the earth, in the mud, it is worthwhile to take up the mud, to become with it master of the pearl. How many pearls lie in the mud! What great value the mud has, precisely because a single pearl can be discovered in it. People sell all they possess to gain this mud together with the pearl. I am only mud! But in this mud God has lost a pearl of love. . . . Do not ever tell me I am worthless. Do not tell it to anyone who is still capable of love.

December 13, 1955
It is worth noting Sister Maksencja's experience on her way to Komańcza. It had been agreed long before with Bishop Klepacz that Sister Maksencja would come before Christmas to look over my clothes brought from prison. Informed ahead of time by a special delivery letter and a telegram, Sister was to arrive at the train station at 5:00 P.M. Mother Superior sent Sister Malwina to meet her. The excursion ended in Sister Maksencja's being taken to the train station at Komańcza, from there to the police station, from there by car to Sanok, and then back to Warsaw. Sister Malwina, sent to meet her, had a policeman for company, who did not leave her side until Sanok. Both sisters were peacefully on their way to Komańcza, when in Rzepedzia four policemen entered their compartment and asked to see their papers. Sister Maksencja presented her identity card and the official document issued by Bishop Klepacz. It stated that on the authority of an assurance by Premier Cyrankiewicz, my

family and members of my household had the right to visit me. The representative of the police told Sister Maksencja that she was to go to the police station in Komańcza. She was not allowed to disembark at the station in Komańcza; she barely managed to hand the suitcases to the sisters waiting for her on the platform. Both she and Sister Malwina found themselves at the police station. The sisters sent to help them were told that if necessary the detained sisters would be returned to the convent. Contrary to this assurance, things turned out differently. At 11:00 P.M. Sister Malwina returned and said that Sister Maksencja had been put in a car, which had just arrived from Sanok, and was returned. To no avail were Sister Maksencja's pleas to spend the night and warm up. The policemen were uncompromising and urged her to hurry so that they could catch the Warsaw train.

December 31, 1955

A formal expression of trust is due You from Your servant, Eternal Father of the future ages. All that You have done for me is mercy and truth. All that I have done for You in the past year is a child's compliance and infant's trust. You are love, grace, and power! I am selfishness, sin, and weakness. You take all of my weakness into Your holy Hands and leave on it traces of mercy and understanding. You alone cause me not to lose faith in Your wisdom and goodness. You alone transform before Your eyes my will and my thoughts. You alone bring me to recognize Your justice. You alone awaken in my soul a desire for sacrifice and martyrdom for Your Church, for Your glory. You alone assuage my fear and an unwillingness to suffer. You alone fill my soul with calm in face of the unknown and with gratitude for anything that might befall me. You alone cause a sensual, egotistical man to want to become his own enemy in order to understand Your friendship. You cause me not to be able to recognize myself, that I begin to wonder at myself, that I ask myself: *unde mihi hoc* [whence this for me]? . . . Now when midnight strikes, I declare to You, Father, in this last moment of the old year and the first of the new, that You have not failed me, it is I who owe You a debt that cannot be repaid. I have worked at a loss.

... But You know how to forgive Your debtors. . . . Perhaps only in this way will I be able to realize the motto of my life—*Soli Deo.*

January 16, 1955
Even if You presented me with nothing else, my Most Perfect Father, but a stone cast by an angry hand, I want to accept it as an expression of greatest mercy; I wish to kiss it so that—just as to Saint Stephen*—it may appear as a blessing to me. And even if You had no good word for me, Father of Love, only an insult from the enemies of the cross, only buffets and mockery, I would still consider it the only mercy of which I can render myself deserving. And if there were no longer any room for me at Your altar, Father of the Eternal Priest, I still wish to see in this the holiness of the Trinity, which alone knows the value and dignity of priesthood and knows who is able to serve You worthily. If You were to close my lips so that I could no longer publicly profess faith in Your Son, I would, professing faith in You in my heart, adore Your power which is capable of bringing stones to life to proclaim Your glory, to shout to the deaf.

Yes, Father, because everything that comes from You—that You permit—is the greatest grace for me, is a sign of Your love, all of this merits my trust in You.

January 21, 1956
The feast of Saint Agnes. The antiphon *Ad Laudes: Anulo suo subarrhavit me Dominus meus Iesus Christus, et tamquam sponsam decoravit me corona* [My Lord Jesus Christ has given me his ring as a pledge and has adorned me with a crown like one espoused]. And the Psalm, filled with longing for the espoused Jesus: *Deus, Deus meus es: sollicite te quaero. Te sitit anima mea, desiderat te caro mea* [God, you are my God: I seek you anxiously. My soul thirsts for you, my flesh longs for you]. . . . (Psalm 62) These words must disturb my peaceful comfort as I wait for God's grace. This is the

---

*Saint Stephen, the first Christian to be martyred for his faith (Acts 7: 57–59; 58–60 KJV) was stoned to death.

true greed of a God bound to me by a ring. Everything keeps me by His side; I see this clearly in time of temptation, which tried hard to undo this bond. The measure of one's resistance in the struggle against temptation is the measure of the strength of one's bond with God. If it does not give way easily, that means my vows are a lasting bond. There will come a test in the fire of temptation, and a person will emerge with even greater desire for You, My Beloved, who hold me by my wedding ring. *Ad Te levavi animam . . . Te sitit anima mea* [I have lifted up my soul to You . . . My soul thirsts for You]. . . .

January 29, 1956
Septuagesima Sunday.* "The Spirit of Truth will remind you of everything and will teach you everything, whatever I have told you. . . ." This Spirit speaks ceaselessly in the praying Church. Today the Church speaks to me through the richness of its thoughts, when it begins the period of Redemption in the liturgy. It reveals God's world, created by the Father—*In principio creavit Deus* [In the beginning God created]—a world blemished by sin, a world cleansed by the blood of Christ. . . . *Circumdederunt me dolores mortis* [The afflictions of death surrounded me]—this is a world made weary by sin. But God so loved the world that He gave His Son. . . . The Son begins the work of renewal. And so we must follow the example of the Father, we must love the world. . . . And so very much . . . We must not call it evil, since God saw it as good. . . . I listen carefully to the Spirit of Truth, Who today reminds me of this. I follow Him step by step, every day, since the Church of the Holy Spirit speaks to me every day. It always has so much to say! It is like a tree that bears bountiful fruit for every day. I am to eat this fruit today and not save it for tomorrow, because tomorrow the Church will serve me new fruit. I must be well fed, because God does not like starveling souls. His children must be satiated with good, as He is himself. Every day I sit down to His feast. . . . Every day I am obedient to the Holy Spirit. . . .

---

*Septuagesima Sunday falls on the ninth Sunday before Easter.

Cardinal Wyszyński walking in Komańcza, rosary in hand.

January 31, 1956

Protect me, Father of Truth, from haughty words. When I pray to You in silence, You alone know my truth; do not allow my words to surpass my truth. You alone know man, and there is no need to tell You anything about man. Do not allow me to say anything grand, anything exaggerated, anything inordinate about myself to You. When I tell You that I am the greatest sinner, You know whether I am thinking of anything for my own justification, whether in my soul I do not see greater sinners than I; do not let there be a gap between my words and my thoughts. When I tell You that I love You, do not let me lie to You. When I tell You that I am sorry, do not let my heart remain cold. Let my word be in truth, let it be true, gentle but sincere. Protect me, Father of the Word, from abusing words. Enter the world of my thoughts and put them in order so that I may not attempt to deceive You by word and thought, to impress you. Protect me from all this "literature," from imagination, from creativity, from a plethora of words. . . . Would that I could fall silent even in my thoughts, when I stand before You, who look into hearts and read thoughts . . . *Scrutans corda et renes, Deus* [Probing our hearts and our emotions, God].

February 19, 1956

The first Sunday of Lent repeatedly returns to us the tragic scene of the Great Temptation of the Son of Man. To this day it is repeated in the history of man, in the life of Christ's Church, in the soul of every Christian. It is a great blessing that Christ let it be shown on Him what methods the tempter uses, what his seductive traps consist of. Do I not observe in myself how susceptible I am to the temptation of "bread," to the temptation of an easy life, to the temptation of being left in peace? Did the tempter not identify my weakness well? If I have not succumbed to these temptations before now, it does not mean that I am safe. If I have persevered, it is not because God has waged battle for me? But doesn't the very suspicion that "one can try to battle him" put me in the ranks of so many others who are being tried just as I am? Today the struggle against the Church succeeds in many people precisely because they bake their bread from the stones cast under the feet of the Church; because they allow themselves to be borne on the arms of evil spirits, because they constantly fall flat on their faces, paying servile homage to all tempters. These are the contemporary "progressive" Catholics. "Progressive" in what? In evil. They make constant progress in succumbing to all, increasingly weak, temptations. Am I to be scandalized by them? No, rather I should grow wiser, so that I myself will not be tempted by the devil. To protect me from temptation the Spirit of God has led me to this desert. But even here I am not free from temptation; there are struggles with myself—no longer to think that there might be roads other than the ones over which the Spirit of God has led me for these past two years.

February 20, 1956

And one of the holiest temptations? Today I studied the new regulations for Holy Week services. How much of Christ's spirit is in them. My heart bleeds at the thought that I will remain here idle, unable to enjoy the experiences of the Church, which has prepared so much happiness for all its children when it tells them to honor Christ the King on Palm Sunday, when it wants to delight them with the love of the Eucharistic God, when it wants to kidnap them up to the Cross, when it wants to infuse into them the hope of the Resurrection. Who will open the eyes of my children to these wonders of God's thought shining through the Church's liturgy? After all, it is above all I who have the state of grace for my children. And the duty and the understanding and the readiness . . . And all this is to remain silent, to be denied a voice, even though the soul is boiling over? Let my stones become bread! Father, for them! "Throw yourself down!" Already now! . . . Unfathomed God! And yet, stones will remain stones. And yet, I will not come down from the clouds—I will remain in my Komańcza pit, jealously peeking from the organ loft at the priest who is privileged to serve his people. . . . Father! Give me the strength also to overcome this temptation —the holiest temptation to "serve You *coram populo*" [in the presence of the people]. . . . Are not holy renunciations—the apparent purposelessness of such a life, sacrificing to Your will the most noble impulses, crucifixion of one's ardor, submitting one's pastoral zeal to Your prodigality—are not all these things greater glory to You? I am to be silent once again, to close my lips, bind my will, restrain my priestly impulses. But the holy is due You more than the sinful. I betray myself for You.

February 22, 1956
Intellige clamorem meum [Discern my cry]. . . . Who will understand me better than You? There is more knowledge in one impulse of Your Godly thought about me than in all the thoughts of my whole life about the history of the world and its people. You know more about me than I know about the whole world! You discover more in me than I discover in the whole world. You alone do not need to ask what is within man, since You yourself know what is in man. I am constantly losing myself within myself, You constantly find Yourself in me. I am always doubting myself, you never doubt in me. I am always over- or underestimating myself, You always see the whole truth in me. I become proud when I understand something of You, You always let me realize that I am an illiterate. I fall into despair when I lose, and You constantly whisper to me that Your grace is sufficient for me because power is made perfect in weakness. I am always searching for my way, my truth, my life, and You always are my Way, my Truth, my Life. One thought of mine about You reveals to me the whole truth about me. I see myself well only in You. I recognize myself through You. I find my whole reason for existence in You. If I had already perished and disappeared into the depths of hell, I would still be able to regain my footing with one beat of the heart toward You. I am nothing without You, I am power in You. "I, dust, will dare talk with the Lord. . . ."

March 9, 1956
You incline me, Father, to become my own enemy, to pray against myself, to ask You for everything that I fear, which might be necessary for Your Church. You demand of me that I give myself for the Church, that I offer my life and my wish to work for my nation's

fidelity to You. You expect me to pray that all terrible things befall me so that they bypass Your Church in Poland and its faithful Catholic people. You have the right to demand this too. I want to become my own enemy, so that I may submit to You. I wish to ignore myself so that You can be considerate toward the Polish Church and its bishops. I cannot do their work for them, but You can say: "Your misery is enough for me, I will forgive you the rest." You could be satisfied to take only twenty pieces of silver, like the brothers did from Joseph, instead of the full price of the ransom for the People of God. Take this little bit, but forgive the rest. Do not look at the great imperfection of my sacrifice, at these internal expressions of resistance which You allow me to place under Your holy Feet.

How I love to officiate at the altar, how I enjoy proclaiming faith in You before the people, how fond I am of the adornment of Your House, how I long to live in the shrine of the Lord! What happiness could be greater? And I am also to deny myself that? If this will add to Your glory, if it will protect you from your unworthy servant, accept also this self-denial, the most terrible for a priest! But You know how to take it, since you freely granted Your grace. You can reclaim it. You have the right.

March 11, 1956

We did not have to wait long for the consequences of Khrushchev's attack on "the cult of the individual, incompatible with the spirit of Marxism-Leninism, which transforms this or that leader into a hero-miracle-worker" (Twentieth Party Congress in Moscow). It was easy to guess that Khrushchev had Stalin in mind. Today *Trybuna Ludu* (No. 69) carried an article "On the Cult of the Individual and Its Consequences"—absolutely unbelievable in its formulations. Underscoring the "outstanding role" that Joseph Stalin played after Lenin's death, the anonymous author adds: "Gradually, however—in the thirties—Stalin began to lord it over the party, to impose his will on it, along with his individual decisions. Collegiality of the party leadership was increasingly diminished and finally disappeared entirely. All this was highly injurious to the Communist Party of the Soviet Union and to the international labor movement." The article is unsigned, which means that it is to be a prototype for the press, which will now begin to expand on it in many other articles. And indeed, in *Ekspres** some author explains to a fictional Janka "brought up in the cult of Stalin" all of Stalin's faults and misdeeds. One must be a Communist to have waited for this so long. Non-Communists knew long ago that something undemocratic was going on in this cult of the individual. When, on the occasion of the May celebrations, Warsaw was plastered with huge portraits of Stalin à la Nicholas II, all thinking people saw in this "adoration" a sin against official Communist atheism. But then only the Communists were right; others went to prison, even though they protested out of nationalistic motives, as citizens of a sovereign state. Who should be going to prison today since it turned out that it was the non-Communists who were the better Communists, who understood better the spirit of Marxism?

How rapid is the decline of gods wrought by human hands! And it is for such a god that the Living God is to step aside—this God for whom there is no room in a Marxist state and who remains "always the same—yesterday, today and tomorrow." And for such deceptive vapidities the Church was to enter into the service of a doctrine that today condemns and rejects what yesterday it raised to the altar?

March 12, 1956

"The crimson of the Church which you desire is the crimson of Christ before Pontius Pilate. You will be burdened with the duty of carrying it," said Pope Honorius to the young Leo (G. von Le Fort, *Pope from the Ghetto*).

Christ wore the first crimson zuchetto† when a crown was forced onto His holy head, piercing it with its seventy needles. It flowed

---

*The Warsaw evening daily that usually includes all the sensational news, e.g., murders, etc.
†Prelate's skullcap. A cardinal's is red.

copiously with holy Blood. My zuchetto is only a symbol of this sanguine and crimson head of Christ.

The first crimson cape was an expression of the soldiers' derision. Just as Christ's cross has become the pride of God's Church, so the crimson cape is the pride of His sons. But it does not cease to be a sanguine symbol of Christ's Blood. My crimson cape, presented to me by the Polish clergy of Rome, was given by Minister Bida to the theater for derisive performances, to be draped around actors who mock cardinals.

March 13, 1956

I awoke at twenty to five in the morning, tormented by a dream. . . . Perhaps it is not worthwhile to note one's dreams, but by way of exception I will write down the one I had today. In my dream I was leaving some huge building, after a difficult conference with Bolesław Bierut. We said good-bye in the hall. As I was leaving, Mr. Bierut joined me, with the obvious intention of going with me. I was embarrassed by this and distressed by the thought of what people would think seeing us together in the street. We were walking along a lengthy street, perhaps Aleje Racławickie, in the direction of Krakowskie Przedmieście in Lublin. We were carrying on a conversation; I still wanted to tell Mr. Bierut something. As we waited to cross the street at the corner, Mr. Bierut turned left and jaywalked across the street. I remained alone with the thought: He is allowed everything, even to violate the rules for street traffic. He soon disappeared from sight somewhere on a side street. I crossed the street at the crosswalk, filled with a fear of two malicious-looking goats that stood in my way. But I passed them without incident and continued to look for Mr. Bierut, to see where he had disappeared. I was looking for him because I still wanted to tell him something. I was surprised that he had disappeared so suddenly. My companion, some priest, wanted to explain something to me; should one be looking around? With the feeling that the meeting had not been complete, I set off straight ahead, down Krakowskie Przedmieście. Then I woke up. . . .

I forgot about this dream during the day, as I do all other dreams.

But I nagged the Good Father more intensively than usual, in my prayer *super populum: Miserere, Domine, populo tuo: et continuis tribulationibus laborantum, propitius respirare concede* [Over the people: Have mercy, O Lord, on Thy People, and mercifully grant them relief, who labor amidst continual tribulations].

Shortly after breakfast two priests arrived.* "Guess what happened?" I did not venture a guess. They told me themselves. The radio had just reported that Bolesław Bierut had died last night in Moscow. A Christian views every death very seriously. He *cui omnia vivunt* [in Whom all things live] enters every life, He *aufert spiritus principum* [Who takes away the breath of princes]. Today all polemics fall by the wayside, because by now Bolesław Bierut is convinced that there is a God and that He is, after all, Love. He is, therefore, definitely on our side. On the opposite side remain those whom he led on earth, who in recent weeks have mounted a "progressive-scientific attack on the superstition of religion." Recently we heard that teachers had received secret instructions to keep the youth so busy that they could not take part in the spiritual retreat exercises.

God has put an end to the life of a man and a head of state who was the first and only ruler of Poland to dare to organize a political and state campaign against the Church. What frightening courage! And Bolesław Bierut managed to muster the nerve. The terrible wrongs inflicted on the Church will always be associated with his name in the annals of the Nation and the Church. Whether he did it out of conviction or for political reasons, the future will judge. Possibly he did not want an open and crucial struggle, but he condoned such a perfidious plan—to use progressive Catholics to destroy a spirit of vigilance—and a consistent, gradual destruction of so many Church and socioreligious institutions.

During the regime of Bolesław Bierut, despite the Mutual Understanding, the Catholic press was destroyed, nearly all periodicals, bookstores, and publishing houses, not excluding the official organs of the diocesan curias were shut down; church charities were de-

---

*Probably Bishop Choromański and Father Padacz.

stroyed, as were many educational and care centers; Catholic schooling and hospital services were destroyed; many convents and monasteries were liquidated, together with their schools. The dreadful outrages committed against imprisoned priests and monks during their detentions, at interrogations, excessively severe court verdicts that resulted in prisons full of cassocks and habits, as they hadn't been since the time of Muraviëv*—this is a long and painful chapter of this regime.

In recent years the Holy Church was bound by the shackles of the Office of Religious Affairs and the decree on filling church posts. This great Church apparatus became immobilized to a great extent, and if they did not succeed in destroying it completely, perhaps it was because the stand of the Catholic community was unified enough, because the power of the Church was great, because the prudence of the Episcopate led to the Mutual Understanding even if it was meaningless, because, after all, times were changing, because new inspirations came from above (Khrushchev's method). These painful experiences will from now on always be associated with the name of Bolesław Bierut. Perhaps history will whitewash him? Today, as he departs, he leaves behind a grim impression.

Bolesław Bierut died on the anniversary of the coronation of Pius XII, a man whom he had allowed to be defiled by the party press. Whenever we drew attention to this method of combat, exceeding all bounds of decency, our objections were ignored, even though Bolesław Bierut's authority in the party was so great that he could have put an end to it or placed some appropriate curbs on the struggle. God sought redress for the lack of respect shown to His servant Pius, before a Catholic Nation so offended.

Finally, still another Finger of God. Bolesław Bierut died abroad,

---

*Michał Nikołajewicz Murawjew (Muraviëv) (1794–1866) was Russian governor-general of Lithuania from 1863 to 1865. During his command in partitioned Poland, after the unsuccessful Polish insurrection of November 1861, he sentenced thousands to death or exile in Siberia, especially priests and religious, burned whole villages, confiscated Church goods and properties, and earned universal hatred among the people for his barbaric methods.

in Moscow—in a place where he had agreed to give away one-third of Poland's territory,* a place from which he had drawn his inspiration for the struggle against the Church. Apparently God wanted to show here that if you live by the sword, you die by the sword. Certainly, it can be assumed that the death was of natural causes, since he suffered from a serious heart disease contracted a few years earlier, and since he worked very hard. But the Nation's public opinion will always have a lingering doubt and will always call for "clarifications."

One thing more. Bolesław Bierut died under the burden of Church excommunication. Not because he was a Communist, but because he participated in the act of force against a cardinal as he was deported from Warsaw. The decree of the Congregation of the Holy Consistory of September 30, 1953, clearly states this. He might have made nothing of this decree, as he did of so many Church laws, but for me this circumstance is especially hard to bear—that on my account another obstacle arose between the just Judge and the deceased. How difficult it is to be a true Christian in such a situation. The violated law of the Church calls for punishment. Proper respect must be shown to God's will. I must recognize this and desire it; I must desire God's justice—a God who fights in defense of His anointed. And yet, I wish this last obstacle did not exist. All the more I wish to pray for God's mercy for the man who harmed me so much. Tomorrow I will offer Mass for him; already now I forgive him who trespassed against me, confident that the just God will find better deeds in his life that will secure for him God's Mercy.

In the evening I recalled my morning dream, which I recounted to the priests at supper. Not only does *sanctorum communio* [communion of the saints] exist. There exists also in the world communication between human spirits. So often during my imprisonment I prayed for Bolesław Bierut. Perhaps this prayer bound us so that he

---

*In the 1945 post–World War II exchange of territories, Poland gained 9,600 square miles in the west (the Western Territories mentioned in the text) and was forced to cede 69,300 square miles to the Soviet Union in the east. Its present territory is 120,700 square miles, about the size of New Mexico.

came looking for help. I looked around for him in my dream—and I will not forget about the help of prayer. Perhaps everyone will forget him soon; perhaps they will all denounce him, as today they denounce Stalin, but I will not do it. My Christianity demands this of me.

March 16, 1956

The novena honoring the moment of the Annunciation in Nazareth leads me to ponder what was accomplished in Mary and in human history. The Holy Trinity is at the side of its Chosen One, discovered in the infinity of the universe. The Father sends His Angel and awaits an answer. The Word Everlasting repeats to the Father: *Ecce venio, ut faciam voluntatem Tuam* [Behold, I come to do Your will]. The Holy Spirit calls upon all His love to embrace the one full of grace. Humanity knows nothing about this moment so important to it. Mary alone stops this moment by asking, *Quomodo fiet istud* [How will this come to pass]? Her *fiat* [Be it done] causes all three Persons of God to begin to act. The Father of the Word becomes the Father of the Son of Man. The Eternal Word unites human nature to Himself. The Holy Spirit unites the divine with the human. Mary becomes the Mother of God, God's Temple, the Sanctuary of the Holy Spirit. She embraces the Unembraceable. *O Beata viscera* [O Blessed Womb] . . . Among us stood the One Whom we do not know, but Who is already among us. But Mary knows Him, the only creature on earth who already knows that the Word was made Flesh.

March 17, 1956

It has come to my attention that the government has "expressed a desire" that the program for the Year of National Vows on the occasion of the three hundredth anniversary of the Vows of King John Casimir* in Lwów be cancelled. This program was prepared by a commission convoked by the Episcopate; it was accepted by the Central Commission and distributed by the Secretariat of the Epis-

---

*That is, the vows dedicating Poland to the Virgin Mary.

copate for implementation. It was of a purely pastoral-religious character. It even covered such points as are the common concern of the government and the people, for example the struggle against alcoholism, promiscuity of youth, and so on. Nevertheless, the government, despite the obvious advantages of cooperation between the Church and the people, preferred to reject this help; what is more, it attempted to paralyze the activities of the Episcopate. What was the chief cause of this? One could assume it was fear of some widespread expression of Catholic opinion under the leadership of the Episcopate. One could assume it was fear that the Episcopate is, in a way, the [true] leader of the Nation. One could suggest a protest against the intrusion of religion, "which is a private matter," onto the social-national scene. Whatever we take to be the reason, the sad truth remains that in its work the Church cannot reap the benefits of the broadly touted détente. The press is already taking advantage of it, coming out more and more boldly with criticism of various economic programs; the so-called Catholic press is taking advantage of it, in a much more timid way, on the moral level. Satirical publications, which have been granted the greatest freedom of opinion, are taking special advantage of it (e.g., *Szpilki* [Pins]). It seems that they have the right to ridicule everyone except the ministers and party secretaries. *Trybuna Ludu* even allows itself to undermine a little "god." But the Church not only cannot imitate these critics, despite protests against the suppressors of criticism, but cannot carry out freely its socioreligious work, even if this is to bring definite benefits to the Nation.

March 25, 1956*

On Palm Sunday, which today for the first time is a celebration honoring Christ the King, the Holy Church sings: "And they stripped Him, and put on a scarlet cloak. . . ." The Church wants its servants to remember this event and so vests seventy of its servants† in crimson. The color can sometimes be the symbol of covet-

---

*In 1956, March 25 was both Palm Sunday and the feast of the Annunciation.
†The number of cardinals in the College of Cardinals in 1956 was limited to seventy.

ousness or pride. . . . But in reality it is a symbol of the blood that flowed copiously from Christ the God-made-Man and from Christ the Mystical Body. Therefore one must destroy in oneself what might have remained of pride, even if it were not associated with covetousness. . . . There was verily no covetousness in me and—I hope—no pride. But I was not free of a peculiar shade of it. How many times have I sparred with the Lord when I had to take upon myself the insignia of the will of the Church? How many times did the kindly Sister Maksencja have to repeat to me, "But this is for the glory of the Church." And yet I avoided this crimson as much as I could; I rarely wore the sash, the red cassock, the cape I took only as protection against the cold after a sermon. I did not wear the red stockings. . . . I noticed that some of the other bishops began to imitate me. . . . And yet this was a form of pride, because there was more thought about myself in it than about Christ's crimson. Indeed, in order to wear the Church's insignia in a worthy manner, it is not enough to wear it with humility, but one must learn to appreciate it for the sake of the Church. Christ did not hesitate to accept the scarlet robe. And I constantly sparred with the will of the Church. Everyone knows that in this crimson there is more of the Church's blood than of human vanity, so that human pride would never be able to overshadow the truth of the Blood. I must, therefore, prize the slightest thread that proclaims to the world the Most Holy Blood of Christ and the Church. . . .

Since I am to confess to You, Father, my pride, probably one of the last sins of my pride was the resistance I offered You ten years ago when Primate Cardinal Hlond told me I was to become a bishop. Even though I knew that it was the day of the Annunciation in Nazareth, I had forgotten that on this day Mary had said, *Fiat mihi* [Be it done unto me]. And my *quomodo fiet istud* [how should this be?] lasted the whole night. When I came to the Primate's residence the following day, it seemed to me that on this day I was more worthy of this grace than the day before, that it was I who had prepared myself for becoming a bishop, through this modest night-long prayer in the chapel of the Common Work Sisters. In this precisely lay my pride. But You knew me, Father, even before that prayer. You had penetrated my heart. You were aware of my short-comings, bad habits, and faults. And yet You wanted the Church to sing to me: *qui in diebus suis placuit Deo* [who in his days pleased God]. In my pride, I failed to notice the delicate reproach that Cardinal Hlond made to me: "One does not say no to the Holy Father." My pride lay in the fact that I thought more of my sins than of the power and the mercy of God. Today I understand this better than ten years ago. Today it seems to me that this was my last sin of pride. Today it seems to me that since then I have not committed the sin of pride. Or perhaps such a thought is, in itself, a sin of pride?

I thank you, Father, that the announcement of my becoming a bishop was made on the day of the Annunciation in Nazareth, that through this act of additional grace You gave me to understand about Mary: Behold my Mother.

March 26, 1956

Ten years ago today I expressed by *consensum canonicum* [canonical consent] in Poznań to Primate Cardinal Hlond to take over the orphaned diocese of Lublin. The Holy Spirit demanded at that time that I go to the clergy and people of Lublin.

Today I received a letter from Father Padacz informing me that "despite efforts, clarifications and explanations, he was remaining in Warsaw for the holidays." I asked Father Padacz, as my chaplain, to come at least for Easter to Komańcza, so that I could have the joy of having at least one of my priests with me. I know how fervently Father Padacz wanted to be with me. And I was looking forward to this visit. A bishop without his clergy—what a terrible renuncia-tion, especially on Holy Thursday. But the UB authorities, who perceive in Father Padacz an old politician, did not agree to this visit. Beginning with January of this year all passes to Komańcza have been suspended. The following people tried to get them: Father Jerzy Modzelewski, Father Stefan Piotrowski, Father Jan Sitnik, Monsignor Kulczycki of Kraków, Father Ziemiński of Warsaw, Prior Jerzy of Jasna Góra from whom an issued pass was taken away, and many others. All requests were rejected outright. It is difficult to determine the reason for this new chicanery, which contradicts the declaration made to me before my departure from Prudnik. According to the assertion of the official who was sent to me, I was to be allowed to see anyone who wished to see me.

Apparently the reason for this stringent course lay in the fact that my personal letter addressed to the Father General of the Pauline Fathers, as an associate of the Order, in some mysterious way was made public and distributed by some "unknown" agents. The letter was very personal in nature, so that mimeographing it and sending it all over the country was most tactless. But the author of this thoughtless act, whom everyone the least bit informed in Church affairs in Poland knows full well (and whom the UB also knows), does not admit to his action. As a result of this dishonorable deed, many people must suffer, burdened with the suspicions of the authorities. The letter was embellished with very fuzzy and unclear comments by unknown parties (perhaps through repeated recopying).

It might also be supposed that the measures taken had become so stringent because of a letter from the Holy Father, addressed to me on the occasion of the anniversary of the Royal Vows. The letter did not reach me in the original, but I know that copies of it circulated around Poland. Maybe this displeased our authorities.

Whatever the cause of this "new procedure for Komańcza," it is a fact that I am completely cut off from my priests. I am condemned to the company of the nuns and my own sisters, who are supposed to come. But Miss Maria Okońska and Miss Janina Michalska, who came here on March 24 from Jasna Góra, managed to secure passes. They brought me some news about work on the Year of the National Vows. I have already made a sacrifice to God of these joys that the presence of close ones brings, but God has accepted my sacrifice in part. He took the priests from me and left me the women. He allowed a similar thing with His Son on Calvary: all the apostles left, but the women, who followed Mary there, remained with Him. Saint Matthew emphasizes this fact so eloquently: "And many women were there, looking on from a distance, who had followed Jesus from Galilee, ministering to Him. Among them were Mary Magdalene, and Mary the mother of James and Joseph, and the mother of the sons of Zebedee" (Matt. 27: 55–56). One can fail to appreciate this gift, can long for work among "stronger" people. And yet God began His task of saving the world with a woman. Once He foretold her in paradise, and the second time he sent the Angel Gabriel to her in Nazareth. The fall of the world began with a woman and the renewal of the world began with a woman.

I once bragged to Father Korniłowicz that I worked with men: I taught the students at the seminary, was the moderator of the Kujawy-Dobrzyń Sodality of Farmers, I worked with the trade unions. Perhaps Father K. took this as a personal criticism, because he said, "If you don't have what you like, then you like what you have." This was in Dratów, at the home of Mrs. Kleniewska, during a retreat for a group called Viola,* conducted by Mrs. Halina Derna-łowicz.

Today I understand this perhaps even better, when all the men of my closest circle have grown silent. I had no sign of life from them during the years of my imprisonment. My sister, Stanisława Jarosz, supported me with her vitality. The girls in Mrs. Okońska's group did not cease in their prayers for me; it was they who found a way in Stoczek to let me know about themselves by sending me a crèche for Christmas, *pisanki* [artistically decorated eggs] which were like eloquent letters, a pall for the chalice with rosaries, and many other signs which no one [outside] understood, but which I could read, since they had been our common language for many years. Today I know that my students from "the Eights"† were

---

*After the flower. Between the World Wars various areas of Poland organized special groups whose purposes were educational, cultural, spiritual, etc.
†*Ósemki* [the Eight], an informal label given the members of Prymasowski Instytut Ślubów Narodu [the Primate's Institute for the Implementation of the National Vows] which was officially called into being by the Primate in 1956, on the occasion of Poland's Christian Millennium, as a women's lay institute and which had existed

capable of crossing the square at Jasna Góra on their knees when they went there with the Warsaw Pilgrimage (1955). The Good Lord saw this dedication, by which even the priests taking part in the Pilgrimage were amazed. How was I not to remember this and to express my gratitude?

Today again I have proof that when none of the priests managed to overcome the obstacles in coming to Komańcza, the *devotus femineus sexus* [the devout feminine sex] courageously admitted to suffering along with me. Nuns come to my aid, giving me material support. I have to rely almost exclusively on the help and support of the Sisters of Nazareth, who stand to suffer great material losses because of my stay in Komańcza, since they cannot accept vacationers. And with constant prayers in the chapel of Jasna Góra, the Eights support me. If it cannot be otherwise, then in this also I must see an expression of the will of God.

The illustrated weekly *Świat (The World)* commemorated the three hundredth anniversary of the successful defense of Jasna Góra in a unique way. For the past few weeks it has been publishing the memoirs of the indiscreet public prosecutor Kazimierz Rudnicki, entitled *The Stepmother Trial* (March 25, 1956). The author himself admits that he is in conflict with his professional ethics "writing not too flatteringly about his client." But perhaps an even greater lack of tact is exhibited by the approval, or maybe even encouragement, of the powers that be, which casts a painful reminder of the distant past into the face of the Catholic community at the very moment when the whole of Poland is preparing to commemorate one of the greatest expressions of social justice, the Vows of Casimir. The editors do this in the same issue in which they honor the memory of Bolesław Bierut. This is really a "new culture."

---

informally before that. The number refers to the fact that the members were to live in communities of eight.

March 29, 1956

Holy Thursday. *Desiderio desideravi manducare hanc Pascham vobiscum* [I have greatly desired to eat this Passover with you]. Eternal Priest, You wished fervently to eat Your Passover with Your disciples. Your fervent wish is so very priestly; it evolves from the unity of the family of the priesthood, of which You are the Beginning and the Source. And I "desire with the desire" the agony of a priest to whom You also gave disciples. But despite so fervent a wish, this consolation, which You experienced during the Last Supper by the will of Your Father, is not granted my priestly heart. You were fulfilled as You distributed the Eucharist to Your disciples. My priestly agony will not end so joyously. I must endure it alone, without the participation of my disciples. It seems that You demand more of me than of Yourself. You gave way to Your heart, succumbed to the needs of Your Heart. But You did not want to indulge my heart even today, the third dreadful Holy Thursday that I must endure. Everything can be borne, but at a moment of true priestly torment, You know how very difficult it is. . . . If Your strength does not sustain me in my weakness . . .

Do not take pity on me, do not feel sorry for me—but look at my agony. Let it continue to the end. It is terrible, Father, terrible. . . . But apparently You need my priestly suffering. . . . I will not give You to my disciples. . . . Today my cathedral is without a bishop whom the Holy Spirit desires for the Church. . . . *Quia peccavimus Tibi* [Because we have sinned against You]. . . . After the Last Supper, You had Your Gethsemane. My entire Holy Week is a Gethsemane, anew. . . . Let this suffering of Your servant cleanse my disciples and the sheep entrusted to me. . . . Do not spare me, do not feel sorry for me, do not sustain me. . . .

April 4, 1956

It is worth noting the holiday adventures of my sisters, who determined to make their way to Komańcza for Easter. First I received the news that Father Padacz, my chaplain, had not been granted permission to come. On Thursday, March 29, both of my sisters, Stanisława and Janina, were to come. In fact, only Stanisława ar-

Komańcza. "The shepherd without his flock."

rived [on that day]. Janina did not get a pass, even though they had made their efforts to get passes together, at the same county office in Piaseczno. Stanisława was handed the pass at the last moment when she had come for the seventh time and stated emphatically that she would not leave the office until she was given the pass. On the next day, Good Friday, Janina came; she was given a pass at the last moment when she appealed to the chairman of the People's District Council (PRN).* The vice-chairman received her and expressed surprise that Janina was the sister of the Primate and claimed that he knew nothing of her efforts. Finally she was given the pass. But on Monday after Easter it turned out that the document was valid "from March 29 to March 10." No one had noticed this clerical error. Only in Komańcza did they discover that the document was not in order. In the morning the Commandant sent a soldier and demanded that my sister leave Komańcza at once. Explanations did not help. By comparing the two passes, issued by the same office, it was easy to see that Janina's pass must have been issued later than Stanisława's pass. Thus there could be no question of "falsifying a document." This did not help either. My sister was to leave the next day. She had to appear at the train station. And here, in the presence of twelve soldiers, who came out in full force, she entered the train and left bureaucratic Komańcza earlier than planned. Besides expressing sympathy, nothing more could be done.

April 14, 1956
On the side of the hill by the railway tracks, we entered a magnificent field covered with snowdrops. What a moving sight! All the flowers opened their pure hearts, as if looking at the unexpected visitors with confidence, certain of their own irresistible charm of purity and beauty. I looked back. Along the path of my footsteps were crushed flowers, trampled leaves. This is my handiwork. This is how my life looks, and my work. I stopped under a hazelnut bush. I did not have the courage to go on.

Only Christ can pass safely over virginal fields of hearts. *Qui*

---

*Powiatowa Rada Narodowa—a level of county government.

pergis inter lilia, septus choreus Virginum, sponsus decorus gloria spon-sisque reddens praemia [Encircled by the Virgin band, / Amid the lilies Thou are found, / For Thy pure brides with lavish hand, / Scattering immortal graces round]. Only Christ will not trample anything, will protect everything with his delicate, masterful ability to lead. And I? This always turned out wrong for me, the unfortunate "father." Perhaps I succeeded best in my work among students in *Odrodzenie* [Rebirth].* But today? I have lost some great ability to exercise influence, my soul and heart have grown hard. From what? I gaze in fear at the patch of snowdrops in the field that my foot has not touched. How beautiful it all is! I will not go farther, my foot will not pass this way, will not touch any tip, will not trample any flower.

I turned aside and saved the flowers. I preserved my soul. But perhaps this was only pride?

April 20, 1956

Bishop Choromański left today, together with Father Goździewicz and Father Bronisław Dąbrowski. They had been here since the sixteenth. Bishop Michał Klepacz, who was supposed to have come, did not, because he was still in the hospital recovering from a hernia operation. Among matters discussed at length, the bishop brought up "the most important matter"—my return to Warsaw. I broadened the base of the discussion. For me "the most important matter" was respect for the rights of the Church, and my own problem was only a fragment of the whole. That was why I expressed the conviction that this matter could not be brought up separately, but it can be brought up together with other matters. In my opinion, the Episcopate should call for a meeting of the Joint Commission with the Premier† or with Edward Ochab. In this meeting it must be shown that the proposals of the Episcopate, presented in September 1953 at the request of the government, had not been accepted. It was

*A large organization of Catholic university students interested in social, religious, and cultural causes.
†Józef Cyrankiewicz.

Komańcza. Wyszyński with his father, Stanisław
Wyszyński. The cardinal had requested permission
to see his ailing father. One and a half years
later, and after his recovery, the father was
allowed to visit.

necessary to bring them up again. On the basis of the present call for law and order, we could try to call for a reconsideration of the case of the removed bishops: Adamski with his suffragans, Archbishop Baziak of Kraków, Bishop Kaczmarek of Kielce, and me with my suffragans. I would not want to return to Warsaw while other bishops remained outside their dioceses. I could return as the last but never as the first. If it developed that my return would be impossible, an effort must be made so that at least Bishop Baraniak could return to Gniezno. The discussion should close with the presentation of a memorandum in writing.

April 26, 1956
Father of Life, today I saw them plowing on the uplands, I saw them sowing. This sight breaks my heart. You granted Your favor to the tillers so that they could cast Your seed into the earth; they take it out of the emptying granaries and, filled with trust in You, render it unto the earth, God's life giver. They return Your seed to Your earth. You will reward this act of faith in Your providence. Father, the seed You have gathered in the granary of my soul still remains in a heap. I cannot sow it. I lack a field. My granary has been sealed. I feel confined, Father. My soul laments. I understand the Apostle: "Woe to me, if I do not preach the Gospel." Today's Gospel said, "Ask the Lord of the harvest . . ." Father, Father, can I ask for myself? Open my granaries. I see how some of Your sowers stint on the grain, how frugally they measure it out. . . . You know that I did not stint on it. . . . Today I withhold my hand and cannot raise it to sow. . . . How much humility I need to accept the fact that the seed You have given me will not be used for sowing. Father, this is terrible! But this manifests Your power, before which I humble myself. I watch the tillers—and envy them. I know their joy, to feel the more deeply Your power over my unworthiness. . . .

April 27, 1956
And yet my misery and unworthiness cannot diminish Your power. After all, my misery cannot be a god. And so, even if I stood before all my sins, even if I took upon my shoulders all the sins and crimes

of mankind, I can still stand with trust before Your power and mercy, just as did the Son of Man. You would have every right and all the power to reject it, but evil does not rule the world—love does. And that is why You, Father, cannot reject. You are not "almighty" because You cannot act against Your nature, against love. I see all my suffering, and through it I see all Your power, which conquers the greatest evil through love.

May 2, 1956
I received a letter from Bishop Choromański today, reporting that he had appealed to the Speaker of the Sejm, on the suggestion of the Chief Commission of the Episcopate and Bishop Klepacz, for my release from prison. The letter, very poorly drafted, was addressed to the Speaker of the Sejm, with copies sent to the Head of the Council of State,* the Presidium of the Party† and to the government.‡ The Speaker passed the bishop's letter over to the procurator general [attorney general]. The bishop made the comment that the letter probably went this route because the procurator general was responsible for law and order, which in my case were very seriously violated by the decision of the Council of Ministers. The bishop expressed the hope that the answer of the procurator general would be positive. It is to be supposed that the procurator general would examine the decree of the government of September 1953. Personally, I would prefer that the matter take a different course.

May 3, 1956
On this the day before the tenth anniversary of my consecration, I begin a novena of gratitude to Christ through Our Lady of Jasna Góra—to Christ, the Eternal Priest, for the grace of my call to be a bishop. I wish this gratitude to be fully a joy for experiences of life past—*qui in diebus suis placuit Deo* [who in days past pleased God]. All the more since there has been so little in my life that could have

---

*Head of state, equivalent to the office of President of the United States.
†Central committee of the Communist Party whose head is the First Secretary.
‡The Premier and his cabinet.

*Komańcza. Wyszyński and Bishop
Michał Klepacz during one of the
permitted visits.*

been pleasing to God. I wish to express thanks for the fullness of priesthood, that it came to me at Jasna Góra. I wish to express thanks for everything that flowed down upon me together with my episcopal state. And, most joyfully, I wish to express thanks for the grace of imprisonment in the name of Christ. I do not wish the Good Lord to regret anything that He did for me, that He chose me and consecrated me. I do not wish Him to be disappointed in me even now as I remain in this diminished prison, while I cannot return to my fold. I do not wish my Heavenly Father to see any trace of sorrow and suffering in my soul. The more something is sad and painful, the more it must be returned to God with thanks. In this frame of mind, I wish to remain on the eve of my episcopal consecration. And all of these consolations I offer into the hands of my Lady of Jasna Góra, who allowed me to be born into episcopacy in her capital.

Your glory is my joy, Queen of the World, Queen of Poland, Mary. This is how Saint Peter Damian harangued you in the breviary lessons we read in the public prayers of the Church. He reminded you of everything: the nature you share with us, your power, and your uniqueness. He wanted to win you over for us. Certainly, the hungry children of a feasting Mother cannot be completely happy, even if they behold all her glory and beauty. Of course, of course, Saint Peter Damian . . .

But your unholy reader still experiences a bit of happiness even from the fact that he has a Mother so richly praised. My people are still in agony. They stumble from one slavery into another. But the truth still remains—even in the grimmest of slavery—that the Queen of the enslaved Nation is Mary.

And your slave, O Queen, wants his slavery to devolve to your greater glory. If my Nation's suffering has brought you glory, then perhaps the enslavement of one of the sons of this Nation will bring you more glory than his freedom.

I will not make reproaches to you, even following the example of Saint Peter Damian. But I will praise you with all that I have at this moment, by the will of the Heavenly Father. Forgive me that the gifts are not those befitting a Queen, that they are the gifts of a slave. But maybe they are more precious to you than the generosity of the blessed of this world.

May 8, 1956

I have been called the Marian Primate. I fervently wish to justify this name by my life. I can do this perfectly only when I become like you, Queen of my life. You became the Handmaid of the Lord; help me so that at last I may be the servant of your son only. You gave your most pure blood to the Son of Man. Help me so that I may not spare my blood for Christ.

May 12, 1956
From the other corner of Poland I call to you, Queen of Jasna Góra, to remind you of the grace imparted to me ten years ago in your house. *Sufficit mihi gratia Tua* [Your grace is sufficient for me]. Today I live by this memory, as I call to you *ab extremis terrae* [from the ends of the earth]. More than three thousand Masses were offered today for the Marian Primate. It is all due to you, Queen of Poland, as a Primate's tribute, on your three hundredth anniversary. I add my modest gift of these ten years of my shepherding and my imprisonment. Let everything of "mine" praise you. Your slave places everything in your queenly hands, happy that he can strip himself for you. I ask but one thing—that, having taken everything of mine, you will be willing to protect Christ's Church, offered to you, to your Immaculate Heart, ten years ago. Protect it with your maternal mantle, enfold it within your heart. If you need, take my life so that the Church of your Son may live in Poland. It appears that, after all, you do need willing sacrifices so that you may preserve the integrity and purity of the Church, so that you may grant the gift of courage to its servants. They are still timid in their obligation to profess the faith. They remain silent even in times when they should be shouting. Grant them courage; let them understand that the strength of the Church depends on public profession. Your slave begs you to grant this gift to the Church and its bishops, as he offers into your maternal hands, fertile and generous, all that the good people have supported me with on this tenth anniversary of my episcopal consecration.

I thank you, Mother of Jasna Góra, that my tenth anniversary has come in the year of your three hundredth anniversary, that it came on a Saturday, that I could offer a votive Mass to honor you, Lady of Jasna Góra.

May 14, 1956
Soli Deo! People have shown me so much affection during these past few days. I know that it is through You and for You. And yet I wish

Komańcza. Visitation privileges gave an illusion of freedom. Wyszyński was given permission to walk within the town limits.

everything only for You, O Christ, and for Your Church. Take away this affection and these emotions and keep them only for Yourself. Take from the people their affection and their feelings for me. I surrender them. Otherwise everything will not be *Soli Deo.*

In Your holy service, I wish no advantages for me. Take the people's hearts; they don't belong to me. Take them for Yourself. I want nothing for myself. Let them all despise me, so as not to squander one iota of love and affection on me at Your expense. Everyone and everything that draws toward me take for Yourself. Help me finally to bring about my *Soli Deo.* I fear everything that is still for me, even in You. Let everything be in You and for You. Protect the people from me. I will do everything I can so to alienate people that I no longer draw any consolation from them, so that I may know that everything is for You. I give them all to You—*Soli Deo!*

I will cease to think of myself—it is enough that You think of me.

I will cease to speak of myself—You are the Word of Life, not I.

I will cease to listen about myself—let them speak to You about me.

May 20, 1956

Descend, O Holy Spirit, on the Vatican and enkindle the Pope's white into burning red; grant him all Your gifts. Visit the hearts of the crimson-clad with Your flame that they may glow like their robes. Embrace all the bishops of the world that they may bear witness to Your truth, not only in sincerity, but also in a life that has its source in truth.

On Pentecost, the Holy Spirit filled hearts and minds with such power that the disciples spoke in various tongues about God's great deeds. They spoke, they cried out, they shouted. . . . They could not contain their words, thoughts, feelings. They seemed to reel with the intoxication of words. This is an awesome power, bearing witness to truth. It is a blessing for anyone who can open the door to this power, when it flows from mouth, through word, through apostolic deed.

But what a tragedy for an apostle when he must thwart this great power in himself, when he cannot speak, shout, rage in a divine way. This is my state! "Woe is me," because I cannot release Your power from me . . . *Loquebantur variis linguis* [They were speaking in various tongues]. This is the apostolic spirit. . . . What is the purpose of silence when dealing with the great deeds of God? What an inconceivable mystery of God's power that can prevent a bomb from exploding even when fires rage within it. Truly, You display greater power when You grant the gift of silence than when You grant the gift of prophecy.

May 22, 1956

You have left Your redemptive signs on the face of the earth, which to this day give forth fruit a hundredfold. I observe these signs with gratitude, as my soul grows rich in the soil made fertile by Your blood. Should we not want to follow in Your footsteps? If they were to bear fruit? My seed is from Your seed. My desires flow from Your deeds. My hopes flow from Your victories. My blood is given life by Your redeeming blood. To give my soul for my brothers, for the Church, for Your cause—this is my need, the voice of Your blood, the hope of the Church. Everyone in Poland is happy that there is someone who can suffer. They are afraid lest this someone flounder, lest he fail. As Christians, we all have a desire for the need to suffer, to sacrifice ourselves for the Church. Almost all of them want me to return to my labors, but they also feel that someone has to continue to sacrifice himself, to bear witness to God's power and to give witness by suffering. Should I look around? Why should I want to look for a substitute? I want to be Your sign in Poland, a sign that would bring the fruit of faith and love for You, O Christ, into men's souls.

There is someone who wants to share this fate, who also wants to be God's sign. . . . I accept this desire because I know it is from God.

Father, this cannot be easy. When I do not feel the burden, it all seems like poetry, like a void. When it is difficult, I feel I have received something tangible, something I can take in my hands and give back to You. I want to give, to take and give. I want to feel this burden, so that I can feel that I have something to give.

May 24, 1956

How often there passes over my soul the shadow of Moses' feelings at the crossroads: *Audite . . . numquid possum deducere aquam vivam de petra hac* [Listen . . . will I ever be able to draw living water from this rock?] So often You speak to me through people who desire Living Water, who tell me that I am to give it, that I must give it. Because who could do this? But people speak to me of issues so great that it is hard to believe that they could have any connection with me. "It is speech addressed to someone else, speech of the hungry for the Unknown One, who is to come and renew the face of the earth." But it is not meant for me. Perhaps because I know my own worthlessness too well, I subconsciously struggle against grand words. I know that this is a sin of pride—so great a pride that it deludes itself into thinking it can take God's place. I fear grand words, whenever people associate them with me. I am too realistic, too sober, too well-informed, knowing the situation too well, to ignore this in my awareness. My sin is precisely the sin of presumption in which there is no room for that impossible word which only God can always utter. I accuse myself of the sin of presumption. The Communists say that I am a mystic. I am not; on the contrary, I am a realist. My greatest sin is realism, the enemy of spiritual eyes. I believe that God can do anything and at any time, but not through me. I believe that God can draw water from the parched stone of the persecuted soul of this Nation. But do it through me? I still lack the humility that would enable me to believe that. Moses' sin repeats itself in me.

May 26, 1956

Today, Father, I received the grace to understand what an inadequate and miserable servant of Your children I have been. It had seemed to me that I was serving them well, that I did not refuse them anything I could give. Today I understood that I had been giving more of myself and less of You. By Your Will I had millions of children; today You leave me only two. But through them I have discovered how imperfect was my service to the millions. After two years of separation from my sheep, I see that I have not yet succeeded in separating myself from myself, since I am not even able to serve these two in You. And my failure is all the worse because they believe that I am leading them to You; they think that I am giving them You. Perhaps because they are too good and compensate for my clumsiness with the grace You are giving them. It is they who are leading me to You, and not I leading them to you. I follow them, instead of leading them. Can I expect the grace of returning to my fold, to my work? It would be brazen on my part to think so and to desire it. You must diminish me even more, so that I may be freed from myself, so that I may know how to lead souls to You. *Ne respicias peccata mea, sed fidem Ecclesiae Tuae* [Look not on my sins but on the faith of Your Church]. . . . Do not allow me to frustrate in souls the grace You have already given them. Do not allow me to minimize their potential and their vocation. Allow me to understand Your greatness in people, and grant me the power to respect it.

May 27, 1956
The Feast of the Holy Trinity. In the heart of Your unfathomable Being, O Holy Trinity, I seek support for my feet. Only there do I feel as if I were in the nest from which my life sprang. Only when I return there through faith and love do I feel as if I were returning to the House of my Father. Only before You, Holy Trinity, do I feel the fullness of my faith. Only the love drawn from here seems pure and free of what might still be too human. I feel a deep need to pay homage to You in Your threefold unity, in Your depth, in Your source of threefold divinity. Only as I look into Your depths do I feel that I worship You for Your own sake, that my love is unselfish, that I forget about myself, about my little concerns and requests. I then see clearly how all that is mine is so small, how useless it is to think about one's own concerns, how little meaning there is to a request, how all my strength should be dedicated entirely to worshipping You. When I look into Your Heart—exis-

tence and essence—I feel Your presence more deeply within me, I desire it, and I abide with You full of humility and joy. Be praised, O Trinity, who are in me.

May 30, 1956
The eve of Corpus Christi. Today I experienced the privilege of working for the glory of tomorrow's celebration. I used to get blisters on my hand from the monstrance; I am still not worthy of this privilege. But today You granted me the privilege of getting blisters from the pruning shears with which I cut fir branches in the woods for tomorrow's feast. This will probably be the greatest effort You will allow me to make for Your glory. Tomorrow I will lurk in the choir loft so that the people who come for the procession will not see me. But I already know today that I will rejoice. Truly, I am not worthy to be Your priest, but You have allowed me to be your lumberman and gardener. Thank You, Father, for this proof of Your understanding the needs of my heart.

May 31, 1956
Catulus leaenae [whelp of a lioness]. I wish to eat at this table where the crumbs fall generously to the ground. I know, O Mother, that you give birth not only to the Body of Your Son, but also to me. I know that You have nourished not only Jesus, but through the Body He received from You, You have also nourished me. I repeat so often: *Ave verum Corpus, natum de Maria Virgine.* This real Body satiates me so fully that I am conscious of your maternal blood, which beats in your Son and through Him beats also in me.

Motherly lioness, who nourished her Son, who endowed Him with everything He needed to feed billions of His children at the eucharistic table. As I observe Corpus Christi today, I also praise your body, this source of the Body of Christ. I am a pup that fawns under the table of your Son's eucharistic Feast. You will not reject me because you remember what your Son heard from the Canaanite woman, that even the pups will feed on the crumbs falling from the Lord's table, from the table set with the Body taken from you. I cannot participate in the joys of the Church, which today pays public homage to your eucharistic Son, but you have not denied me the nourishment that has its source in the Mass. And now, Mother, accept the homage of my submission to the Father's powerful will, which now demands for the third time that I not share in the joys of the Church. Even this I consider a grace, a crumb that today fell from the table of the Church, rejoicing because of the Eucharist. I am your pup, O motherly Lioness, who gives birth to the Body so that your sons may be nourished.

The Angelus on the feast of Corpus Christi is most nourishing. The *concepit* [she conceived] is like the consecration which, from the Body of Virgins, gives birth to the Bread of Life, which, in turn, gives birth to virgins. The Body of Virgins—of Mary the Virgin and Christ the Virgin. *Ancilla Domini* [Handmaid of the Lord], who yearns for a human body in order to feed human bodies and souls with the Body. *Verbum, Caro* [the Word, Flesh]—that is the beginning of the transubstantiation that henceforward will be born from the word spoken at the altars, so that through the Word bread becomes the Body. *Factus cibus Viatorum* [Made the food of Pilgrims].

Today we celebrate for the first time the new feast of the Queen of the World. This is the will of the Holy Spirit, who wanted to teach us that the Woman giving birth to the true Body of the God-made-Man (the Body being Nourishment, *qui pacem ponit fines Ecclesiae* [which establishes peace as the purpose of the church]), must be the Queen of the World. This divine granary, nourishing humanity through her Son, carries Life in her womb, without which we would all die of starvation. Every kingdom must satisfy the most pressing needs of its subjects. Our Queen feeds the world forever by giving us the God of Life.

June 2, 1956

You grant me, Father, the grace to see the delicate point at which converge the two camps of Your children: the one that is with You and for You, and the one that is without You and against You. When I try to understand where the heart of this problem now is in Poland, I must see it in relationship to me. You wanted me to be your David, who would take a stand against the mightily armed Goliath. There can be nothing in me that resembles Goliath's self-confidence. I must be humble like David. I must put my trust in the tiny glistening pebbles in a stream, this nonentity in the struggle for You. I must press forward in the name of the Lord of Hosts and not my own. With deep humility I must understand that You have chosen me for this contest in which Your Name and Your rights on Polish soil, the rights of the Nation to come to You, the rights of the Church, are at stake. There is nothing I can do about the fact that, although I regard myself with humility, I must recognize that the most delicate point in the struggle of faith and disbelief turns within me and on me. I am this point of intersection, this barometer, this seismographic needle. This is the tragic truth that demands heroic humility. At the moment the situation does not depend on the Episcopate, does not depend on Piasecki's racketeering nor on the "patriots"; it depends on how I respond to the challenge. They all—the government and the Party included—now look toward Komańcza. This is not conceit, it is the gift of understanding a situation as delicate as the ways of God are unfathomable on the pages of history. And so I must be a David for God, I must trust in the name of God, I must be as pure and humble as the pebbles in a stream. This is the revelation of the day.

June 5, 1956
Whoever has managed to visit me has sensed a reservation present in alert public opinion: why could he [get in to see the Primate] when others couldn't? He's probably a "secret agent" of men with blood on their hands. People who have managed to get here must endure these conjectures. The sensitive nature of these opinions reveals how the public fears lest I weaken. They need a sign of great strength, perhaps because they themselves have succumbed to weakness. They do not want me to be subservient because they themselves are subservient. My true friends today are torn: they want freedom for me, yet feel that I need to suffer. The struggle between these two feelings is a measure of the value of friendship and Catho-

lic thinking. I must desire suffering more than freedom, if only because there are fewer of those who are willing to suffer.

June 7, 1956

Vere consumpti sumus ira Tua [Truly we have been consumed by Your wrath] (Psalm 89:9; 90:9 KJV). When I look around, Father of Nations, I see that You have provided a bit of a respite for everyone after this terrible war. Even for the sons of the "nation of blood,"*even for those who spilled our blood so wantonly in so many concentration camps, You have prepared a place where they can feel at home and safe.

Only Poland has been denied a moment of respite. We choke on an excess of suffering, anguish, and violence. One group of ravagers has gone, but those who fill the camps and prisons with their own brothers are infinitely more cruel. There is an amnesty now. Hundreds, thousands of people are being released from camps and prisons. But the torment does not cease.

Father, *O Clavis David* [O Key of David]! Allow us some respite to recall what it is like to live a life of God's children, of free people. You have given freedom to nations, have given them the desire and need for freedom; You have infused into their souls powers that can develop for Your glory only in an atmosphere of freedom. Do not allow so many gifts of humanity to go unused in us, do not force us always to live like cattle.

After all, You have created man in Your image and likeness, O Father of freedom, and through Christ have lavished mankind with freedom. Let my people be heirs to some of these gifts. Today You give freedom to Your children in Dahomey. Remember Poland.

June 7, 1956

"Blessed is the Fruit of Thy Womb," Nourishing Mother. If ever He is "sweet on my lips," it is now, during the octave of Corpus Christi. You are an inexhaustible ciborium from which millions of

---

*Nazi Germany.

priestly hands, billions of lips draw [nourishment]. You continue to give birth endlessly from the time you became the Mother of the ever-increasing Body of Christ. Ark of the Covenant, in which is preserved the manna given by the Father. Your Fruit is ever fresh, ever life-giving, ever bountiful on the table of the Church.

Every altar is a Bethlehem where you keep vigil to feed the servants of your Son at the appropriate time. In this Fruit I can taste the flavor of your immaculate grace. I know that He gives birth to virgins, because he was born of a Virgin. O You, my Peace . . .

June 8, 1956
Sanctissimi Cordis Jesu [Most Sacred Heart of Jesus]. I read at None, *Serenum praebe vultum Tuum servo tuo* [Show Your serene countenance to your servant]. . . . My childlike heart seeks Your serene countenance. But the will of a mature person who knows the needs of the Church and his own worthlessness restrains the heart. Show a serene countenance to Your Church. But turn away from Your servant, O Father, so that the burden of abandonment and loneliness may cleanse my heart, which still continues to seek consolation. Once I sought Your serene countenance. Today I know I do not deserve it. The greatest wisdom of Your Heart will be to let Your servant understand that only You are happiness, peace, and quiescence. But Your servant has not yet deserved happiness, peace, and quiescence. Your servant must be tormented until he drops, until he is debased, until he is forgotten by everyone. All human hearts must abandon me, even those that do not want to stop loving me. All must stand afar and shake their heads at my absurdity and my defeat. Only then will my heart be healed. You have already given me a taste of this understanding when I suffered the greatest disappointment from people who had long claimed that they were my friends. But that is still not enough. Those who have remained steadfast in their love and friendship must now leave me. Only then will I become like Your Son, whom even You, most Affectionate Father, abandoned. Perhaps such suffering will win Your Fatherly favor for the Church and for the Nation that You have christened and given over

into the hands of godless men and traitors. Do not spare me, O Father, even if You must deny the strength. Let all my friends be scandalized.

June 15, 1956

In montibus Dominus videt [In the mountains the Lord sees]. When I stand on the top of a mountain, I have the feeling that I am alone on earth, alone on its highest point, closest to heaven. Alone closest to God. Alone with God, face to face. It seems to me then that God sees only me, and I feel His very eyes on me. Only on me . . . Then I feel truly great. Even if I see my nothingness against the immensity of space spreading out beneath me. Man's greatness lies in ever climbing upward, ever higher, ever unhampered. He wants to reach the peak, to feel above it all. And when this "all" finally pales, then he feels his greatness. And it is just then, at the height of his greatness, that he feels he has stood face to face with God. In Him he saw his smallness. My smallness is truth in the eyes of the One who sees me. God sees into me. That is why I climbed to the mountaintop, so that God could see me perfectly.

I climb like a lad onto the knees of his Father, to tell Him: You and I. No obstacles, no intermediaries.

> *Dio—Io* [God—I]!
> Impudent fellow!
> Father! . . .
> Son! . . .

When, in the evening, carnations send their fragrance from the top of a high hill, and fill the heavens with their perfume, I know what You need, Father of Life, from the earth. If You so enjoy the fragrance of the earth, how much more that of man. You are the Lord of mesmerizing beauty and charm. You, Father, are capable of unusual refinement and subtlety of feeling. I know why You demand incense in Your churches. The fragrance of these flowers is your ultimate pleasure. Who would come here in the night to indulge in earthly joys? We are afraid of wolves and of the dark. But the carnations who do their duty in the dark by delighting the heavens with their fragrance fear nothing. It is they who pray to You when the earth sleeps. It is they who open their flowery—though modest—hearts and delightfully glorify You by the song of the perfume of their souls. Be praised by all the plants and greenery, by all the fragrant flowers that pray to You with all their souls, as best they know how.

Have I created a fragrance for You, my discerning Father? What fragrance comes from my soul? Am I able to intoxicate You? How much less I am than a little plant. My poverty renders me a debtor.

As night falls, I will give my soul to You, Father. *In noctibus extollite manus vestras in sanctitate et benedicite Domino* [At night lift up your hands in holiness and bless the Lord]!

When will I tell you, *Nardus mea dedit odorem suavitatis* [My nard has given an odor of sweetness]?

Benedicite, montes (Bless Him, you mountains)! Mountain of fragrance, be the cause of my envy, as you intoxicate the Lord nocturnally with your perfume!

———————

June 16, 1956
I am beginning a thanksgiving novena of Masses and prayers today to thank you, Queen of Poland and Mother of Jasna Góra, for being with us, for consenting to be our Queen for these three centuries. Thank You for inspiring us to remain faithful to you, for aiding us in remaining faithful to the Holy Trinity, that through you we could be called the bulwark of Christianity, for taking our hearts in bondage, for enlivening our love for you, a love we cannot and dare not lose. I wish to thank you, Queen of Jasna Góra, for my trust in you, for watching over me from the beginning of my priesthood until now, for giving me your emblem for my episcopal coat-of-arms, which emblem became the spirit of my work. I thank you for everything, especially for these years of prison, during which I have grown to understand that I am your slave and your hostage. You

will free me when the whole Nation realizes the duty of fidelity to the truth of your Son.

In this jubilee year of the three hundredth anniversary of the Vows of the Nation, I feel that I should be with the whole Nation, with my clergy and people, on Jasna Góra, at your feet. It is so obvious that the first Primate who rules the Church under your sign, Our Lady of Jasna Góra, should himself be before you to repeat the renewal of vows. And if I cannot fulfill this sense of duty, then there is some great mystery, O Mother, some great secret between you and me. Perhaps I will not comprehend it, but it is enough that you know what is necessary. I surrender to this secret in humility, although as Primate of Poland I cannot surrender my rights. I act not only in my own name, but in the name of the whole Nation. Mother, do not let our secret diminish your glory in the eyes of the weak and not understanding.

Et ego sicut herba aresco. Gloria Patri et Filio et Spiritui Sancto [And I dry up like grass. Glory be to the Father and the Son and the Holy Spirit]. Thus I conclude the psalm for Saturday Terce. I dry up like grass for Your glory, O Holy Trinity.

Yesterday on the hill I saw a lofty spruce that had been struck by lightning. There remained only a white, broken stump, its branches broken to splinters, scattered about. It stood in wonder over what had happened. The whiteness of the stump reflected with light all around. A tree laid bare.

Is this how You lay bare a soul, when You want to engulf it with Your light, when You wish to brighten it lighter than snow?

The robes of empty pride are scattered about, the whitened heart remains. The tree will no longer live its own life; it has dried up from Your lightning. And yet people stop and gaze with wonder at Your might. *Vox Tonitrus Magni* [The Voice of Great Thunder]. This tree laid bare has become an apostle of Your might. It too voices its *Gloria Patri*.

I am not a spruce, only grass that longs to wither for Your glory.

Sicut herba aresco. Gloria Patri et Filio et Spiritui Sancto . . .

And yet you are magnificent in your blinding whiteness, shattered by the Finger of God, so suddenly brightened. . . .

Perhaps you recall the Immaculate One, when God's Lightning coursed through her to take on flesh within her earth.

June 20, 1956

I often think about how very poor I am; I look around me and see that I have no material security for the future. It seems to me that my circumstances are similar to Your life in Nazareth. I lack even the simplest aids to my normal work. Your poverty, Jesus of Nazareth, was richer, because in Nazareth You were the Word. My library remains on Miodowa Street, and it is so hard to live without it. But those are external things, words on paper. You are the living Word, my Word of Life. I have You; why do I need a library? You are my library.

A week before my arrest You asked me, in such a distinct voice: "Would you know how to be poor?" I answered then, "I think so, Christ." I now answer Your question with my daily life. Now You certainly know whether I know how to be poor.

And if at this moment You would demand of me even greater poverty, I would leave everything I now have, without regret, and follow You.

When I left Lublin, I left behind at my residence all I possessed, even my purple cassocks and personal gifts. I did not wish to "make a fortune" through my pastoral work. I did the same thing in September of that well-remembered year. Nothing that I possess at this moment has been gained through my efforts. It is the simple fruit of human sympathy.

You gave me everything, everything is Yours. O Christ, You, being rich, became poor. I want to be as poor as you.

June 22, 1956

I thank You, O Master, that You have made my fate so similar to Yours, that by Your Passion You have given me such a good ex-

*Komańcza. Wyszyński was
fond of dogs. His own white
sheepdog, Baca, tried to defend
him from the security officers
who came to arrest him in
the Miodowa Street residence.*

ample for my suffering. Your Apostles deserted You as the bishops have abandoned me; Your disciples deserted You, as my priests have me. They all succumbed to fear. There remained with You but a handful of women; I also see them at my side. Only the laity, the weak, the sinful remained: the Thief, Mary Magdalene, the Centurion, Nicodemus, Joseph of Arimathaea, and Simon of Cyrene. And there remains a handful of the laity with me, not at all the strongest ones, who have the courage not to disavow me. That is all. When I compare my limited suffering with Yours, I rejoice that You have endured everything You ask me to imitate. Be praised in my suffering.

June 23, 1956
Stabat Mater [The Mother was standing]. I cross out the word *dolorosa* [sorrowful], even though it has its historical meaning. Certainly Mary was *Socia passionis* [Companion to the passion]. But no artist has depicted Mary bracing herself at the cross. She stood on her own. Everything about her trembled! But whoever looked at Mary saw that she did not tremble! She was always *Virgo Auxiliatrix* [the Virgin who helped]—by her demeanor she helped those around her. And she prevailed!

June 24, 1956
John the Baptist, most sensitive to the voice of Mary, leaped in the womb of his mother Elizabeth upon hearing the greeting of the Mother of God. This inspiring sensitivity shakes the whole existence of man.

Grant, Mary, that I may always be sensitive to your voice, as the precursor of your Son was sensitive to the first word of your greeting. How blessed to have heard you from within the darkness of his mother's womb. Even then he was prepared to fulfill his task.

Awake in me, Mother, the readiness to foretell the coming of your Son. I am still in prison like John. But let my readiness substitute for the deeds I am prepared to undertake.

*July 1, 1956**

Sanguis Christi inebria me [Blood of Christ, inebriate me]. . . . So much of Your Blood has already flowed down on me! When I consider that one drop would be sufficient to wash away the sins of the world, I am amazed by Your generosity. What streams of Your most precious Blood have flowed through the chalice of Your blessings on the altars of the world. What a powerful wave of Blood You have directed at me. How much of Your Blood have I already had before in my chalices? How necessary it is for me to draw daily refreshment from the chalice of Your Blood. Every drop You have poured into my chalice is a gift beyond measure. And what of the superabundance of Your Blood that has flowed through my hands, onto my lips? I am bathed in Your Blood. I am awash in it within and without. I live by Your Blood. I cleanse and wash myself in Your Blood. It is my daily fare.

How eloquently the Gospel speaks today on the sixth Sunday after Pentecost: "I have compassion on the multitude." Your compassion opened Your veins for the people, to feed and nourish them with Your most precious Blood. Your heart surrendered the very least drop of that Blood, so that Your compassion on Your people would not only be an emotion, but would be translated into action.

I am ever on my guard to live in the spirit of gratitude for the streams of Your Blood that flow on me from Your side, from the chalices of the whole world, and from my own priestly chalice.

Nourished by Your Blood, can I stint on my blood which comes from Yours?

July 2, 1956†

On the birthday of the Most Blessed Virgin Mary, I give thanks to the Queen of the world and the Queen of Poland, and offer the homage of my prayers of the past two weeks. I thank You, Mother and Queen, for the fact that you exist, for being our Queen and our

*Feast of the Most Precious Blood.
†Feast of the Visitation.

Mother, for reigning on Jasna Góra and for reigning over Poland for three centuries, for being our intermediary of all the graces that have flowed from the Holy Trinity onto our Christian Nation, for having adopted the Church in Poland under your care and for embracing it with your immaculate heart, for having taken both of my dioceses under your care; for allowing me to labor under the sign of your countenance on my episcopal coat-of-arms, for reigning over my heart in absolute unity, for inspiring all my dear ones to love You, Virgin of Jasna Góra, for having united all of us in this love.

All my Masses, prayers, and works, all suffering and joys I lay at your feet, Mother and Queen, as a tribute of gratitude. I add these three years of prison fate and through them wish you to be especially praised.

I willingly renounce all attempts at freedom, voluntarily accepting further suffering only so that you, O Mother, may fully reveal your glory.

In te, Domina, speravi, non confundar [In you, Mary, I take refuge; let me never be put to shame].

July 20, 1956

The most humble priest in Poland must be the Primate. Dear Sister Stanisława reproached me today for directing the gift sent to me by the Sisters of Nazareth in Rome to the chapel of the convent of the Sisters of Nazareth in Komańcza. Perhaps this was not very tactful; perhaps it should have been directed to someone else. But I felt better when I rid myself of this possession. I am not as yet so perfect that I do not feel the burden of ownership. It is easier for me not to possess, easier to give up things than to keep them. A proper degree of virtue is necessary for everything.

July 25, 1956

Stephen, my Patron, First Martyr! So often your mystery repeats itself in my life. I was born on the day your martyr's remains were discovered, I was given your name, and I was ordained on that same

Komańcza. Father Hieronim
Gózdziewicz, Wyszyński, his
father Stanisław, and his sister
Stanisława.

day. Thus I am bound to the mystery of your life. Today I begin a new novena of thanksgiving as preparation for the day of my fifty-fifth birthday, for the day of our name days, for the thirty-second anniversary of my priestly ordination.

I spend this time in giving thanks: to the Heavenly Father for the gift of life received on your day; for the gift of your name and for the gift of a new birthday—into the eternal priesthood.

I thank the Father for life—under your sign of the open heavens and in your prayer, for your enemies. I thank God for such a name, which obliges me to imitate you. I thank God that my priestly life begins under the banner of your sacrifice and witness to the Truth —a martyr's blood.

I am sorry for having used your name so unworthily, that my life perhaps has cast more than one shadow on your name, that perhaps I have uttered your name more than once in anger, malice, and outrage.

I wish to make up to the Father for the imperfect way I used the gift of life. And for carrying your name so unworthily— perhaps using it for my vanity, insignificance, and abasement.

I wish to renew my resolutions of will and heart—of my readiness to dedicate my life, following your example, as witness to the truth. I wish to pray most fervently for those who want to consider themselves my enemies.

This is the spirit in which I will spend these days of the novena preceding the feast of the finding of your remains. Would that I could find you with all my life.

August 1, 1956

It is the anniversary of the Warsaw Uprising. Love does not know what slavery is. It will always find some escape by which to sacrifice its sincere and loving blood. And that is why there was an Uprising in which the blood of free spirits flowed lovingly into the Polish earth and made it fertile for new seeds.

We pray for the Insurgents. This is probably the first anniversary that we are allowed to speak about the blood of the Insurgents and its merit for freedom. But the Church prayed for Insurgents from the beginning, regardless of their outlook on the world or political views. After all, they all spilled blood that was red: those of the Home Army (AK) and those of the Peasant Battalions, as well as those of the People's Army.

Today we offer this scarlet blood of our brothers to the Father of all blood, in the hope that He will accept it as He accepted the Blood of His Son and for this Blood full of love will graciously open His fatherly heart to our tormented nation.

Suscipe, Sancte Pater [Accept, O Holy Father] . . .

August 6, 1956

I am "setting out" today with the Warsaw Pilgrimage that annually walks to Jasna Góra.* I will pray together with the pilgrims. For their intention, I will offer my Masses until the feast of the Assumption. I hope that the hardships of the pilgrims will bring much glory to the Father, that they will be a thanksgiving for Mary's reign over Poland, and that they serve as preparation for the renewal of the Vows of the Nation.

In spirit, I accompany my children who are privileged to be called to Jasna Góra.

August 26, 1956†

It is the day of the Vows of the Nation at Jasna Góra. Now I truly know that I am your slave, Queen of the World and Queen of Poland. Because today, on the day of the great feast of Catholic Poland, everyone who wants to can stand at the foot of Jasna Góra. And I have full right to this, a holy obligation, and who could possibly wish it more fervently than I? And yet, having such a powerful and benevolent Mother, I am to remain in Komańcza.

But that is your will! No one is able to oppose such power. Only we two, O Mother, can wish the same thing. At this moment all of Poland is praying for me to be present at Jasna Góra. Only we two know that the time has not yet come, that your will is to be done. In this lies your great power to which I humbly succumb, as a total slave of the most powerful Queen. Be praised in this power which you give me, so that I can fully concede that the greatest power and love is in my submission.

This is your reign over me. I have done what I could for your glory. On May 16 I prepared the text of the Vows, I wrote special prayers for priests, for youth, for husbands and mothers. These

---

*The walking pilgrimage begins on the feast of the Transfiguration (August 6) and concludes at Jasna Góra on the eve of the feast of the Assumption (August 15). Up to 40,000 pilgrims take nine days to walk the more than ninety miles from Warsaw to Częstochowa, using side roads and trails.
†The feast of Our Lady of Częstochowa.

*Komańcza, May 16, 1956.
Here, on the feast of Saint
Andrew Bobola (the
martyred Jesuit who
witnessed the Vows made by
King John Casimir), Wyszyński
wrote the Vows of the
Nation for the celebration at
Jasna Góra.*

words will speak to the people in my name. And I will speak only to you, in their behalf. I prayed for your greatest glory for this day. I wanted to gain it by the price of my absence. I trust that the Queen of Heaven and Poland will enjoy great glory at Jasna Góra today. I am now totally at peace. A great deed was accomplished today. A great weight, a stone fallen from my heart. May it become bread for our people.

August 29, 1956

When you bow your head today during the *Gloria* at the words *Gratias agimus Tibi* [We give You thanks], do it as if God your Father could see your neck ready to receive the blows of the sword with which He once honored John the Baptist.

Make all the priests of the Warsaw archdiocese as happy today, O Mary, as you once made John with the sound of your voice when you visited his mother Elizabeth. Let the priestly hearts rejoice *in vocem salutationis tuae* [in the sound of your greeting].

September 1, 1956

One drop of the Most Precious Blood sufficed to wash away the sins of the world. The sea of Polish blood, spilled during the war, blood which has not ceased to flow from the open wounds of our Nation, may it obtain for us from You, O Father of Nations, the grace of peace and respite for which we have waited so long. Queen of Poland and Queen of Peace, bring before the throne of God all the prayers which our Nation has brought to your throne on the day of its vows.

September 3, 1956

The Feast of Saint Pius X. Saint Pius X consecrated Adam Sapieha, bishop of Kraków; and Adam consecrated Teodor Kubina, bishop of Częstochowa; Bishop Teodor consecrated Stanisław Czajka, his suffragan bishop; and Stanisław Czajka, suffragan bishop of Częstochowa, coconsecrated Stefan, bishop of Lublin.

In the apostolic succession, I am the great-great-grandson of Saint Pius X.

*September 25, 1956**
Omnia bene fecisti [You have done all things well]. . . . After three
years of imprisonment, I consider this conclusion final. I would
never give up these three years from the curriculum of my life.
. . . It is better that were spent in prison rather than on Miodowa
Street. Better for the glory of God, for the position of the Universal
Church in the world, as the guardian of truth and freedom of
conscience—better for the Church in Poland and better for the
position of my Nation, better for my dioceses and for the strength-
ening of the attitude of the clergy, and certainly better for the good
of my soul. I finalize this conclusion, at the hour of my arrest, with
my *Te Deum* and *Magnificat.*

The Church was born in Christ's regenerative Blood on the cross,
just as every one of God's children enters into the world. The child
is healthy when his blood flows; a blood clot is dangerous for the
human body. In the same way, stagnant Blood is dangerous for the
Mystical Body of Christ. It must always flow somewhere, not only
in chalices at Mass but also in the living chalices of human souls. The
bleeding of the Church must take place somewhere, so that it may
remain in good health, filled with vigor and strength. And that is
why the Church is forever bleeding, in the endless persecutions ever
present in the history of the Church.

October 4, 1956
Lack of courage on the part of a bishop is the beginning of disaster.
Can he still be an apostle? Bearing witness to the Truth is essential
for an apostle! And this always requires courage.

The future belongs to the brave who trust and act forcefully, said
Pius XII—not to the fearful and the undecided. The future belongs
to those who love, not to those who hate. The mission of the Church
on this earth is far from complete; it requires, therefore, new ordeals
and new endeavors.

On the day of giving thanks for the victory at Chocim, only the
Church in Poland offers its prayers of gratitude to God for His

---

*The third anniversary of the cardinal's arrest.

protection. Who among the great patriots recalls this event today? And yet it was probably decisive in determining the course of events in the development of culture in Central Europe. Certainly it is the duty of the Primate of Poland to remember and to give thanks to God in the name of his country that has relegated the event to its archives, even though the fact continues to live in the annals of this country's history. I praise *Victricem manum Tuam* [Your conquering hand], Father.

I thank You for the power of that faith which withstood force. I thank You for that ultimate idealism which carried entire tribes to the field of battle and sacrificed almost all the sons of many a family. Thank You for the power You breathed into the wings of the hussars. I hear its song and sense the rush of victory. Let this all sing for You, O Father of Nations. And as I thank You for the past, please remember our struggle of today to keep Poland from being overrun by foreign perversity, by materialistic brutality, by half-educated pride and insolence. It is a terrible force that triumphs through fear even over the brave and the decent. Please intercede for Your Nation whose Father and Master You are. Let those who are made weary by oppression and struggle find some peace.

Even if I should die unheard, O Mother, I shall consider it a true grace to have been able to speak to you.

October 26, 1956

At nine in the morning Vice-Premier of Justice Zenon Kliszko and Sejm member Władysław Bieńkowski appeared at the convent in Komańcza on the orders of Władysław Gomułka and told Sister Superior of the Sisters of Nazareth that they wished to speak with the Primate. After more than fifteen minutes, I received the two gentlemen in the parlor downstairs. They declared that they had come on behalf of Comrade Wiesław,* to present certain matters for consideration. The new Secretary of the Polish United Workers' Party took the position that the Primate must return to Warsaw as soon as possible and resume his duties. They described for me the

----

*That is, Gomułka.

socioeconomic situation in the country, as well as the domestic and foreign political situations. All of these observations called for a speedy return to complete pacification in the country. Władysław Gomułka felt that in the area of Church-State relations, the people were most disturbed by the present situation of the Primate. And that is why they were delegated by the Party Secretary to solicit the thoughts of the Primate. My answer: "For three years I have maintained that the place for the Primate of Poland is in Warsaw."

We analyzed the situation as it related to the most pressing needs of the Church. Then they went to the village of Komańcza to call Gomułka by special telephone and inform him of the results of our discussion.

They returned for a small meal, which we ate in the parlor. The sisters wanted to prepare a more elaborate dinner, but I was of the opinion that it should be the usual everyday meal.

After dinner the two emissaries bade us farewell. They left behind mixed impressions. Mr. Bieńkowski was open, cheerful, with a human approach. Mr. Kliszko had the mind of a lawyer and saw difficulties and reservations everywhere. He thought in categories. I foresaw difficulties with him in the future.

The basic conclusions of the two-hour discussion could be summed up as follows:

(1) The Primate was positively disposed to the changes occurring in the internal life of Poland which are designed to calm the situation and break with the errors of the past.

(2) To define this position more precisely, the statements of Comrade Gomułka at the Eighth Plenary Meeting and at the Warsaw Rally* were considered authoritative within the framework of differences that may occur in philosophical outlook.

(3) Gradually to appease Catholic opinion in the country, which

*A spontaneous celebration took place in Warsaw after the selection of Władysław Gomułka as the First Secretary of the Party. He had just been released from prison.

Awaiting the return of the cabinet ministers on Saturday, October 27, 1956, Wyszyński walked through the fields and on the forest paths he himself had made the previous year. He quietly recited the rosary. To the surprise of those around him, he did not appear animated. "All is mercy," he said. "There is the mercy of imprisonment, and there is the mercy of liberation. I do not know for which I am to thank the Lord more. . . . You must thank Him with me for one as well as the other. . . ."

has been deeply affected by the government's past activities, it was absolutely necessary to abolish the decree on the appointment to Church posts, and this should be done as quickly as possible. Both men said that Comrade Gomułka was negatively disposed toward this decree. Both said that, though they were not thoroughly familiar with the decree, nonetheless they were both negatively disposed toward it. It was to be the business of the appointed Joint Commission to draft a new statement of this problem.

(4) It was considered a basic point that the filling of bishops' posts should have the approval of the government, as it was agreed under the Concordat. As to the filling of other church posts, it was not essential that these be approved, although some form of an exchange of opinion might be necessary. Of course, a great number of church positions could not be subject to approval.

(5) It was urgent to begin anew the work of the Joint Commission, in which specialists met to discuss matters. On the part of the government, the composition would be entirely new. On the part of the Episcopate, Bishops Klepacz and Choromański would remain. Bishop Zakrzewski, because of the state of his health, would not be able to take part in the work of the Joint Commission. Other problems, of which many have accumulated, would be directed to the Joint Commission.

(6) To calm public opinion, it was vital that Bishop Adamski with his suffragans and Bishop Kaczmarek of Kielce return to their posts. The government representatives mentioned difficulties regarding Bishop Adamski, about whom they had had reservations for a long time.

(7) The return of the Gniezno suffragan bishops to their posts was considered obvious and was related to the case of the Primate, all the more because for three years the Primate's diocese had been without bishops. It would be impossible for the Primate to carry out his duties without their help.

(8) To calm public opinion in Silesia and to instill confidence

*Bishop Zigmunt Choromań-
ski (right), the secretary of
the Episcopate, escorts
Cardinal Wyszyński back to
the capital on Sunday,
October 28, 1956, the feast of
Christ the King.*

in the new chain of command, changes must be made in the
positions of the administrators in Wrocław and Katowice.
Both should leave.

(9) For an appropriate ideological structure to exist, it was absolutely necessary to restore the Catholic press in the full
meaning of the term.

(10) In the opinion of the government representatives, this was
still not the time for a Concordat with the Holy See.

A communiqué for the Polish Press Agency was drafted as follows: "As a result of a conversation held by representatives of
the Central Committee of the Polish United Workers' Party with
the Primate of Poland, Stefan Cardinal Wyszyński, the Primate returned to Warsaw a few days ago and resumed his
duties."

The cardinal on his first visit since his imprisonment to the chapel at Jasna Góra (November 2, 1956).